TWO GOLDEN AGE OF
FLYING SAUCER CLASSICS

DIANE -- SHE
CAME FROM
VENUS
BY DANA HOWARD

AND...
WHY WE
ARE HERE
BY GLORIA LEE

INTRODUCTION BY
REGAN LEE

Cover by
CAROL ANN RODRIGUEZ

Global Communications

Two Golden Age of Flying Saucer Classics

Diane : She Came From Venus
By Dana Howard

Why We Are Here
By Gloria Lee

Introduction
by Regan Lee and Timothy Green Beckley

EAN: 978-1-60611-095-9
ISBN: 1-60611-095-0

Timothy Green Beckley: Editorial Director
Carol Rodriguez: Publishers Assistant
Sean Casteel: Associate Editor
Cover Art: Carol Rodriguez:

Printed in the United States of America
For free catalog write:
Global Communications
P.O. Box 753
New Brunswick, NJ 08903

Free Subscription to Conspiracy Journal E-Mail Newsletter
www.conspiracyjournal.com

"THE INSTRUMENT" SACRIFICED FOR A DARK ENTITY?

By Regan Lee

PUBLISHER'S NOTE: It is the given role of this publisher to keep in print as many as possible of the rare UFO books from the classic, so-called, Golden Age of Flying Saucers. Even though the UFO contactee movement of this period is still considered to be highly controversial in nature, we do believe that reputed contacts between humans and off-world intelligence are an intricate part of the history of the UFO phenomenon. Regardless of a person's individual suspicions regarding the legitimacy of the subject matter, it can't be denied that the reports of close encounters, mainly coming forth from the western regions of the United States (circa 1950ish) resulted in the birth of the New Age movement as we for the most part recognize it today. In essence, long before there was Shirley MacLaine, there lived Dana Howard and Gloria Lee, two star-studded ladies who set their sights high and traveled to the stars, either for real or in their ahead-of-their-time imaginations.

As it turns out, one of these two women who involved herself in these ultra-terrestrial escapades seems to have attracted something incredibly beautiful and very extraordinary into her life, while the second individual's days ended tragically, either at her own hands due to her lack of responsibility, or because her alien contacts were not what they represented themselves to be.

Dana Howard's contacts may well have been angelic, "from the light," while those of Gloria Lee might best represent the demonic rustlings of a fallen angel. Indeed, some see the UFO phenomenon in terms of a heavenly battle between good and evil, taking place on Earth as well as in the sky, the forerunner of Armageddon for all of humankind. In fact, it is Dana Howard who states early in this book: "The 'coming of the angels' has been shouted from every pulpit over the face of the globe. *Who* and *what* are these angels? Are they sprightly ethereal beings, winged like the birds and with a passion for harps? Or are they other-planetary teachers, clothed in celestial splendor – beings who have come unbidden to our beleaguered planet that they might better serve us, a lesser order of life?"

Dana was convinced that many alive today "will live to see it emblazoned across the morning skies commingled with the dazzling radiance of the sunrise. With trumpets and fanfare the New Age will be ushered in. When that wonderful moment arrives, those from ON HIGH will descend earthward. They will help to release all the human family to a new octave in living. 'And He shall send His angels with a great sound of the trumpet, and they shall gather together His elect from the four winds. . .'" (Matthew 24:31.)

Gloria Lee maintains that she was "trained" by the space visitors for a total of four years. She learned that they were invisible because they were "etheric" in nature and could not speak directly but only through telepathy because they had no vocal cords, not being flesh and blood like humans. Our favorite blogger Regan Lee (no relation to Gloria) tries to put the whole matter in the right perspective. Wherever your sentiments may rest, these two classic works from the Golden Age of Flying Saucers need to be preserved in an age that has lost a little bit of magic that can best be revived only by returning to the non-spoiled tone of a bygone era when space beings were, in spite of great frustration with our collective slowness to receive their message, attempting to guide us along the path to personal and universal salvation. Time alone will tell if they were in any way successful.

Now let us hear from Regan.

Timothy – "MR UFO" – Beckley

* * * *

Like contactee Ida Kanneberg, who channeled Sasquatch among the space beings, contactee Gloria Lee communicated with her space entity via automatic writing. And like contactee Elizabeth Klarer, Gloria Lee was also a pilot (though she was employed as a stewardess, as flight attendants were called in Gloria's time.) But unlike the majority of the contactees, Gloria Lee suffered a dark fate: she died while awaiting her space brother friend J.W. to arrive and remove her spirit/soul/consciousness from her self-inflicted coma.

Reminiscent of many of the contactees, male and female, in purported communication with Venusians or Jovians (Jupiter) or some other planet or star system, the message given to Gloria Lee echoed the messages of so many other entities from outer space. They were messages of universal love, of care for the Earth, of banishing fears and greed, of striving to reach a higher vibration. Only when humanity does all of that will we be saved from ourselves. These messages are the messages of the space aliens – if they are space aliens – that have been given to contactees over and over.

J.W. told Gloria he was from Jupiter. While Venus is often the home of Space Sisters and Brothers – contactee Dana Howard, for example, had magical meetings with Diana, whose home planet was Venus – Jupiter hosted Gloria's space creature, a space creature who remained unseen but whose words were "heard" in the mind of Gloria Lee who, as "The Instrument," as Gloria called herself, recorded his words for our world to read. J.W. could not communicate with speech for, as he told Gloria, he lacked vocal cords. Telepathy was the mode of information sharing between entity and human, which seems to be the preferred method for space aliens in many other instances as well.

And while Jupiter was home base in the relationship between J.W. and Gloria, Venus still played her part. For, as Gloria reported, "J.W. has mentioned that I incarnated from the planet Venus," and promised that when "the Instrument is finished . . . she will return to Venus." This contrast in planetary symbolism is interesting. Jupiter represents the paternal, the "father," and an authoritative voice of consciousness (as J.W. portrayed himself), while Venus represents the female, love, a feminine spiritually. Gloria's space brother communications were of both worlds. The moon also figures in Gloria's adventures, as a sort of limbo or holding area for consciousness.

There were warnings of doom and death, humanity in the cold grip of fear at what was to befall Earth and her inhabitants, who could not, or would not, raise themselves up to the proper vibratory state. That would require love and the rejection of fear and greed. It would require knowledge of the seven ethers, that all is one, that the flesh is a mere husk that houses spirit. Openness to the higher: the higher state of being, of consciousness, of mind, of desire. We've heard it before from so many of the contactees. All the Earth's ills and humanity's woes are due to our own fears, mistrust, and blindness to something greater than ourselves. We can only be raised up (literally, in saucers) when we raise our consciousness. And, while these tenets are nothing different from the usual contactee lore, and are thinly disguised religious doctrines, one obvious parallel can be made to The Rapture. There is some truth in these paternal platitudes. (Jupiter as male energy.) As we've seen with other Contactee messages, their relayed prophecies are often eerily accurate.

Gloria Lee was driven to share her message, and she was a popular contactee with a large following. Her Cosmos Research Foundation continued after her death. And in the morbid and mercenary aftermath of Gloria's death, others claimed to be in contact with her postmortem. The Mark-Age Metacenter in Miami, Florida, published small books of Gloria's channeled words, which were communicated to a woman calling herself "Nada-Yolanda." ("Nada" means nothing in Spanish.)

Gloria took her channeled designs of a space station platform, along with her message of a new spiritual life for humanity, to the United Nations, where she was rejected. And it was then that Gloria Lee's life energy began to slip away. She began a "protest fast," telling her followers that when she entered the coma state, her consciousness would be taken over and released to higher realms. After starving in a hotel room for sixty-six days, she was admitted into George Washington University Hospital where she died on December 3, 1962.

What to make of Gloria Lee? It is easy to dismiss her story as one of UFOlogy's darker episodes, and to see her as nothing more than an unstable individual who believed herself to be in communication with an alien. Maybe so. However, it is possible J.W. was "real" and an entity – though not necessarily from Jupiter or any other planet – but an entity nonetheless, one who entered our world via the invitation of a seeking mind. In our haste to dismiss those who find themselves lost while seeking hope as they try to escape the daily horrors they see around them, we also dismiss the possibility that there are non-human entities afoot who manipulate us and have been doing so for thousands of years. Some are idle manipulations, almost harmless, even entertaining, but seemingly pointless. Others are malevolent, either by their intent or by some negative symbiotic interplay with humans.

It is interesting that Gloria Lee was a pilot and a flight attendant, sharing with many contactees professions that involved either flying or its mechanics. Gloria saw flying saucers before her contacts with J.W. (Like many other contactees, she heard a voice telling her to look up; a flying saucer was waiting for her to notice its presence in the skies above her.) Her husband, William H. Byrd, was an aircraft designer. Did the saucers, or the intelligences operating them, respond to Gloria's psyche in some way, allowing whatever who, or what, "J.W." was into her mind? Was this energy known as J.W. created in part by others as well? Gloria had joined a "psychic development class;" some of her fellow psychics said they had seen J.W. near Gloria via telepathic images. Gloria herself wrote that she never saw J.W. except as "a manifested light form, by my own psychic power." A common interdiction in myth is the idea of invitation: the entity cannot enter unless it's invited. Did Gloria Lee unknowingly invite (for such invitations do not need to be overt) J.W. into her life, and thus into her mind?

What was this energy experienced by Gloria Lee, and other contactees? If not literal space aliens, is it possible these beings have nothing to do with ETs but are posing as space aliens for our benefit? Or, for their own entertainment? Forteans and UFO researchers such as John Keel, Jacques Vallee, Philip Imbrogno and Nick Redfern have theorized that spirits – call them what you will, Djinn, Ultra-terrestrials, tricksters, demons – are responsible for what we call "aliens." Was J.W. one of these darker entities who ultimately gave Gloria Lee not love and peace, but a cold and lonely death on December 2, 1962, at the age of 37? Or does the airplane-engineering-contactee link have something to do with the manipulations of shadow government groups? Who was Hedy Hood, the woman Gloria met in Washington and who was present during her hunger strike? The contactee realm is sometimes fraught with much intrigue.

There is a poignant irony to Gloria's story: on the back of the dust jacket of the original Why We Are Here! is a black and white photograph of Gloria; in that photo she is wearing a large Egyptian ankh. The ankh has many meanings but its main symbolism is clear: life.

Regan Lee - orangeorb.blogspot.com/
April 2011
Eugene, Oregon

DIANE

SHE CAME FROM VENUS

by

DANA HOWARD

DIANE
She came from Venus

DANA HOWARD

DIANE

SHE CAME FROM VENUS
BY DANA HOWARD

Dana Howard's fame as an authoress is based on her profound mystical knowledge of this age. Her deep and true understanding of many of the problems that beset mankind and the amazing experience she has had in her contacts heralding the coming of interplanetary communications are told in the wonderful story of Diane—She came from Venus.

CHAPTER I

ALL over the world an auspicious *new day* is dawning. A triumphant spiritual victory is soon to be won. Many earthlings will live to see it emblazoned across the morning skies comingled with the dazzling radiance of the sunrise. With trumpets and fanfare the New Age will be ushered in. When that wonderful day arrives those from ON HIGH will descend earthward. They will help to release all the human family to a new octave in living. "And He shall send His angels with a great sound of the trumpet, and they shall gather together His elect from the four winds . . ." Matt. 24 : 31.

The " coming of the angels " has been shouted from every pulpit over the face of the globe. *Who* and *what* are these angels? Are they sprightly etherial beings, winged like the birds and with a passion for harps? Or are they other-planetary teachers, clothed in celestial splendor—beings who have come unbidden to our beleaguered planet that they might better serve us, a lesser order of life?

Since 1947 when so-called *flying saucers* began to appear in great numbers in our skies, many intelligent earthlings have had a radical change of mind. Static viewpoint has given way to wonderment. Many of us like to think of these superior ones as being human like ourselves . . . perhaps further along on the roadway of life. It is possible they have been supervising our growth and development from the days of our turbulent beginnings to our present state of civilization. Perhaps the lights from their candles have never ceased burning . . . or buried deep in the archives of their holy temples our own New Age Charter was drafted. In other words : " Are they not all ministering spirits sent forth to minister for those who shall be the heirs of salvation? " Heb. 1. 14.

We are living in momentous days. There is a supreme moment in the heart of each new cycle, and many believe that moment is here now. Anything can happen from a little miracle to a big miracle. It can happen today, it can happen tomorrow or it can be postponed for many more centuries. It is up to us. Those who were accorded an earthly existence at the beginning of this great epoch, and those who will be permitted to live in the shadow of its close, are indeed the favored ones. It is at the commencement and conclusion that the universal dials are set.

The time between is filled with the loitering expansion of the forward march.

At the gateway to every major cycle there is a beacon light to pilot the way. Throughout the long centuries of recorded events a few earthlings have watched the flutterings of that celestial candle. Today signs and omens are coming to us in ever-increasing numbers. The minute hand of destiny is leading us toward that exalted goal. Mystics aver that the coming of strange spacecraft to our skies is the most significant event since the birth of Christ.

Think what it will mean to this muddled world when the avenues of space have been conquered! When we can be certain other planets are peopled with beings like ourselves! But more memorable than all, when we can embrace their wonderful way of life.

Always out of the great mass of humanity there are the challenging few who must go on ahead. They are the torch-bearers. These chosen ones, the weavers of destiny are the ones in whom we must place our faith and our trust. They make up the warp and the woof of the fabric of *tomorrow*.

There is a turning point in every human life . . . a time when some paramount decision must be made. The turning point in your author's life came sixteen years ago when she first stepped out of a holocaust of sacred fire and was " ostensibly " teleported to the Planet Venus. That this might be more clearly understood by new readers, I quote a passage from the first book recently published —MY FLIGHT TO VENUS.

" I leaped to my feet as if to herald in some cosmic drama. Then IT came, starting at my ankles like a gorgeous display of lighted fireworks . . . a transcendant violet flame that fanned out until it enveloped my body like an aura of sacred fire. As the flame grew in intensity, extending over a wide periphery, it raced through every cell cleansing and purifying as it went. Channels of my mind that had been tightly closed before opened up like an enchanted lotus flower. I was vibrant, magnetic and I could feel the effervescence of an enthusiasm I had never felt before. My heart beating in rhapsodic rhythm was tuned in now with the heartbeat of the universe. I was no longer a citizen of a little inhibited world, but a guest in the World Universal. I was no longer a separate entity, a human personality, but a part and parcel of every inch of God's glorious creation. In that moment I knew as others before me have known, the true meaning of the UNITY and the ONENESS of ALL."

6

Since the inauguration of the "flying saucer era" many have claimed to have made contact with strange spacecraft. Some contend they have met these visitors from other planets, face to face. Sightings by the thousands have been catalogued in public records. Countless more thousands have seen "something" in the skies, but have never reported the happening. It is apparent of course, a large percentage of these accounts can be discredited but this still leaves a substantial number of sightings unaccounted for. Countless hundreds of intelligent persons could not easily mistake whirling silvery discs and brilliantly lighted craft travelling at lightning-like speed, for cosmic vapors and frivolous seagulls. Yet, this is just what our would-be superiors would like to make us believe.

Today, even the "sightings" have had to go underground. Spectacular happenings in our skies seldom reach our newspapers or other news-dispatching mediums. The reasons are apparent and some of them are justifiable and sound. We earthlings have not been cultured to meet a superior order of being. We have waded through centuries of conditioning weighted down with the warring instinct. A traditional chip on our shoulder, a gun and saber in our holster, we deem it would not be proper and fitting to meet them as friends.

This could be the reason they are seldom seen except in the barren wastes of the desert and in other lonely, isolated spots. It might also be the occasion for them being seen by the lowly ones and not our top-bracket "brass". The lowly ones have played no great rôle in the "bomb-happy" world. The lowly spirit has been their "shield and buckler" against the ego's hateful seeds coming to fruition. Those who claim to have seen the saucers at close range, or allege they have ridden in them are grateful and appreciative for these golden nuggets mined from higher lands. These moments of other-worldly grandeur could not be wrenched from them on the highest hangman's rope. The discs in the skies might disappear forever, but in their hearts their own singular experience will never be erased. The skeptics and the die-hards will shout to the heavens it is all a myth but those who have seen for themselves will never change their minds. They go around with a smile on their lips for they know when transition time comes; perhaps long before that day the skeptics too will have seen for themselves. They will quickly forget they ever doubted or ridiculed.

Skepticism is always present when changes are eminent. To be jarred loose from preconceived convictions is vexing and painful.

Fearing both God and man the die-hard groups hesitate to venture over virgin soil. They are skeptics only because they refuse to weigh the evidence. They are with us now and they will always be with us and so we can forget them. Over the face of the earth today, thousands are beginning to embrace the hopeful thought that in the not-too-far-distant-future we will be travelling from planet to planet. Then we will no longer be obliged to depend upon visions, inspired messages, hit-and-miss physical contacts. That which seems mysterious to us now will be commonplace. We are a people prone to dub all revolutionary happenings as fantastic, but in the end this illusionary phenomena usually turns out to be the genuine reality.

Your author's first eye-view experience with flying discs occured one day in mid-August 1952. I quote from an addendum attached to the back of MY FLIGHT TO VENUS.

"Driving my car out on the desert near Cabot's Old Indian Pueblo, Desert Hot Springs, California, my attention was suddenly captured skyward. Silhouetted against the red and gold of the fading sunset I saw the exact replica of the gem-studded spaceship that years before had flown me to Venus. It was of leviathan size and perfect in every detail. Some distance above the mother ship and making a pragmatic square in the heavens, were four silvery discs. Out over the broad expanse of violet-tinted desert they looked like shiny moons. From my vantage point high above the village I could clearly discern lines of radiation extending from the larger craft to the smaller discs. It was quite apparent the discs were being re-fueled by means of solar radiation."

Surely this offers some ray of hope in our world of magnified atom madness. How much more secure we would feel knowing these superior ones have been sent to us to help absorb our nauseating stupidities? To assist us over the threshold of the new cycle ahead.

These are the sparks from the central flame. As we march onward toward the New Age we will witness the spectacular and the bizzare in epic proportions. Transiting this cyclic change means changing everything upon the earth . . . perhaps transforming the face of the earth itself.

CHAPTER II

EVERY great sage has said: "There is nothing in the universe impossible of accomplishment." Every philosopher and mystic has declared: "Whatsoever the human mind can imagine, it can ultimately achieve."

Creation and re-creation is as simple as that. The will to create is actualized throughout all Nature. It is behind the science of all predictive arts. We know that every psychical experience comes to us from the reservoir of the unknown, but it is none-the-less real for it portends the coming of future events. When the mind is properly attuned it captures the universal flow of life. One day science will realize there is nothing supernatural, but only higher arcs of the natural exemplified.

The coming of Diane, that lovely lady from Venus, the world might call an experience in the "miraculous", yet this strange happening proves there are points of specialization somewhere out in space. While the *modus operandi* of such a phenomenon is still beyond ordinary comprehension it can be intelligently explained.

Your author first made contact with DIANE in June 1939. I quote from MY FLIGHT TO VENUS:

"Still wrapped in the warm intoxication of the spirit, my vision was directed to a gnarled old tree overlooking the antedeluvian hills. Leaning casually against the grotesque trunk was a woman being of unsurpassed loveliness. Her head was radiant with a crown of fire, strands of golden hair cascading gently over her beautiful, slightly olive-tinted shoulders. The strange mystic light flooding her dark, prophetic eyes, added a wistful something to all her other charms.

"I seemed to glide on rhythmic feet toward this lovely creature as though she were expecting me. She smiled her welcome.

"'Have no fears, Child of Earth,' she intoned. 'Let the doors of your mind be opened and we of the faraway planets will speak to you in poetry and song. . . .'"

"It was then I observed for the first time a beautiful rocket-shaped ship suspended in mid-air about three hundred feet from the earth. It was beyond mortal words to describe. In the main it seemed to be constructed of some sort of translucent materials, but trimmed in gold, and gem-studded. An almost invisible ladder extended from the ship to the earth, and I obediently followed the radiant being up the filmy stairs without questioning. Once aboard, my sacrosant companion vanished, and I never saw her again."

On April 29, 1955, DIANE returned. This is how it happened:

Reverend Bertie Lillie Candler, proclaimed by many as the greatest physical medium of the world was holding a private seance at the Church of Divine Light, 837 South Parkview Street, Los Angeles, California.

I had never attended a materialization seance before, and my inquiring mind asked all sorts of questions. As my cerebral atoms whirled with curiosity toward the close of the meeting the "little white church" seemed to me, electrified with a powerful vibration. Then—some ten or twelve feet from the draped-off area where Reverend Candler was in deep trance I saw a rising glow of phosphorescence. It was very tall at first, but out of this phosphorescent substance a form began to manifest itself. She was definitely different from the other "spirit" manifestations, a solid, fleshly being, delicate in charm and manner.

She called for DANA. Overwhelmed with emotion I could not choke back, I went up to her, standing only inches away from the manifestation. While I did not recognize her instantly, I knew there was something quaintly familiar about her. Standing like a sylph-like goddess, and bowing low in greeting to the twenty-seven persons present, the rich tones of her voice vibrated through the little church.

"I AM DIANE. I COME FROM VENUS."

Once adjusted to the vibrations she dwindled in size until I judged her to be about five feet tall. As she tossed back her well-shaped head revealing her perfectly chiseled features, there was no mistaking her identity. She was the same "being of unsurpassed loveliness" who sixteen years earlier had escorted me to the waiting spaceship.

I was speechless at first, my thoughts tumbling over one another. I finally managed to say:

"Are you my mentor . . . the person who has been giving me those wonderful discourses?"

She answered: "Yes. *This is the first time we of the greater planets have been permitted to come to beings of earth.* From now on we *shall be with you, always.*"

Diane then went into a few moments of profound discoursing the content of which I could not recall later. Before taking her leave, as if to reassure me that she was *not* an imposter, she placed a corner of her jewel-bedecked garment in my hands that I might feel the texture of the fabric—materials I quickly identified as Venusian.

She then went into a beautiful, rhythmic dance described by one onlooker as " The rhythm of the ocean waves." She finally bade us all good night and with her fragile hand on my shoulder she melted into the nothingness.

Lucile Points, of Los Angeles, one of the questers present on that memorable night says of the event:

" I have had the opportunity of sitting through many materialization seances, but I shall *never* forget one particular evening this Spring when Reverend Bertie Lillie Candler had one of her very interesting and inspiring seances.

A beautiful, fleshly being came, rather hesitantly at first, then saying, ' I am Diane. I come from Venus.' Since I was sitting next to the draped-off place I greeted this beautiful one asking : ' With whom do you wish to speak? ' She replied softly : ' I wish to speak with Dana.'

Dana Howard stepped up to her, but recognition was not instantaneous. Dana asked : ' Do I know you? ' Diane replied : ' Why yes, my dear. I have been with you before. I came for you when you made your flight to Venus.'

Mrs. Howard then asked her if the discourses she had been receiving since the publication of her book had been coming through her. Diane answered :

' Yes. I have been trying to help you write the experiences you had on Venus.'

She gave such an interesting talk with so much love and with a soft, yet powerful voice. She then gave us somewhat of a Butterfly Waltz as if floating on wings, her full-flowing jeweled gown shining in the phosphoresent light.

Yes, truly I can say this was the most outstanding experience of my life."

Lucile Points.

Mrs. Gladys Campbell of Alhambra, California and her friend Mrs. Maude Haas both of whom were present that night have made a joint statement.

"On April 29, 1955, the writer, Mrs. Gladys Campbell and my friend, Mrs. Maude Haas, attended a materialization seance at the Church of Divine Light, 837 South Parkview Street, Los Angeles, California . . . the medium being Reverend Bertie Lillie Candler of Florida, one of the foremost materialization mediums of this country.

"I am more than happy to give an account of what I witnessed to the best of my recollection, and you will recall when you spoke at the Pyramid Church in Alhambra the following Sunday after the visit, I was the one who got up and verified your statements concerning the visit of Diane.

"It was truly a marvelous thing to be present and see for myself such a wonderful personality, and I know you must be very humble and gratified to have the facts that you brought before the public in your book—'My Flight to Venus', substantiated in such an unexpected manner."

Mrs. Gladys Campbell,
Mrs. Maude Haas.

The following letter from L. M. Cahill is still more explanatory :

Dear Dana Howard,

"I have for many years, engaged in private research entirely separate and apart from my profession, into the possibility of the existence of many natural laws that effect or control the earth and its people.

Such investigation and study have occasionally brought me into contact, during their lifetimes, with many persons engaged in various scientific activities, including Millikan, of the California Institute of Technology, Whitmore of the University of California and Father Rikard of the University of Santa Clara.

I have also carried my investigations and studies into the works of or records of many persons, including Jeans, Flammarion, Thompson, Kahn, Crookes, Lodge, Crandon, Prince and of Jesus of Nazareth as reported in the New Testament.

I have occasionally given some thought to the possibility of greater scientific proof of the existence of the earth entity after death and that there may exist a law of communication which would have application not only to persons living on other planets, but also to those who once were known as persons here, but who might be living in a different form at places not known to us now.

Upon being informed last winter that the great materializing medium, Rev. Bertie Lilly Candler, had agreed to leave her church at Miami, Florida, for several weeks in April, 1955, for the purpose of acting as visiting pastor to the Church of Divine Light at Los Angeles at the request of its pastor Rev. Beulah Englund; I decided, in furtherance of one stage of my work, to seek permission to witness one or more of the materialization meetings that it was believed would be held while the Reverend Candler was here.

Such permission having been granted, I was privileged to witness over a number of months, the materialization of many so-called " dead " entities who appeared in Reverend Englund's church through the power of Reverend Candler, and not only talked audibly to their relatives, but who walked and danced and sang songs.

After viewing and listening to 500 or more of such materialized spirit entities, and after talking personally to twenty or more such entities, I am of the opinion that the entity " DIANE " that appeared to you on April 29th, 1955, during a meeting where Reverend Candler was functioning was an entirely different entity than the others. The difference is hard to describe but I will do the best I can.

She was in human form. A beautiful female dressed in white. Yards and yards of soft flowing material that gave the impression of chiffon. I was soon to realize however, that underlying the white material or possibly underlying part of same was a distinct blue effect.

I heard the entity speak your name and saw you move out of the group of approximately thirty men and women present and approach her. The first word I heard her say was " Diane ". Then followed some conversation in low tone and as I recall it she said : ' Diane is my earth name '.

The entity then moved very gracefully forward and toward the center (from the side lines) of the church and performed a dance of a type or style of which I had no previous knowledge. The motion was rolling, as of ocean waves; the body was moving in a rolling motion and in what appeared to be an arc, or a series of such. The dancing continued for about one minute and the entity after what appeared to be a final word to you, disappeared as suddenly as she had appeared.

I would be very foolish to attempt to describe the beauty of this entity or the graceful rhythm of her dancing or the perfume that so definitely followed her. I do not care for the commonly used phrase 'out of the world' but that is what it appeared to me and to those present.

I believe I am well on the road to being able to place before others, if requested, a scientific explanation of all of the other entities, but as to this one I do not have even a sound theory for the present.

Sincerely yours,

L. M. Cahill.

A final statement from Reverend Beulah Englund should prove conclusively that Diane was not an ordinary materialization—but something beyond the scope of knowledge of all those present.

Dear Dana Howard,

This is to state that I have known Reverend Bertie Lilly Candler for many years and can honestly vouch for the authenticity of her work. She has worked in my church many, many times and has drawn her audiences from the highest brackets of society, doctors, lawyers, educators—and just plain every day folks.

I consider what happened at my church on April 29th a miracle. I no longer look upon it as a church but as a shrine that will help many people with their problems.

My only regret is I missed part of Diana's appearance. It was growing late and two or three of my guests had to leave by way of the back door to go home. When I returned I saw the beautiful woman standing there, and knew that nothing like it had ever come before. I sincerely believe it was not a spirit apparition as the others had been—but a physical being from another planet. Whether she was teleported direct from Venus or whether she came from one of the spaceships seen by members of the Air Force over Mrs. Howard's home town at the same time she appeared in my church . . . I do not know. I *do know* this is the greatest privilege Rev. Beulah Englund will have in this lifetime.

Sincerely,

Reverend Beulah Englund.

The appearance of the lovely Diane in the "little white church in Los Angeles" is only one side of the miracle that occurred on April 29, 1955. Out on the desert where your author resides during resort season, another miracle had happened. Mrs. Barbara MacDonald, a member of the Ground Observation Corp, a civilian agency attached to the Air Force reported that her skywatchers had broadcast four strange ships seen high in the desert skies during the week of Diane's visitation. There was no chance for error here . . . no exaggerated rumors, for all sightings were the result of observers detailed to duty, Air Force volunteers whose task it is to spot and report any unusual happening or any alien ship seen in the skies. These skywatchers, working different shifts, all gave the same account. Mrs. McDonald reports that H. A. Mooney, a young man well trained in sky phenomena and only recently out of the Navy, stated he saw a huge ship very high over the desert skies and travelling at a startling rate of speed. Although the ship was of gargantuan size there was no tail fire and it was absolutely noiseless. Mooney stated it revealed a long row of odd-looking portholes from which streamed radiant fire. It vanished into nothingness before his eyes.

Mrs. McDonald further relates that a few nights later, Jan Carlyle, secretary of a prominent Palm Springs attorney, another duly appointed skywatcher, reported a similar happening. This ship was virtually the same in appearance. It was described as unusual in size—the same long row of portholes and travelling at fabulous speed. It too was noiseless. Repeating substantially the same story as young Mooney, the ship vanished into thin air while the watcher's eyes were upon it.

Again Mrs. McDonald tells of another similar incident. Rickey Anderson, another skywatcher and a decided unbeliever in the "saucer theory", reported a few nights later the appearance of two such ships traversing the desert skies. He described the light streaming from the portholes as a luminous blue-white light. The ships were travelling in an easterly direction and he followed them over the little town of Thousand Palms, California, but like the others they disappeared into the invisible beyond.

Your author has been reliably informed that all four sightings have been duly classified by the Air Force as "unidentified flying objects."

Again, a few nights later the townspeople of Desert Hot Springs, California, a health resort located ten miles from Palm Springs, were alerted by a different kind of craft. Flying the skies, almost directly over my home, Joe and Marian Merrick made this sighting report: /

" It was 7 o'clock in the evening," say the Merricks. " We were sitting on our front porch when suddenly we saw a strange object in the sky, the forepart of the ship a huge orange disc, the tail portion made up of blue-green lights which seemed to flash a luminosity over the desert sky. It was broad daylight and visability over the broad expanse of open desert made the sighting stand out in *bas relief*.

" We watched it for quite a long time. There was no wind. A quiet still desert evening. Then as suddenly as it appeared it took off at great speed and disappeared into thin air."

Joe and Marian Merrick,
Desert Hot Springs, California.

This sighting was confirmed by countless other individuals but I quote from the lips of Mrs. Agnes Gentile who has been a desert resident for many years and familiar with desert sky phenomena.

" I was out of doors with the children," says Mrs. Gentile. My little granddaughter saw it first. She looked upward and screamed. There was this fantastic thing—a huge ball of orange fire with a long tail of brilliant blue-green light. It so frightened the children they ran screaming into the house."

Alice Gentile.

Now comes the poser, where did these strange ships come from? Are there transporting currents in the atmosphere about which our scientists know nothing? Will voyaging to the stars be a commonplace when we learn these secrets? Again . . . was the lovely Diane " teleported " from one of these ships or did she come over the clouds from Venus? Are the ships equipped with some sort of mechanism capable of rendering them invisible as it would appear? Perhaps teleportative methods is the answer to their sudden appearance and the same abrupt disappearance. There seem to be no differing accounts in this particular. Their speed and maneuverability is beyond our comprehension. They seem to flash through the skies with lightning-quick velocity, then without a wave of warning, dissolve into nothingness.

Is this the way God works his miracles? Is this something we might hope for out of our own illimitable future?

CHAPTER III

WHERE are these strange sky ships coming from? This is a question I am asked repeatedly. From many and varied reports they seem to range in size all the way from a child's toy to leviathan craft. It is not wholly convincing to earthlings that the smaller ships at least, could battle air waves across millions of miles of space. Science cannot answer the question any more conclusively than the layman. At this point we can only theorize. To be able to think without prejudice we must be able to view psychism, not as some sort of bewitching magic, but a genuinely real science . . . the doors of perception opened up to the flow of divine vision.

It is ever the urge of the soul to know itself. If we remain fair to ourselves it is not difficult to believe that buried deep in the heart and soul of every living being is that unconscious desire to penetrate the deep abyss of the unknown. This means we must let the seers and the mystics lead the way. They *know* because some time in their lives they have made touch with *knowing*. The mystic sees through divine binoculars. He is discerning in his knowledge of the universe for his perceptions have been enlarged to embrace the unknowable.

The story of Mount Shasta has been told and re-told but to this day it still remains the unsolved enigma of the north-west United States. Perhaps even this riddle can now be solved through the coming of flying saucers. It is not only possible, but probable that Mount Shasta and other high consecrated points on our globe are the actual conditioning stations for visitors from outer space. It would seem like sound reasoning logic to assume that voyagers from other planets upon first coming into our earth's orbit would have to be conditioned to our atmosphere. They would need to adapt themselves not only physically, but they would need to accomodate themselves to our thought processes. We earthlings learn to conform even in small ways. Interplanetary visitors would necessarily have to harmonize and fit into the lowered vibration of our earth.

I quote another passage from MY FLIGHT TO VENUS:

"I recall distinctly when I first put my foot on Venus I was attired in the robes of earth, but it was all so different. My whole being seemed to be made up of rarified essences. My personal appearance had changed. With the heightened vibrations there

17

was a radiance, an alphabet of quality I had never known on earth."

While this is extraneous to average intelligent thinking, we must realize we are living today in the greatest era the human race on this planet has ever known. This takes us out of bounds of the usual and forces us to round new corners. It brings us ever closer to events that make the stars stand still. However, once we are irrefutably convinced these so-called flying saucers are coming from outer space, we will then be able to accept the star-standing-still events without quibble or question.

This is where the hitherto unsolved mystery of Mount Shasta might shed some small measure of light over the broad scope of doubt. For several hundred years past, the tall, pine-treed cliffs of Mount Shasta have held inviolate a secret believed by many to embrace a long-dead tradition. There are geologists and other men of science who proclaim it the oldest land on earth—a consecrated plot cut off from that mythical continent known as Lemuria. It is believed by many that in some miraculous way this plot of earth escaped the cataclysms of long ago.

For many years Mount Shasta has been the object of serious investigations not only by the few steeped in occult lore and traditional romanticism, but by scientists, the press, educators and just good neighbors living in the valleys beneath the high peaks. Untold numbers have given evidence that on occasions too numerous to mention they have seen streams of blue-white light emanating from the Shasta heights. These lights appeared long before Thomas Edison gave us the electric light and it is said they often extended a beam as far south as the San Francisco Bay.

This ties in perfectly with the words of my charming Venusian host:

"There are many contact points on your Planet Earth," he said. "Points of ingress and egress from planet to planet. These are the pivotal points in universal consciousness because here the fragmentary remains of great continental histories are stored away in secret archives."

Researches assert the State of California is posited on very old land. In fact it has often been called "the cradle of humanity" and not a few believe it to be the actual site of that fabulous Garden of Eden. Relics have been unearthed from one end of the state to the other that take us back into an almost extinct past. California's rare old trees, the Sequoia and the Redwoods, to say nothing of an unusual specimen of Frankincense Tree found growing a few short years ago in the Borrego Desert. Enough substantiating facts can be gathered together to bear evidence that California might well have been the scene of the original paradise.

Mount Shasta is part of California's Noahian soil. This would make the peak of Mount Shasta the cone of an antedeluvian volcano. At the foot of the mountain buried deep in the rocks searchers have found more than twelve hundred feet of hieroglyphics that to this day have not been deciphered. These rock writings are said to be totally different from anything known to the long red line of American Indians.

In recent years, many persons living in the lower areas declare that in days gone by they often saw men of strange appearance in their midst. They have been described as tall and stately with an aura of maturity and wisdom about them that set them apart from other men.

The neighbors report blue-white lights glowing through the tall pine trees. For a time these beams of light created considerable excitement in press circles. In fact they were almost as provocative as flying saucers. Fabulous yarns have been spun about them— how, when the wind blew in a cetarin direction they often heard strains of wierd music and loud chants. Many of these same persons have gone on record as stating they have also seen fantastic sky ships floating in the skies around Mount Shasta. They have been described as " peculiar silver-like vessels " that appeared and disappeared. Occasionally one of these ships flew out over the Pacific Ocean. They have been seen by seamen all the way from the California coast line to the Aleutian Islands. And again, investigators by the score have been turned back from their investigative treks by some powerful invisible ray, always encountered at a given point in the high mountain climb.

It would seem within the scope of possibility that Mount Shasta and other pristinely clear points on our globe would be the conditioning areas for visitors from other planets, if in fact they are calling on us. While we may look upon them as a superior people, they are still human. Any foreigner coming into our country and land would have to accomodate to living conditions and the language. They too would have to do likewise.

All of this poses another question . . . were these strange-appearing men so often seen below the cliffs of Mount Shasta actually Venusians? Has Mount Shasta been one of their bases for more years than we know anything about? Your author challenges the fact that these strange beings are the direct descendants of the Lemurians. The pattern of our earth is one of ascendancy and descendancy. That which goes up, must come down. A flower blooms at its maturity; then it fades and dies. In other words, we must use a natural premise from which to springboard our reasoning. It would seem by the very laws of consanguinity they could not safely survive the decaying hand of time. In the course of thousands of years they would have ceased to evolve and would have degenerated. Though they may have survived tidal waves, earthquakes and whatever other catastrophe the earth had in store for them, they could not have escaped tradition's natural heritage.

In 1930, shortly before the passing of that grand Old Indian Chief, Francisco Potentio, your author interviewed him in the hope of discovering something new about the mystery of Mount Shasta. Chief Potentio, founder of the fabulous village of Palm Springs, and one of the surviving remnants of the old Cahuilla Tribe was then one hundred and eight years old. From him I first learned about the silvery ships that came and went from the highest point of the mountain.

" Sky ships come from Morning Star," the old chief said, pointing to the Planet Venus.

Again, if these strange people were in reality the last surviving sparks from a long lost continent now sunk beneath the waves, would they disappear for years at a time? Today one hears nothing about wierd music emanating from the Shasta Peaks, nor is there any mention of the odd-looking men seen a few years ago around Weed, California located in the valley below. If they are still there hidden in the deep-recesses of the mountain why do we no longer hear about them? Why have they gone into seclusion?

Then there is another point of view. If these people are in fact the last survivors of the Lemurians who can say how much or how little Lemurian blood flows in our own veins? During their long sojourn on this continent it is possible many of them deserted the little band and travelled into the valleys. It is even conceivable they might have comingled with the Red Men of that day. When the Pilgrim Fathers landed on our shores they were met by a highly evolved and friendly race of Indians. Perhaps they were the sons of the seeds left over from The Morning Star.

Sixteen years ago, when my soul embarked for the Planet Venus the point of departure was an equally enigmatic peak—Arizona's

Superstition Mountain. A so-called curse has hung over Superstition since our earliest recorded histories. Today it is impossible to count the numbers who have met with an unfortunate demise attempting to wrench from this mystic mountain the secrets of her gold and her treasures.

Superstition Mountain like all other hallowed spots on the earth appears to be always protected by some invisible mantle of power —a ray that in some strange manner prevents the footsteps of man from violating sacred soil.

Today we are bending our efforts in many directions in an effort to solve our world problems. If our issues are too difficult for us to solve alone it is logical to believe a superior order of life would be sent to help us. It is hard for most of us to realise that the very fabric of our earth's civilization is threatened. When we scoff and jeer at something we do not understand we are only holding back the hands of the clock. In the past our own stubborn fixations have prevented us from looking into the far horizons. Today the whole world is space-minded. We are beginning to realize we are all part of the same universal pattern. Whatever we are capable of " thinking " we can become proficient in *doing*. Whether we are aware of it or not we are ably equipped with invisible extension cords with which to make a definite tie with all the domains of existence.

If other planetary beings have come to endow us with new strength and a resurgence of faith it is not necessary that we wear some badge of identification. As strangers coming into our earth's orbit they would naturally exchange the robes of their sojourn for the robes of earth. While they might be instantly teleported to our planet unless they had been here before they would have the same adjustments to make as the newcomers. If they intended to remain for any lengthy stay they would have to adjust to our lowered vibrations. This might require years, hence they would need conditioning bases of the nature of Mount Shasta.

Let us not discredit that which we have not learned to understand. Perhaps the message they have to bring to us—is the very message for which we have been waiting these last two thousand years.

Interplanetary communication and travel would soon become a reality.

Whether we know it or not we can hasten that day. It all depends upon the consciousness we put into it. Do we want these wonderful Venusians to look upon us as undeveloped children? That we haven't grown up? If we will only give them the chance they can help re-mold our lives. From them we can absorb new strength and new faith.

Once we start working toward this new order we will find it the greatest thrill we have ever known. When we know *where* we are going we will be filled with new enthusiasm—new driving power. We'll race forward pushed by the rushing winds.

We can fall again, of course. Our histories prove we have failed many times. If we fail this time, when transition time comes our friends from ON HIGH will be forced to take over and finish our job. This would mean repeating the long cycle all over again. It might mean starting over again in a darkened world.

The keynote of Venus is *beauty*. The Venusians live for the beautiful in life. They believe that even the profane forms can be transformed by splendrous living. This should be good news for us. It means we need make no sacrifice to gain the greater values. It means only enhancing the luxurious and the grand.

If my extended vision can be used as a measuring rod, Venus is a pageant of fairyland—a fairyland filled with beautiful overtones and a pulsating vibrancy known only to the heightened consciousness. It is that ecstatic consciousness that is known and realized when time and space have been transcended.

I sincerely believe the coming of DIANE is in the interests of our destiny—that she is one of the chosen sent to this earth to help usher in the glad tidings prophesied long eons ago. Every person present that night at the Church of Divine Light is in agreement that she was *not* the usual spirit manifestation. That she appeared at a public gathering is also understandable. Jesus said: "Where two or three are gathered together in MY NAME, there I shall be also." Diane appeared in a house of worship. Our churches are dedicated to the uniting of consciousness in prayer and devotion.

Reverend Bertie Lillie Candler bears an inter-national reputation. She is among the elite in her class. Fortunately there were no doubters present to spill a negative influence. It would seem pre-destined this place had been selected to prove to earthlings that it is possible to manipulate consciousness in the same fashion a potter

worn out concepts and unfold the creatively new. I sincerely believe the Venusians can help bring a new spiritual significance to the Planet Earth. As a matter of fact, this is their plan and purpose. If we are willing to put forth the proper effort we will doubtless wake up some fine morn and find the adamantine walls between the worlds dissolved into nothingness. The dawning of that wondrous future is no more remote than the day Christopher Columbus set out across the deep blue waters, new worlds to conquer. The people of that day were fearful of the outcome. They pondered over this mad adventurer's perilous journey. Columbus did not find the lands he set out to discover—but he did find America.

The oceans of the world have been conquered. World sights are set on conquering the airways of space. But the same apprehension exists today as in all times past. Thousands are seeking the same question. Can it be done? Will it come in my lifetime? These and a myriad more questions are on every tongue.

They are questions that can only be answered by those who have developed the faculty of "looking beyond". Only they can reach over the invisible horizons where designs and plans are cached away. Only they can draft the new-age patterns.

It is much easier than we think, really. When we look down the long vista of yesterday and see the feats man has accomplished in a short few hundreds of years, we know that any new goal is just another challenge. If we can mutate a cycle without the grinding of gears, without sorrow or bloodshed, then anything at all can happen because we will have opened the door to miracles. However, should this change in cycles come while we are ill prepared, like in other times past, it will almost inevitably end in cataclysm.

Our Venus friends assure us of a better way of life. We are well aware of our great social need. If there is a more advanced way (and I am sure there is) why drag along on this beleaguered planet with its miseries and woes? Once we build a constructive consciousness it can happen in the "twinkling of an eye". The same rich experience known to the Venusians can be ours. But it must first be embraced vicariously. When we can embody the entire universe in consciousness we will then feel a stirring deep within for we will have opened ourselves up to the universal flow. This fresh challenge is the first major step forward. When that day arrives inventive genius will be awakened in countless individuals.

CHAPTER V

SUPREME moments come to us, but supreme moments are fleeting. They must be captured at the peak of the tide woven into the fabric of the garment of the day, else centuries may pass before conditions are right for them to come again. Supreme moments follow on the heels of prophesy.

When we piece together both facts and symbols we are reasonably assured that these intelligent ones from faraway planets have cast their influence over our earth many times in the past. But as DIANE said :

"THIS IS THE FIRST TIME WE OF THE GREATER PLANETS HAVE BEEN PERMITTED TO COME TO BEINGS OF EARTH." Does this mean there are many Venusians among us, walking the streets of earth?

When we research into the past we find that thirteen centuries before the birth of Christ the voice of Venus spoke through Ich-na-ton, known to historians as the mad Pharoah of Egypt. Aton, as his devout followers affectionately called him, tried mightily to impress the Egyptians of that day : there could only be peace when and where the brotherhood of man prevailed. Egypt was then in the childhood of the cycle. The preponderance of weight was on the side of evil. The Egyptians failed to heed their prophet. One of the bloodiest times in all history followed, bringing to dust one of the greatest civilizations our earth has ever known.

Before this time the ancient Egyptians had worshipped many gods. They had a god for every day in the week. Just as many of us today need images and symbols as a spiritual crutch, they too needed something before which they could prostrate themselves. They wanted to believe there was a divinity ready to grant every trivial wish and desire.

Ich-na-ton was perhaps one of the greatest psychics who ever lived. He received his divine instructions through the medium of vision. Each day he would go out into the blazing, sun-clad desert where he offered prayers to his ONE GOD. He knew there was but ONE GOD for his visions told him so. This God was everywhere present. He was in the trees, the flowers, the hills and the seas. He was buried deep in the hearts of the people. While many deemed Aton mad, still they loved him. As their ruler, Ich-

molds his clay. Diane possessed the ability to materialize and dematerialize at will. This should be a lesson in symbolism to us. For does it not symbolize that they are here to help us tear down our old structure and erect the new? They are the message-bearers of things to come. " I now create all things new. Former things shall not be remembered nor come to mind." Isa. 65 : 16.

CHAPTER IV

IN the vast scheme of life every level of manifestation is just as God meant it to be. But God never intended for us to become slothful and static. The value we take from life is the value we put into it. The sum total is the experience that is gained. We can only *know* as we *experience*.

In the past eight years a new type of being has come into existence. The flying saucer era has sharply divided the human family. There are those who believe whole-heartedly that we are nearing a complete mutation, and those who do not accept the fact that radical changes are in the making. The believers are the self-delegated pioneers. The wealth of consciousness generated by the devout can rapidly expand the scope of our objective. It can spread like a gargantuan mushroom into something far greater than any of us realize.

We dare not sell any of our pioneers short. Even that which seems to be sheer fiction can prove to be the spiritual threads that go into the weaving of greater things. From these golden threads new patterns are woven. Nor dare we ignore the fantastic or the illusory things of life for in so doing we are shutting out valuable knowledge and experience. We might not reach the identical goal we are seeking, but if we remain open-minded, ready to look and listen, investigate and outreach, at least we will have gained something valuable in our attempts. Outreaching toward the fantastic helps to develop senses long dormant. New senses are brought into play. There is greater accuracy in the reasoning processes when there is a conscious awakening and cooperative interplay between spirit and matter. In the final analysis who are we to say that our earth plane is all there is? Our Bible says: " In my Father's house are many mansions." In one of these mansions we are sure to find the plans of a new design for living and a still surer design for winning.

The Venusian concept is ONE UNIVERSE. In all of her marvelous discourses DIANE has inspired your author with the fact that by means of extended vision we can project to any part of the universe at will. In so doing we can touch the source-spring of " universals ". By extending our " thought forms " and acceding to higher and superior forces we can overthrow the old

na-ton gained many converts to this new belief. It wasn't easy.
For each believer there were two disbelievers. Then as now the
majority wanted to cling to that which they were used to. They
resented change and were willing to spill blood to keep the *status
quo.*

This did not deter the devout Aton and his zeal grew to boundless proportions. Day by day, true to his visions, he continued
his trek into the lonely desert for moments of sacred quietude with
his God. As he preached to them, for a time converts came rapidly.
He pleaded with them to believe in him.

"There is but ONE GOD," he preached fervently. "All others
are but His manifestation."

The harder he prayed the higher the evil gods reared their ugly
heads. The converts were separated from the incredulous by the
symbol they wore on their person, a symbol known to us today as
the *crux ansata* or *cross of life*. This circle with a cross beneath
it signifies that God is a sphere within which is embraced every
living thing. It was this *cross of life* that first brought your author
to the realization that the Venusians had brought their influence
to bear on the ancient Egyptians. In "my flight to Venus" I
noted this symbol in evidence everywhere. The Venusians display
the *crux ansata* as we display our national flag.

Aton told his people this new God would deliver them from their
fears. He would take away the darkness. "The heart of man is
dark," he said. "Many think they believe, but they do not know
the light when they see it."

The reign of the "mad" Pharoah was short-lived. In the end
much blood was spilled. The dark forces won out, and Aton went to
his couch of death a sick and disillusioned soul. Before he passed
into the beyond he told his people :

"My eyes have pierced all barriers as if they were barriers of
pure water. I behold the world that will come after me. In that
world is neither hatred nor fear. Men share their toil with one
another and there is neither sick nor poor among them. All are
brothers and war is banished."

Many centuries have passed and the words of Egypt's sage have
not yet come to pass. The seeds we are reaping today were sown
in the soil of Egypt at the beginning of this present cycle. Hearts
were "twisted and shadowy" then. They are "twisted and
shadowy" now. Each generation has gone around on the same
treadmill, the forces of good speared against the forces of evil.

By the same token, truth is the same yesterday, today . . . forever. It should mean something to us to see that as far back as the reign of Ich-na-ton, the Venusians, our next order of life, have been trying to impress and inspire us. In our hearts we know they cannot do the job for us. We must do it for ourselves.

Egypt fell because she refused to listen to the voice of Ich-nat-on. She fell because evil overpowered good. The Egyptian cycle was ushered in. It ran its gamut of destruction ending in the woeful downfall of a great empire. But we believe sincerely the dying words of Egypt's prophet will one day come to pass.

The Great Ich-na-ton was true to his ONE GOD to his dying breath but at the end he had but few loyal followers. These few remained loyal in their hearts but they were always careful to conceal the holy symbol away from the profane gaze of their enemies.

The spirit of the great Ich-na-ton is with us today. The seeds garnered from his unswerving faith have been born and re-born, generation after generation. His was a loyalty generously and honestly given. These self-same seeds are struggling to germinate in the little handful of believers today.

As in the early Egyptian times, Venusian influences are all about us. If we will but place our faith in that influence we will fly on wings of splendor to the domains of success. With belief in our hearts we will find the power to accomplish that which we set out to do. To those whose perceptions have been acutely awakened this sky pageantry is not a myth. It is a miracle in the evolution of progress. It is one of the wonders of our age. It can change the pattern of events drafted in our man-created universe. It will one day revolutionize our world.

This places the burden on the few who have made contact, either physically or otherwise. They should be relentless in their efforts to put the message across to the less fortunate. Many will listen if they are approached in the right manner. It is a wonderful feeling to know we are reinforced from beyond.

Henceforth there will be those who will come close at times, then again they will seem to be far away. Those who earnestly seek will receive help from beyond.

If the pattern of past times is followed out we cannot expect this help to continue forever. While they will always be there beyond the visible horizon to be contacted by those in tune, we cannot expect to have the continued warm camaraderie of their presence

those dreams come true. As the High Priest in the Temple of Venus told your author:

"Only this—our Planet Venus has known the fullness of perfection. But step by step each and every planet in the broad universal system must climb the golden stairs. Child of Earth . . . your America is the hope of your planet. She will rise to her greatness, a haven for all who seek rest. With the coming of the New Dispensation—America, the land that has housed so many races shall rise. Her banner of freedom shall wave in all its glory."

the glorious inheritance we shall one day enjoy. Few of us would want to go into their beautiful, nature-woven world with the scales of our own filthy debris clinging to our aura.

The Venusians came to the "mad Pharoah" in vision. They are coming to many in visions today. When we are prepared for them they will come in physical manifestation. They will come in numbers. They will walk among us, they will be one of us. Who can say, just as I was joined in holy matrimony with the noble LeLando, perhaps the women of earth will wed men of Venus, and vice-versa.

In the long interim of waiting some will heed, but we can still expect the majority to scoff and jeer. In the time between perhaps thousands of space ships will be built in readiness. And who can deny that perhaps thousands of human beings will be borne over the air waves just as countless millions were borne over the ocean's waves in the long forgotten days before our earth was destroyed. When that time comes perhaps millions of interplanetary beings will descend to earth. They will come in "the twinkling of an eye". "Whereupon are the foundations thereof, when the Morning Stars sang together and all the sons of God shouted for joy." Job 38 : 6,-7.

Those earthlings who are today ready and willing to make a place in their hearts for the teachings of Venus, should know no more anguish, no tear-stained struggle. They should thrill to the strange elixir coursing through their veins. Those who are willing to labor for a better way of life just as those who have toiled for the glittering stuff we call gold, will know the meaning of friendship and love. Each and every one of us will know that the span of our lives is not the measurement of existence—that it is only a tiny dot in the great whole. When we are cleansed right down to our ancestral taproots, that will be the day we will know brotherhood, not for the few, but for all humanity. It seems beyond the realm of possibility now, but once we set our sails to the four winds we will find we are possessed with a universal driving power that will carry us to the end of our sojourn. Just as the Venusians seemingly have learned to mold the plasms into any desired form, we too can manipulate skilfully the self-same plasms, for in the last analysis, plasm is nothing more nor less than "dynamically actuated consciousness."

Whether we believe it or not, this is all within the chainwork of our times. This means we can have our dreams and we can make

unless we avail ourselves of the opportunity before us today. If we hue to the line, travel to other planets might be much closer than we think.

Many are asking the question—was the Egyptian cycle the only evidence we have had of the coming of the Venusians? Let us think a moment! Midway between the Egyptian cycle and our modern times Christianity was ushered in. Signs and omens were in the heavens then, just as they are today.

Every church tenet has taught that the "birth of Christ cycle" was heralded by the maneuvering of a strange light across the heavens—The Star of Bethlehem it is called. This illumined star led the Three Wise Men to the cradle of the infant, Jesus. This poses another momenteous question in the minds of serious thinkers. Could the Star of Bethlehem have been a brilliantly lighted flying disc? It has been a mute question in the minds of ecclesiasts and laymen alike, for the Bible clearly states that the Star that led the Three Wise Men to the manger of our Lord was visible only over the holy city. It was not seen beyond the limits of the birthplace of Jesus. "And lo, the star which they saw in the East went before them 'til it came and stood where the young child was." Matt. 2 : 9.

Coming down to our own times our whole existence has been dominated by a passion for luxury, for things beautiful. Is this not a Venus-born desire? If your author's experience, whether teleportive or mystical, can be wholly relied upon (and I feel certain it can) we are still a far cry from Venus perfection, but no one can say we haven't made the effort. Men have braved every conceivable torture—they have risked their very lives to obtain gold with which to purchase luxuries. We have obtained ours the hard way, through greed and avarice. We have maimed and killed, then gleefully climbed over the dead bodies left in our wake. In the cycle we have lived through we lost our spiritual core. We have sought one goal that we might escape the goal behind us that was hateful to look upon. It has been progress of a sort but never have we known the true meaning of existence. We are constantly asking the question . . . why are we here . . . and where are we going? We have reached for classical cultures only to see them wither and die in our grasp. Throughout our long existence we have worshipped the superficial rather than the real.

Jesus said : " I go to prepare a place for you." Many want to believe that other planetary visitors are here to help prepare us for

CHAPTER VI

DESTINY is not an act of malice-aforethought. We create our destiny as we go along. It is created out of our thoughts and our acts. We are only fettered and chained as we fetter and chain ourselves. We often do it by accepting tradition's blind errors. Yet through all our gloomy thinking there is always a ray of hope.

The human mind is the open door between that which we *know* and that which we are seeking *to know*. The efficacy of our thought power determines the depth of the imprint. As we open up the floodgates we find that the mind harbors the concepts of fame, fortune and untold success, but it must remain free and unhampered. The mind is the conduit through which beneficient influences flow from one world to another. It is from these other worlds new knowledge streams in. If we are limited in one world—then we must learn to cooperate with the greater worlds.

Thoughts are the obsessing demons that take their toll at night. It is in the darkness of the unborn the destructive seeds germinate and are finally born into the light of day. This is where unity of thought comes in. When numbers can be gathered together in ONE THOUGHT—then there is power. When the world consciousness is impregnated with ONE THOUGHT, then slowly the world picture begins to change.

As we have noted in a previous chapter, the Venusian influence made its first deep groove long before our histories began to record. The casual threads woven then are still in existence today. When we can learn to distinguish the gold from the lead we can pick up those threads and weave them into the new fabric. World progression will be speeded up. Advancement will be rapid. If we are to believe the seers, those who came to birth at the beginning of this long cycle have already taken up residence on another planet. Is it not reasonable to assume that the new life is being made ready for us, too?

If we do not make preparation now we will have to repeat our lessons. Other cycles have been wiped out by terrestial floods. They too had to start all over again.

We have come a long way since then, but it has been a hard struggle. We have reached high water marks and we are headed for still higher marks. Today we have an opportunity to enjoy an

c

came from the lowly. He began life in a manger. Mohammet's world-spreading religion was inspired under the desert's white moon. Moses led the multitudes into the desert wilderness seeking for the Promised Land. All great religions—every long-lived philosophy has been born and bred in obscurity. Inspiration comes first through the lips of the prophet but it is the heart-shouts of the masses that keeps inspiration alive.

The coming of strange spacecraft will prove to be the turning point in many human lives. Many self-evident changes will come. The way will be paved for glorious new values. It is out of soul-fired enthusiasms that new worlds are built. As one cycle of experience is finished, word comes from higher planes. That "word" is with us today. It is the word we must be ready to accept.

One will hear it from the next-door-neighbor. Others will welcome the stranger who knocks on the door. Someone else will sight a "flying disc" or a brilliantly lit spaceship. Last but not least one might meet a stranger who in reality is a visitor from another planet. He might speak in our own tongue, or he might speak a soul language we all can understand. He might vanish before our very eyes—or he might leave by way of the door. No one knows "from whence the stranger cometh," whether from star-spangled space or the avenues of earth. Whether we hear it from the lips of the mighty or the shouts of the lowly, it matters not. If it can untwist humanity's heartstrings that is all we are concerned about.

Spiritual gifts are always to be found under the canopy of the heavens—in the clouds of the turquoise sky—and in consecrated places. "Life, liberty and the pursuit of happiness" is within the reach of us all.

would be sure to follow. Pandemonium would reign over the face of the earth. Many of us have not forgotten what happened when Orson Welles' MEN FROM MARS came over the air-waves. Why should this be so?

How many in our world of today would be willing to meet them peaceably? We would deem it our patriotic duty to start our own little war. This would be a natural consequence, for the warring instinct is stronger in the mass of humanity than the heart-throb of brotherly love.

This then is one of the major reasons why alien knowledge and extraneous experience must first be given to the isolated few. When the word is passed along by them the reception is imperceptibly slow. It infiltrates gradually and mass equilibrium is not disturbed. It is the way of the masses to align themselves with the majority . . . and the plurality in this case are the non-believers.

When the sharp blow of awakening is moderated, day by day the consciousness spreads. A few more begin to believe even if only with a small corner of their minds. Others are more willing to listen. A few more gather up the wisps and the whispers. Though they may be a far cry from being convinced they are beginning to be disturbed and at least they resent this disturbing element. Since they are neither attuned to the concords, nor completely out of tune with the jarring discords, they just want to be left alone to wallow in the *status quo* of their every-day living.

While this might seem like an upsetting state of affairs to those who want desperately to press on ahead this is how it should be at our present stage of progression. Those who believe—those who will accept the message from the unsung . . . they are the disciples. Like the followers of Jesus they become the genuine message-bearers, the sparks that eventually ignite into a holocaust of flame. These isolated few accept because they *know* that hidden somewhere in the arcs of the heavens a pattern for a new and better life has already been drafted. Consciousness is built first by the believing few, then the slow gathering of numbers.

It is your author's sincere belief that when the masses are ready many Venus-sent teachers will come to our earth. They will share with us their wisdom, their truth and their knowledge. In that day human beings will be brought together in a common bond of spiritual interest. This will be the healing remedy for all mankind.

We should never discredit the lowly and the unsung. Jesus

increased dimension in human understanding. We have done it by building consciousness first in the few, then in the many. We have lived within the circumference of the earth. Now we must extend beyond the earth. We can hope for something greater—we can pray for something greater . . . but we can only know it when we make direct contact. When we know it deep in our heart and soul then we can help others to be acutely aware in the same manner.

This means weeding out all negative thoughts. It means getting away from clinging doubts. It means cleaning out our minds, then helping our loved ones, our friends and our neighbors, to clean out theirs. The power of group thought is more powerful than the atom bomb, and certainly without the destructive results.

We can do this more readily when we begin to listen to the sibilant voices from the sky. All too often we have shut our ears to their warnings. Today is no different from yesterday. We still will not listen to the voices of our prophets. Only a scattered few over this broad earth of ours is ready and willing to give even a shred of credence to the happenings in the sky. " They are coming from Russia," many aver. " They're phantasmal illusions," cry others. Rather than trying to inculcate a ray of hope in the doubtful those in high places prefer to call the believers " crackpots " and " deluded fools ". Words of ridicule come from press and pulpit alike. One minister, a friend of your author, when told there might be something to the " saucer theory," became quite indignant. " No! No! " he cried in alarm. " It can't be so? What would happen to *our* religion? " And so it will go on and on until the flying discs in our skies are proved to be something more than meteorological phenomena or sprightly sea gulls.

Another question frequently asked from the platform is : " If flying saucers are real why do they appear to obscure individuals in isolated places."

Before Ich-na-ton, the "mad Pharoah", passed over the borderline, he told his people he had received a message from God. It seems God told him that never again would a world-shaking message be given to a ruler or one in high places. God saw the havoc and bloodshed that had come from bringing such a message to the reigning Pharoah.

Perhaps that is how it should be. Should the news of visitations from other planets be suddenly broadcast from every radio, headlined by the newspapers, depicted in drama on television, panic

CHAPTER VII

ARE we equal to this great task? Will we fall as Egypt fell? Can we this time adjust to the swiftly shifting scenes?

The first step is in delegating authority in those who believe. The sheepskin might be missing from the wall. They may not measure up in many ways, but any worthy human instrument fired with the message will help us get the job done. At the moment it is a job bigger than anything the human mind can conceive. We will proceed blindly at first but as changes begin to take place the road ahead will become straighter. Already the coming of the saucers has helped prepare us for this New Dispensation. When the boundaries between the planets are torn down new thoughts will stream in like sunshine after rain.

How will we know when the great change comes? It will be obvious in many ways. A friendly spirit will prevail. People will grow more tolerant. There will be an attitude of helpfulness that has not existed before. The change will be apparent in almost every person we meet. One day it will encircle the earth like a mammoth girdle. When the new viewpoint is launched in the body of humanity new patterns will be drafted—a road map all can follow.

There will still be alibi's . . . many of them. Some will blubber . . . " I don't know how." Others will cry : " I haven't the proper background." Still others . . . " I can't," etc. These deficiencies are bound to appear but even deficiencies can become opportunities. It means pushing through the decayed and crumbling floors of " world thought ". There is nothing to be lost, but all to be gained.

There are no limiting boundaries to knowledge and experience. That which is within our grasp we can gain and hold. Now that the creed-cluttered surface of the earth has been rent, an avalanche of knowledge is at the disposal of all. One by one we will begin to absorb the heightened influences. Intelligence will take the place of sottish thought. We will be drawn into a cognizant relationship with higher grades of consciousness. With the Venusian influence streaming in we will be able to feel and enjoy these co-operative impulses. We will come to know this is the way the superior ones magnetize and impregnate the lesser orders of life.

How can we make direct contact? It is not necessary that they come to us in person to impress us. Nor do they need words to make themselves known. Thoughts are things. They need only to project their thoughts through space. Thought is the agent of consciousness. We are bound together subjectively by the same invisible cord. Too, we are composed of the self-same elements, one somewhat more rarified than the other. That is all. In other words: " All are part of one stupendous whole, whose body is nature, and God, the soul."

The beautiful DIANE came to your author sixteen years ago. Her melodious voice vibrated through the vastness of the cosmos. This same voice has been heard on many occasions since the release of MY FLIGHT TO VENUS. Sometimes it has followed me over the cactus-studded desert where I love to roam. It has come in silent moments driving along the highways. Time and again the voice said : " You will witness a miracle." I mentioned it to friends. I shouted it from many platforms. Again and again I tried to imagine what this " miracle " might be. Frankly I expected a saucer to land in our midst. That I should make contact with the lovely Diane in person was certainly not in line with my expectations.

We know that miracles *do* happen. They come at the least expected times. " The miracles of earth are the laws of heaven."

Again I am asked : " Are there Venusians among us?

Perhaps ! Since they too would be robed in the accoutrements of earth we would not know them by their appearance. They may not make themselves known to us but if we are in tune with them we should feel the warm glow of their personalities.

Teleportation is perhaps no more a chore to them than driving an automobile is to us. With no more than a powerful concentration of *will* they can be at any corner of the great universe with the speed of thought. Knowing no boundaries of limitation they are free to go and come at will.

It will be a red-letter day in our world when science turns its attention to the conquering of life essences. We will then know we are on the threshold of the New Age. In that day disease will disappear. A way will be found to lengthen the life span. Instead of groping blindly through years of trials and sorrows we will dance through happy glorious years. Youth will reign on a throne supreme. Perhaps spacecraft travel will be as commonplace as the airplane or the locomotive. What a thrill it will be to travel over millions of miles of space with the comfort and ease of a Pullman Coach. A few lines from MY FLIGHT TO VENUS illustrates this point perfectly.

"During flight we seemed to penetrate many dimensions of abstract space. There was no static. No interference. Then something happened. It was like a gentle explosion of gorgeous colors accompanied by an experience akin to an orgasm of spirit and matter. There was no time after that. No space in the usual connotation of space. All was consciousness. *Absolute consciousness.*"

Many times since that memorable date I have tried to arrive at some logical conclusion as to what actually happened. Did I leave my body behind, travelling only in a finer vehicle? Or was it true teleportation and I took my body with me? Did the atoms of my body actually disintegrate at one point, re-materialize in another?

I am sure the form that housed the beautiful spirit of DIANE was composed of pure protoplasm (the essence of all things). It was apparent too that the other spirit manifestations that appeared in the Church of Divine Light were made up of the usual ectoplasms drawn from the medium and the guests. There is as wide a difference between protoplasm and ectoplasm as there is between flesh and spirit.

Many of those present observed the breastplate that seemed to fit over Diane's gown. This was obviously the " hub ", the center point of contact where fusion takes place. From this point the plasms are united and molded into manifestation. From this magnetized center Diane could follow the lines of force travelling over the face of the earth and also traversing every star and planet in the entire universal system.

Plasms are existent in all higher ethers. Plasm is the true creative substance. It is the substance used in spiritual healing. When we learn how to control the plasms we will have done away with ailing bodies.

Universal cooperation is ALL WORLDLY. There are worlds on every level of existence, worlds within worlds each one functioning according to its own fixed rhythm. All are blended or welded into the Greater Universe. When we have conquest of space, like the Venusians, we will be able to reach them, one and all. We will be able to draw on the consciousness of these worlds just as we draw on a bank account. Having no more questioning doubts about invisible force governing a visible world we will know that changes can come with lightning-like rapidity. We will no longer hoard supplies nor try to possess the world with a fence around it. Realizing that transcendental security is our Bank Universal we will know that our potentialities extend beyond the boundaries of world limitation.

This feat can be accomplished in a small way even in our day and age. When the human vibration is raised to a higher level we can tune in harmoniously with the planets and worlds of the universe. When we have mastered vibration, teleportation will no longer be an alien word in our dictionaries. It will be no more difficult than pushing a button to bring forth electric lights. By means of powerful creative thought we will be able to transport our bodies to any point in the vast universe.

This is also true of the strange spacecraft that has created so much furore in this day and age. We will no longer be looking for a saucer to crash that we might take it apart and learn the secret of motivation. We will have the know-how to build the same sort of craft. We will recognize interplanetary visitors, not by the clothing they wear, nor the vehicles they ride in, but by the light of their celestial aura.

When will this happen to us? Perhaps our Bible has the answer:

" And there shall be signs in the sun and the moon and the stars, and upon the earth distress of nations with perplexity; the sea and the waves roaring, men's heart's failing them for fear and for looking after these things which are coming to the earth; for the powers of heaven shall be shaken. And then shall they see the Son of man coming in a cloud with power and great glory." Luke 21 : 25-27.

Again, will flying saucers play a part in this great world drama? Through the long and winding centuries the superior ones have looked down from their exalted heights. They have beamed their beacon lights on our doorstep. In our sorrow-torn days they have been with us in spirit. They have followed our error-strewn pathway not only through the cycles of life, but to the grave and beyond.

The coming of the saucers has awakened us to a new dimension in thinking. Whether real, or a figment of every imagination, they have stirred not only individuals, but governments. I quote from our own Air Force:

" The majority of sightings can be accounted for as misrepresentations of conventional objects, such as balloons and aircraft. Others can be explained as meteorlogical phenomena or light reflections from crystallized particles in the upper atmosphere. Some were determined to be hoaxes. However, there still remained a few unexplained sightings . . . The Air Force has stated in the past and reaffirms at the present time, that unexplained aerial phenomena are not a secret weapon, missile or aircraft developed by the United States."

Does this not suggest that those in high places will one day be willing to investigate more thoroughly? When the governments of the world are convinced, we will all be convinced. If they are sent to us as a means of saving mankind from the error of its ways —if they are here to help weld all the worlds into one—then why not try to hasten that day?

This could happen tomorrow. It might happen next year or the year after. If we can speed it up, why wait?

Above all, we dare not spurn the strange omens and the beacon lights. We know they have come before to guide our erring footsteps. We know that in the past they have been spurned. Through the long centuries only a few have heeded, the many have ignored. If we pave the way for them to come now, we will see the road ahead with clearer vision.

Again . . . why should we wait for someone to guide us—that someone might be just as blind as ourselves.

CHAPTER VIII

RETURNING again to visitors from other planets, we cannot repeat too often, rather than looking upon them as phantasmal, we should try to see them as patterns of our own future. Surely it is neither fantasy, nor illusion to believe other planets are inhabited just as our own. Earthman has always felt himself the "one" superior animal in all existence. Whether he knows it or not this viewpoint has narrowed his horizons down to his own microscopic size. He *wants* to believe there is only one earth. He wants to assume that the stars and the planets are in the heavens to shed light upon his lonely nights. He does not *want* to extend his vision beyond the perceived.

Such "quest-inspiring" events as occurred in the "little white church in Los Angeles" helps to bring about the altering aspects of life. We need not admit such a happening as a reality. Many would not admit it even had they seen for themselves. But at least it compels us to think about it, then plunge into the depths of self for a satisfactory answer. The deeper we go the more interest is generated. Finally a burning desire to *know* is developed. From there on we are ready and willing to give the best of ourselves to the quest. It then becomes The Great Adventure.

There was a day in our histories when the quest for the spectacular was a dangerous pursuit. Men were burned at the stake for believing that which was contrary to contemporary thought. Today the heritage of the ages is ours. If we can gain mastery over these days we will no longer be in bondage to any person or thing. We will be above the caprice of fate.

We can plunge into the task, singly or collectively. We can work toward accomplishment graciously and perhaps be granted an extra ten or twenty years to the calendar of our lifespan. Not just ordinary passing years but a happy, fruitful life continuance.

Your author firmly believes when we are able to overthrow the old and bring in the new we will no longer suffer the misfortunes of living. When we can act together as a vast mass we will be able to obtain the things we desire quickly, for we will be enlisting the help of the "many".

If we can entertain the thought that DIANE is only "one" . . . that there are thousands of Diane's ready to help us, then life can be turned into a living miracle. When such a realization dawns in our consciousness, changes will take place in rapid-fire succession.

The mystery of life need not be an enigma. In the past we have sought to solve a complex riddle when in reality it is all so simple. It is the dramatic happenings along life's pathway that help to awaken our vision and stir us to action. Deep mystical experiences have a transforming effect. They compel us to put useless things behind us.

Human nature is frail; human beings are weak. Only one here and there is willing to venture over virgin territory, even though they know in their hearts that a voyage to another planet would be the most enterprising adventure ever attempted. Even a "psychic" adventure into this realm is a great event. It too is accompanied by many dangers unless we have first learned to use constructively, the great force within us. But most of us do feel for a certainty that one day interplanetary travel will be a fact. This means conquering our fears and *knowing* that we have the power to govern, not only the earth, but the universe.

To do big things we must start with little things. One of the most outstanding human examples in "overcoming" goes back into our own country's history. Many look upon Abraham Lincoln as the greatest President in the long line of presidents. "Honest Abe" had every sort of handicap to overcome. He began life in a log hut far removed from books. He was an ugly, gawkey specimen of man. But today Abraham Lincoln enjoys a posthumous fame, the symbol of the power inherent in us all.

There are many undiscovered "Lincolns" in our world. Once they set themselves to the task they can wield a wand of power over any fixed circumstance. We're a "wonderful people" really. All we need is some paramount issue to stir us. We have proven over and over again that war is not the stirring element to achievement, while "celestials" such as DIANE can give us the success-producing touch. It means only reaching out toward the far-flung goals. When we tie in with the larger plan the smaller issues take care of themselves. I feel sure were we to suddenly meet these faraway voyagers face to face our future would not be dull. Even inconsequential things would take on cosmic importance. It might be sometime before we do meet them face to face, but at least we can be prepared.

We all agree we are now in the midst of earth-shaking events, but they are events of violence. There is scarcely a free moment

44

in any twenty-four hour day. We can transmute this concept of violence merely by making up our minds. When we can view life from one " all-comprehensive whole " then we will experience unfoldment that will insure us of greater progress. If we follow the beacon lights beckoning from ON HIGH we will have no difficulty in our upward climb for our perceptions will quickly unfurl to the larger dimensions.

If we keep our candles burning it can come like lightning from heaven. But we must prepare for it in advance by discovering the hidden resources within ourselves. The veil between the worlds is very thin these days. It will become thinner and thinner as time goes on. When we change our point of view our attitudes will change. When that happens we would never be willing to go back to the false values we have left behind us.

Your author sincerely believes that when we gain the full import of the coming of DIANE we will be able to shed our dwarfed, thwarted thinking. When the weight of the world is lifted from our shoulders, we can help lift the load from the shoulders of others. As a reward we will not only have spiritual possessions in abundance—but matching creature comforts and wealth as well.

These are turbulent times. We need these new contacts to inspire us with new fortitude. If we can believe that DIANE was actually teleported into the " little white church ", this is one example of the power of their skills. Think of being " teleported " from another planet—or even from a spaceship high in the skies ! Added to this was the thrill of watching her materialize before our eyes, bring us a message of hope, then vanish in a flash.

Of course there are those who will argue : " But she appeared at a seance." True enough. Rev. Bertie Lillie Candler's seance corner provided a definite concentration in consciousness . . . all were of one mind awaiting the appearance of their loved ones—but it provided also the perfect setting for a verification of " teleportation ".

Jesus was skilled in the art of teleportation. Did he not say that we too have the same resources within ourselves once we uncork the power within us? The power lies a little deeper perhaps, but it is nevertheless there.

As other planetary voyagers come in greater numbers we will be able to stand by and watch the shackles of our own ignorance drop away. The Bible states : " And these are the signs that shall follow them that believe."

This brings us to the realization that our material quest has been in vain. It makes us know and realize how shallow our earth existence has been. There is no mystery about it. When we have omnipotent unity we have a kinship with all God's wondrous creations. The soul knows no boundaries. It can reach out beyond ONE WORLD. There is no reason on earth why we should be dis-united.

From time to time certain individuals will be singled out of the mass to become the prophetic voice of the new era. It might be YOU. It might be ME. It might be our friend. It might be our foe. Few at best are fitted for the task. Finding the best channels will not be easy. Those in high brackets, our leaders are too comfortably esconsced in their easy chairs and foam-rubber pillows. Those in low places feel the scars of their own inadequacy. This means we must be trained to measure up. We will not be measured by some perfect yardstick, but by the qualities of sensitivity. The mystic sciences furnish a base, a spring-board, but the greatest human ingredient is receptivity.

From time to time warnings and omens will come. These warnings we *must* heed. If we do not wake up that glorious goal might be centuries away. When a solid foundation is built in conscious-ness, then it is bound to happen. How we handle our spiritual controls today, will determine how we are voted in, tomorrow.

We are in the van of the march of events. There are no accidents in life. When the doors to other planets swing open— when their designated messengers come into our midst we know then there is a definite reason for their coming. It could mean we are in graver danger than we think. It could mean we are closer to the transition period than we realize. As we accept in faith, then one miracle after another will follow. With many " Diane's " by our side we can walk the sidewalks of earth, or we can float over the spacious firmament.

This does not mean seeking some cream-puff heaven with angels and musical harps. Venus is not a fantastic Utopia. The Venusians both preach and practice a workable ideology. They are a perfectly balanced people who have sought beyond man-created systems for their enlightenment. They believe there is but ONE and all things are created in HIM.

If we beings of earth had the powers of discernment we would not elect to live in turmoil. We would like to run away from the violent explosions of the world. Deep in our hearts we want to vibrate to the finer forces. We crave the response from the deeper

46

urges. The more enlightenment we have the more we want to *feel* the deep surge of spiritual infusion coursing through our veins. We yearn to sit at the feet of unseen mentors. We want to wet our thirsty throats with nectars from the enchanted cup. All these things can be ours when we know *where* we are going and *why*. Furthermore, we need not wade through a river of tears to reach our destination. We have slipped off into the mire many times, but when we *know* we have these superior ones to shield us from the blows—to guide and to bless us, the way will be easy.

Not all will get there, of course. A few will reach the finish line. Others will start, then turn back. But the torch-bearers will always be in the lead. As one falls by the wayside, others will pick up and carry on. On ahead there will be beacon lights to guide the way.

The power of "mass consciousness" is the greatest power on earth. Thousands pulling on the same rope at the same time can produce miracles. It takes courage to enlarge our horizons, but what have we to lose? The epic rewards will go to the pioneers, whether drawn from the rank and file of humanity or from the high places.

Let us believe that the advent of DIANE can become a red-letter day in our lives . . . our first tottering steps toward universalization.

And now I ask my readers to bow their heads for one brief moment. Let us offer tribute to this visitor from Venus—the beautiful DIANE.

PART TWO

THE DISCOURSES OF DIANE

(Note : Diane spoke to me in a language of the mind
which was instantly translatable into words.)

ON—THE MEANING OF GOD

It was early morning and the golden sands of the desert were breakfasting on the first glow of the sun's actinic rays. I loved to walk at this hour when all the unseen little people were gay—filled with the spirit of the new-born day. I could see them now in my mind's eye as they danced with the rhythm of abandonment, tuned with the orchestration of the *spirit of life*.

Making my way over the wind-swept sand dunes drinking in inspiration for my day of work, I came to a sudden halt. It had happened many times of late—a tingling sensation of my body—bells ringing from afar—the fragrance from beautiful flowers—strains of melody floating in from out of the nowhere.

A patch of soft sand beneath a sprawling greasewood bush beckoned to me. It was an ecstatic moment, that sharpening of the perceptions of my mind . . . then a merging with an " alien " something as though I were being hooked up with all the main lines of the Cosmos. This cosmic clairvoyance I had come to welcome for I knew I would soon be honored by HER saintly presence. Then came the concordant tone of voice I had come to know so well.

" Child of Earth . . . it is with the spirit of gladness I greet you this day out on the clean desert sands. It was from the same clean sands we of Venus found our way to the throne of God. We did not arrive at our journey's end by way of platitudes and dramatic petitions. You will find our footprints one by one over the stepping stones to the arcs of Venusian splendor. Out where the wilderness is wild, you too will come to know the meaning of God. This is the lesson earthman must learn, my child. He has chosen the arduous way through supplication and sacrifice. He has tried to reach God as though he were trying to climb a ladder of gold—rung by rung. Just as your plodding footsteps have moved slowly over the evolutionary sands of time—just so your approach to God's throne has been a slow-paced crawl. Many start, but few arrive. The rungs of the golden ladder are broken before the throne is reached.

Through the long eons of time, from our exalted summit, we have watched the milling masses of earth's children. We have seen them stumble along earth's hills and valleys. Our lights have beamed over the bright spots, they have tarried longer over the areas where tears have rained down upon the bloody paths man of earth has ordained to travel. At times our lights have burned with luminous intensity, at other seasons only a dim flicker could find its way through the fog.

" Yes, Child of Earth—we have watched our younger brethren stumble and fall. We have observed him on bended knee before the altars of earth's temples. How harrowing have been his entreaties for the favors of God! But here has been where earthman has erred. Though ardent have been his prayers, though bountiful has been his praise and thanksgiving not always have his invocations reached the Supreme over them ALL. In fact, rarely does earthman raise his vibrations to the God level.

" Few worship God in the same way. To some God is LOVE. To others God is POWER. To many He is INTELLIGENCE. And so on and on. The way to God's throne is *not* segment by segment. It requires *no* ritualistic drama, but rather it is as simple as turning on your electric light switch—or turning the ignition key on your motor car.

We Venusians *KNOW* that GOD is the *Source* of *all things.* We *KNOW* that HE is everywhere present. That HE is *in* every created thing. We *know* that GOD owns the UNIVERSE. That we own nothing. Human life comes into being unbound by possessions. The harvest man gathers through life he cannot take with him when he departs. All things are *loaned* by GOD. They are treasures to be glorified while we use them, but we know that one day we must give them back to HIM from whence they came. Being eternally aware that we own nothing of ourselves—that GOD's beneficent storehouses are ever open to us from the smallest need to the grandest luxury we borrow freely on a prodigious scale. GOD trusts us to pay our honest debts. HE *knows* we will not misapply HIS treasures. That we will return His gifts at the close of our day.

" Child of Earth—prayers to GOD need not be abstruse. GOD knows the needs of HIS children before they ask. HIS blessings HE has created for their advantage. Does not your Bible state : ' In the beginning was the WORD and the WORD was made flesh.' Do you believe that my daughter? It means does it not, that we have only to tune our thoughts to GOD'S thoughts—to *speak* and all blessings shall be ours. In the conception of GOD, man's daily manna and castles of gold are of the same equal value. When GOD is enthroned in our hearts we are part of the very *breath of creation,* small or large.

"No, my daughter, ours is not a *miracle* existence. We are not what earthman calls . . . magicians. We possess no magical formulas. GOD is our magic. GOD is our formulas. Authors and theologians alike have endeavored to expound this principle, but few there are who have applied it to the worship of their daily lives. Though men of earth have built fences and pillars of marble around GOD'S glorified concepts, at the same time he has never bothered to remove the boulders he has placed in the way of his true understanding.

"Child of Earth—the greater number of earth's children have never learned their mission toward GOD. Earth man has not known the *why* of his birth. My daughter . . . God's children are brought into fleshly manifestation that they might gain needed experience. Man goes out from GOD'S house an infant in understanding. He returns a Sage. He is sent over roads dotted with thorns and thistles—often he must swim through a river of tears, but this is only that he might find himself, by himself. God *knows* that one day he will return mature with knowledge and experience. He *knows* he is but a prodigal son.

"Why has earthman been so blind? Why has he accepted eons of years of suffering? My daughter . . . only because he has persuaded himself that the earth plane is all there is. Earthman has been haughty in his self-importance. To gain superiority over all things earthly has been his vain-glorious ambition. His lordly goal. Earthman has chosen the illusion of growth. He has exalted man-made scientific grandeur over the majesty of GOD'S universe. He swells with pride at the sound of the hammer, he thrills to the blade of the sword. Seldom does he pause in the silence to breathe in God's wondrous sunshine. Rarely does he accept that which his senses have not substantiated. Earthman, believing all is contained within his own plane of existence, has gone contrary to the echo in his heart. He has floundered in the illusions he has built up for himself.

From our exalted heights we have beseeched earthman to listen —to turn his gaze upward. But more often than not his vision has been blinded by his egotistical viewpoint. Our lights have blinded him rather than inspired him. The worlds etherial, the star-strewn heavens—the planets so far away to him—they are all a part of an unsolved enigma. Earthman prefers it that way. A few short years of earthly sojourn, then the state he calls death. Only birth and death and the time between does he comprehend.

GOD knows no boundaries, concrete or etherial. We *know* that nothing is born of man, even *superior man*. Forms may come and go, but that which animates *form* goes on forever.

"My daughter . . . earthman is a born procrastinator. To him today does not exist, only yesterday and tomorrow. GOD dares not procrastinate for one single, infinitismal moment. Should HE do so the very heavens would tumble down. GOD does not slumber. He does not rest. Never for one instant does he relax his vigilance for with GOD there is no beginning and no ending. The crudities of today are the perfections of tomorrow.

"All things stream out from Source. All things go back to Source. We Venusians have learned how to control and utilize this " source material ". It is the taproot of our greatness for plasms are the substance of the soul.

"Child of Earth . . . remember always, GOD preceded all thought. HE preceded all form. GOD is as close to you as breath itself. You have only to throw the switch to reach GOD'S powerhouse. And . . . there is but ONE POWER. It is the motivating force behind all manifest creation. There is but ONE GOD—a GOD to be worshipped in HIS ESSENCE not in his image.

"I take my leave now, Child of Earth," she said. The tap of her long tapering fingers I felt upon my shoulder—the light touch of her holy kiss, I felt upon my lips. DIANE vanished as she came . . . back into the invisible ethers.

ON—THE MEANING OF THE NEW AGE

THE morning light streaming in at my window announced the coming of another new day. The view reaching across the wide expanse of desert helped me hook up with the subjective domains —to extend the dimensions of my mind. The electrical charge going through my body told me SHE would be here in a moment. Would she come in vision? Would I hear the softness of her golden voice? Would I view her shadowy form?

"Good morning, Child of Earth," she greeted warmly, her voice meeting my mind over the ether waves. "Today I shall discourse on the coming New Age. For many long years, my daughter, earthman has envisioned the beginning of the new epoch, a day of transition when all things would be made new. Every inch of earth's creation can feel the deep, unstilled yearning of the cycle ahead.

"The time is not long, now. The dawn of the spiritual dispensation so long withheld you will soon behold. Earthman cannot reach much farther on the ladder of materialization. He has spanned the dizzying heights. Now he must start his rapid descent. His ascent has been slow. His descent will be speedy. From that point he will then start his ascension to higher states of usefulness. No longer will he strive for material eminence, for power over his fellowmen . . . for possessions which soon pall—for he will have seen the folly of his ways. He will seek just as earnestly for truth, justice and goodness as he has sought for the goods of the earth.

"The coming of the New Age is long overdue, delayed by earthman refusing to look beyond his own little self for inspiration and guidance. Though he has preached "the glory of God in the highest, on Earth Peace and Good Will toward Men," this beautiful concept has not been enthroned in his heart.

"No, Child of Earth, when the New Age dawns man will no longer seek the sterile and the barren, all of which he has created in his small mortal mind; he will strive to be fruitful, to elevate himself and those around and about him. He will challenge his contestants to the highest celestial realms. The world he has nourished with sensuality, with greed and avarice, with lust for power, will no longer sprout its despicable seeds. They will fall on arid soil. The banquet table that has fed his pompous vanity will be carried away. His hunger will be a spiritual hunger, his thirst a spiritual thirst. He will offer thanks for every precious drop of spiritual nectar that touches his hot, parched lips.

"Look down the long road of earthman's stumbling past," my daughter. You will be sickened with the nauseating stupidities of human-kind on earth. You will look askance at the greed-built structures. To these earthman must light the fires of destruction that he may not be forced to look upon the monstrosities he has created. I am sure he will not wait for them to crumble into dust, mired down with mud and debris. He will reduce them to ashes as rapidly as he can do so. Knowing beyond all shadow of doubt that he has built his human temple on insecure foundations, he will no longer wish to look upon them. Too, he will view with disdain the ritualistic serfdom he has dared to call equality. Having elevated himself above his fellowmen, he will know that the feudal system of the Middle Ages had never passed into oblivion. It has only been changed in the content of the word. Earthman of today has shown but little more mercy than the feudal overlords of days gone by. When he sees himself in the rôle of the master, whip in hand, ready to lash out at the least provocation, he will then realize that his ignoble urges are no different from the master and slave precepts born and bred in the childhood of the cycle.

"Child of Earth, if there are any doubts left in your mind, go back into your histories and recount earthman's great conquests. These conquests he thought so noble . . . what have they amounted to? Have they not all fallen by their own weight? Have not your great civilizations been reduced to ashes?

"Today the centuries have fled and the sun is again coming up over the wooded hills. The time will soon be at hand for those ON HIGH to descend earthward. You will find it in your sacred scriptures: 'Now have the unstable kingdom of The World become the Kingdom of the Lord and His Christ.' Rev. 11 : 15.

"Yes, Child of Earth, we of the Greater Planets are the messengers of The New Age. We are the angels mentioned so often in your sacred writings. We have come to help wing in the *new* heaven and the *new* earth. We have come to help prepare for that glorious inheritance which will one day be yours to enjoy. It has long been decreed that a roadway should be established between your planet and ours.

"Be it known, Child of Earth, through all the long centuries our watch-towers have never been deserted. The lights from our incandescent lamps have never ceased burning. In your darkest hours our sights have been upon you. Now again we have sent our silvery ships into your atmospherean seas. Your noble Red Man knew us in vision. He saw us in The Morning Star. His own majestic forebears have long since taken up residence on our lofty planet. This has been told to you by our Brother Blue Cloud.

"Today, new conditions confront us just as they confront the Planet Earth. Since we are the upper arc of your planet we too are destined to go on to higher realms. Our work is soul-enfranchisement, our creed equal justice for all the peoples of the universe. This is why we wish to come now in all glory that your sin-clad earth might be purified, that fertile seeds might be planted over every inch of the globe's surface. No longer must earthman harken to the voice of false leaders. No longer must his premise be words that have lost their meaning. In your new dispensation mankind must listen to the voice of his heart. Only then can he exemplify his beautiful yuletide hymn "Glory to God in the Highest, On Earth, Peace and Good Will Toward Men."

"On your unhappy planet, the heart and soul of every man is crying out for a new way of life. Every man is seeking, consciously or unconsciously for something beyond his ineffectual religions to help him toward a larger understanding. He wants something more tangible than the faith he has been taught to embrace. He wants something he can see, and feel and touch. When he finds that which he is seeking, then he will have bridged the gap of centuries.

"Child of Earth, in the New Age, whose dawn you now behold, earthman will be lifted to higher arcs of usefulness. His credo will be: 'Do not fear God . . . but Love thy brother.' When his intelligence is awakened then he can be entrusted with the secrets of space travel. He will be taught in the ways of a greater science.

"Transition time is rapidly approaching. That which was set into motion at the beginning of the cycle will be made manifest and complete at the cycle's ending. 'When will that day come, you ask?'

"Transition is ever sharp and sudden. When the omnipotent moment comes millions will be unprepared. While earthman's knowledge has increased through the centuries, his wisdom has not. Though he heralds the coming of 'wonder drugs' as a panacea for the ills of mankind, he has not yet uncovered a remedy for the greatest ill of all—the pollution of the lifestream of human consciousness. When all this comes to pass—then the transition will follow.

"Child of Earth, we come now that all doubt might be alleviated. Those who are not prepared cannot rise by themselves. They need our help. Signs will be posted along the way. The word of the New Dispensation will be quickly spread. Those who *are* ready will meet us and acknowledge us. We will appear first in vision, then we will walk down the streets of earth together. Our guides and our teachers will be without number. We will be ever watchful that earthman does not stray into the mire of past action. Every effort will be made to keep him from faltering and prevent him from falling. He will not err in understanding for we will speak a language all will understand. Our radiant lights will be beamed over every inch of the earth plane. None shall be able to cover himself nor hide from the glare. One by one those who stray will be coerced back toward the paths of righteousness. It is our hope and our prayer that none shall be lost.

"Child of Earth . . . in that day the sick will be healed. The afflicted will be comforted. The hungry shall be fed. This is the New Deliverance—the pathway into the new tomorrow."

May the blessings of Venus shine upon you, Child of Earth. I am DIANE. I shall come again.

ON—FEAR

It had been a trying, difficult day. One of those days when everything had gone wrong. Frustrations had beset me on every side. Weary with it all I had retired early. But not to sleep. Hour after hour I tossed on dew-wrinkled sheets trying to force my cerebral atoms to give up an answer to my problems. But instead . . .

At the midnight hour my troubled mind grew tranquilly calm. It was a moonless night and only a Stygian darkness prevailed. Unexpectedly a phosphorescent glow swept across my room, followed by a small illumined disc from which streamed a brilliant orange flame. The luminosity moved slowly across the entire length of my bedroom, then out of the window where it instantly vanished.

I sat bolt upright, absorbed with fascination. Then out of the corner of my eye on the opposite side of the bed I caught the faint outline of a white-robed shadowy figure. Although the features were indistinct, I knew it was DIANE.

"I come again, my daughter," she intoned. "This time to allay your needless anxiety. Fear, Child of Earth . . . is *not* of God. Fear is the bondage of your Planet Earth. Earth's children have even been taught to fear God's ireful wrath. What a mistaken concept this has been!

"Fear has damped the fires of inspiration. Fear has coerced the light of reason from earthman's soul. The burning fires of a man-created hell has laid earthman in torment through the eons of time.

"Fear, my daughter is the ashes of sin. It has brought to your unhappy planet a long series of shattered hopes. This would not be so if earthman would be rid of his fears. Because man fears, the evil forces from the darkest dungeons are brought forth. The hateful past lives again and again.

"In the childhood of this long and arduous cycle earthman made images in his own likeness that he might prostrate himself in prayerful supplication. He came to worship the false gods rather than The Living GOD. It was then his concept of the real GOD became distorted. It was then he began to know sickness, poverty and evil. When this erroneous concept occupied the throne where his GOD should have been, earth man became bewildered. He was

61

forced to wade through centuries of despairing civilization. The evil seeds sown in one generation were scattered into the next. And so on. Behind every evil lies the phantom of fear. Fear digs deep into the repulsive passions there to form a sediment of *evil*. The evil-doer, afraid of himself, lives in a world of shadows. Blinded by the fears he has created, he is too weak to rise out of his miseries. And so he lives on in the superficialities of life, his eyes blinded, his soul forsaken.

"Fear has manacled earthman to greed. It has carried him the full gamut of destruction. It has often taken him out of life before his patterns of violence have run to completion. These evils he carries with him into the sub-worlds for others to acquire and give forth.

"Child of Earth . . . the highways and byways of life are strewn with the pompous and the vain. At the root of vanity is fear. In the depths of themselves these pompous ones are repentent and sorrowful. Though it is hard for the good man to understand, sin is quite as repugnant to the evil-doer as it is to the sufferer from the evils done.

"Your humanity is ever asking: 'Can man rise from his hateful sins?' Yes, my daughter . . . let me repeat over and over again, we of the greater planets have come to act as shepherds and shepherdesses to lead earthman out of his chaos. To awaken him from his centuries-old-slumbers. To release the repeated errors to which he has been anchored—errors burned into the chart of time.

"Your humanity must rise again. Your civilization must be saved. Only then can a lasting peace come to the Planet Earth. Only then can there be absolute assurance of man's continuance and growth. If earthman is to dwell in the loftiest realms of the spirit—if he is to listen to the soft melodies of the night—if he is to know a success-crowned existence—he must be rid of his fears. He must be rid of them for all time. Then only can he be entrusted with the secrets of life eternal. Only then will he know the true meaning of unity. Only then will his soul be fresh and cleansed. In that day there will be no more struggle—wealth will flow in abundance. Earthman will be able to tap the boundless sources where life is filled and running over with all things good. Human hearts will sing with gladness for all will be rising on the same note toward achievement.

"Child of Earth . . . man does not make the complete circle in one short life span. Fear and ignorance stifle the germs of growth. The seeds planted in one season germinate and grow in the next. In time the shrubs become the trees waxing sturdy and strong. The tree ultimately becomes the 'tree of life.'

"Great earthly changes are coming, my daughter. The false pyramids that earthman has erected will soon crumble to dust. Materialism and spirituality must blend as one. There will be social competency, for spirit will reach down into the very core of your social system. Adjustments are inevitable. The minds of men must be changed. They cannot be changed all at once. Earthman will seek avenues of escape. When he finds the doors shut and barred, then he will begin to cooperate. He will know he *must* cooperate. Stripped of his pride and his egotism, the like of which he has mistaken for courage, he will gladly toss his false concepts onto the funeral pyre.

"Through his long stream of lives earthman has been a ship without a rudder. Instead of marching forward, true to his God, he has raced backwards toward his own destruction. The day is close at hand when he will no longer worship the tinselled existence he has created but he will have respect for that which God has created, through him. He will give thanks to his divine Source. He will know the meaning of attunement.

"And now, Child of Earth, cast off your fears for all time. If God is with you, there is no room for fears, doubts, hatreds, jealousies, or for the ruthless tramping over human lives. God is the same yesterday, today and forever. There is but ONE SUBSTANCE. There is but ONE ENERGY . . . the eternal, creative LIFE OF GOD. When earthman violates the laws of God he feels deep in his conscience the fears that are his ultimate downfall.

Venusian achievement is rooted in GOD'S glorious truths. This same achievement earthman will one day inherit. Long years has be awaited the Second Coming of His Savior to bring him these same glad tidings. He has prayed that his higher vision would be awakened. When earthman is rid of his fears he will make a noble contribution to all expansion. He will experience in truth, all cosmic reality. He will speak a divine language that will help to lift every heart. When his perceptions have been cleansed he will know the meaning of life's ultimate goals.

"Child of Earth, all of this is within earthman's grasp today. He is swinging between two worlds. His head is bowed at the bar of justice. Once he places his feet on the right path he will travel swiftly to the mecca of greatness. He will then know, that even his dreams have souls, and the twinkling lights of civilization can comingle with the illumined lights from ON HIGH. The concepts he will learn from us will eventually be built into his own social structure. They will become a part of the civil and religious life. Existence then will become a series of miracles. Man will have outwitted time. He will have conquered space. He will worship Principle because he has become a Principle. He will know reality . . . because he is Reality. He will be one with all life everywhere for the wound he has nursed so long will have healed.

"The soul of earthman is eternal. It cannot be destroyed by fire or flood. When his outlook is changed—when his viewpoint is transformed he will then turn his efforts toward transforming the world he lives in. He will rise to the heights lifted to new horizons where he will touch the hand of God.

"And now Child of Earth, again I leave you with our blessings. But I will come in the future, a living witness to Truth."

DIANE.

ON—TELEPORTATION

IT was Full Moon and the desert sands were like newly drifted snow. I loved these balmy summer nights and I often stretched my work-weary body on a canvas cot looking toward the starry heavens as they created a giant canopy over the desert wastes. Alone once more with my thoughts my mind started to wander out into that nebulous world of space. Segment by segment my consciousness was reeled out into the Great Unknown.

Suddenly I felt an amplified awareness that seemed to touch off the sparks of my soul ... then came the echoing melody and sweet scent of perfume I had come to recognize as the approaching presence of the lovely DIANE. Silence prevailed for moments, it seemed, then she gathered me into her warm embrace. The sweet words of her mind floated in over the night waves.

"Again I come to you, Child of Earth ... this time that I might clear away some of the misconceptions about us and the mystery of our silvery discs you earthlings so vulgarly call—flying saucers. Look toward the starry skies, perceive well the vast area of space between earth and the heavens above. There in that sea of space you will find the keys to all knowledge, for space, my daughter, is the mixing bowl of the cosmos. In that great chemical region above one element is being constantly resolved into another. This is the matter in which creation takes place. It is the clue to constant change; to evolution itself.

"In that vast sea above you there is a 'center' ... a 'hub'. Balance is the keynote of all creation. When earthlings find the balance-wheel of the cosmos, they too will become skilled in the processes of creation. They will see the Universe as only a larger pattern—the pattern of accomplishment.

"Many long centuries ago, we Venusians found that key. Since then we have become dynamic creators. Having learned well the art of creation all things are ours for the asking. The cosmos may seem far, far away my child, but it is as close to you as breath itself. Man, whether he resides on earth or on some one of the Great Planets, is a little cosmos within himself. When he finds the wheel of balance he can do anything the larger universe can do. When there is perfect balance between man and God there is concord ... syntheses of the tangible with the intangible. This brings about perfect understanding of all things, manifest and un-manifest. Once you make touch with the 'center' of that great

65

E

chemical laboratory you will know yourself to be an integral part of the Great Scheme of Things.

"In that laboratory all thought is created . . . thoughts are translated one to another. It is there the metamorphosis takes place. Once you have attained perfect balance all knowledge is available to you. You have but to 'wish' to know the answer to the most abstruse question and it will be flashed back in an instant from that vast horizon.

"Child of Earth, you have but to soar into those higher realms as we do, to know the truth. At the center of all, you can look to any part of the universe. This is the workshop of God. Here creations are made manifest. As the center is touched the Greater Universe moves closer and closer. Then as man is skilled in one endeavor he is given greater tasks to perform—tasks that require greater skills. When he reaches the zenith of his skills on one planet—he is re-born in greater spheres. Your present civilization is close to the summit of its earthly skills. A few of God's chosen will soon be permitted to go to that 'center'—experience the glorious heaven that is there—then go back to help others along the way.

"The great masses must come on in sections. They will be banded together by leaders who will attempt to wrap them in one unified thought. As collective units are assembled progress will be rapid.

"This work must start with the weakest links. As the weak links are made strong the strong links are made stronger. The difficult requires great effort to be sure, but vibration will help the speeding up processes. As each one is given a definite responsibility, actuated with 'one idea' new levels will be quickly reached. When the new world-outlook prevails there will be few recalcitrant ones . . . fewer who will fail. Just as flowers appreciate the sunshine and give forth in gorgeous bloom, man when he sees the beautiful new world around him, will likewise try to give back in grateful appreciation. When fertile seeds are sown and dynamic force added all things will begin to move. Static creates the slow-moving times. Static prevents man's working toward the greater manifestation.

"My daughter, on life's pathway there are always two roads—two distinct paths over which earthman can travel. Intelligence only can guide his footsteps in the right direction. On your earth the kind of cycle that looms ahead will be determined by the 'thought force' that is set afloat in the sea of pure dimension you are viewing now.

"Child of Earth . . . you will now see that all this preliminary has been to establish a premise upon which to satisfactorily explain the principle of teleportation, for by means of teleportation we can voyage from planet to planet. For many long centuries we Venusians have possessed teleportive powers. By teleportation I mean the ability to depart from one point and re-appear in another with the speed of thought. It is only possible to teleport a solid body where there is a perfectly balanced interchange between spirit and matter. Only the perfectionist, one who has touched the center of the universe, can teleport or be teleported. Through the centuries a few earthlings have been instructed in the art of these celestial mechanics. There are many recorded instances of mysterious appearances and disappearances, even of whole civilizations vanishing without a trace.

"In teleportation the vibrations must transcend time and space. Time and space is eliminated. There must be intense visualization. When the vibrations are speeded up—raised a full octave above the usual norm, then seemingly lifeless matter yields to the mind's every command. In teleportation there must be but 'one thought' and that thought . . . all powerful.

"My daughter, teleportation is the act of uniting spirit with matter at center. This you have seen in your vegetable kingdom where it is called—spontaneous generation. Again I repeat, in rare instances teleportive powers have been given to earth beings. Teleportation is very difficult for terrestrians, for yours is a planet of slow vibration while ours is instantaneous. Earthman, even the 'greats' more often than not go off balance in their attempts.

"An objective-subjective relationship runs through all things. Where there is perfect balance so-called lifeless matter springs to life merely by the power of thought.

"Again I repeat . . . before teleportation is possible a foundation must be first created. Only then can the creative power of God's inspired WORD be made flesh. You saw the result of this Godly command when I manifested to you and others in teleportive substance. First by means of a dynamic creative will I affirmed that which was *flesh* should be made *spirit*. In an instant the atoms of my fleshly body started to disintegrate. Instantly I was surrounded by an invisible shadow body. In the length of time it takes thought to travel through space I arrived at my destination. Still clothed in a 'thought body' I again gave the command that the invisible should take on embodiment. I spoke the *Word*: ' I

AM DIANE. I AM MADE MANIFEST IN EARTHLY FORM.'
Instantly the fleshly atoms whirled into pattern—and as you saw—
in an instant a state of solidity was reached. I was DIANE . . .
not in *spirit* . . . but in *flesh*.

"My daughter . . . always remember—without inner perfection
there can be no outer perfection. There must be perfect balance
between the realm of spirit and the realm of materiality.

"In this great universe there are worlds within worlds—each
carries its own rate of vibration into higher worlds. Balance is the
keynote. Should one go too far in one direction, not far enough
in another, the purpose is defeated. Skill makes all things possible.

"As I have said—in teleportation solid bodies are moved by an
unseen force. Before teleportation can be demonstrated the power
of thought must correspond with the state of manifestation.
Visualization must be all-forceful. Only in this way can the 'state'
of the life-giving plasms be altered.

"That you might better understand, Child of Earth . . . let me
put it still another way. In teleportation, substance is drawn from
the cosmos and molded into form by the power of thought alone.
This applies not only to animate bodies—but inanimate bodies as
well. A concentration in consciousness is needed for the perform-
ance of teleportation. A concentration in consciousness is likewise
needed for any world-changing event. This is the principle of
direct creation.

"Child of Earth . . . while there have been rare instances of
teleportation on your earth plane it will be many centuries before
earth bodies are sufficiently subtile to make teleportation general.
Perhaps the most outstanding evidence of teleportation on your
plane was that of your Great Teacher, Jesus, The Christ : 'While
they beheld he was taken up in a cloud.' . . . 'And I looked and
beheld a white cloud and upon that cloud one sat like unto the
Son of Man, having on his head a golden crown and in his hand
a sharp sickle.'

"My daughter . . . be not alarmed when a voyager from other
planets comes into your midst. Open up your heart in welcome
for such a one brings you a message.

"Again I take my leave with blessings . . . 'til we meet again."
I could hear the faint strains of a beautiful hymn . . . "God Be
With You 'Til We Meet Again." With the perfume of rare incense
in my nostrils—Diane was gone.

ON—THOUGHTS

HIGH up in the pine-treed cliffs of Pinecove, California, DIANE found me again. The beautiful late summer's morning seemed to put new life into the birds' sweet song. Skinny and Janie, two play-loving squirrels were scolding for their breakfast for it was past their "peanut time". These little grey playsters were more like tree spirits than lively animals. How completely they had come to rely on humans for their daily repast!

There was a slight chill in the air, but it was clean and fresh and redolent with the scents from the mountain's yellow pine. I thought I heard her, whispering in my ear.

"Good morning, Child of Earth . . . let us sit together again for the days are shortening and there is so much to be said."

I could not see her with my mortal eyes, but I greeted her with a smile. I had now learned how to be tranquil when she appeared.

"Your earth," she began, "is swimming in a sea of negation. Negative thinking has come out of the depths of time, and earthman is moored to tradition's negative guillotine. For ages, mass humanity has been steeped in negative thoughts. Wrong thinking has held him captive in the catacombs of suffering. He has lived in a world of despairing hopes because he has not tried to burst the shell of ignorance. The thoughts earthman has so carelessly planted, have ripened on his tree of life.

"Child of Earth, to think error is to breed error. "Thought" is more powerful than your armies, for if it were not for wrong thinking there would be no need for armies.

"The world man abhors he has himself created through wrong thinking. But it can be quickly re-made when he replaces thoughts of error with thoughts of truth. Remember, my daughter, behind tion emanates from these thought patterns. In the realm of thought all things visible are the molds of thought. All visible manifesta-all things are created whether for good or for evil. If earthman so wills he can change from a being of decaying flesh to a healthy vital individual by the power of thought alone. He can likewise change from a state of impoverishment to a rich and abundant life. Throughout these eons of time earthman has been bound to the lower prisons by the bonds of his erroneous thinking.

"If it were not for the scattered few true thinkers, my daughter,

69

your world would soon wither and die. The time is coming when you too will have the power over circumstances through thought. You will be able to mold the primordial substances into solids by means of thought alone. It has been our great privilege to have direct and semi-direct creation for many long years. The time is close at hand when we will be able to bring all manifestation through the mental planes.

"Thought is creative, my daughter. Thoughts are the healing blocks. Thoughts are the building blocks. The power of thought is all-powerful.

"In your world there is a saying : ' murder will out '. A murderer is caught not so much by clever police tracking, but the murderer is usually trapped by his own thoughts. He is discovered because the poignancy of the ' thought stuff ' has registered in the universal ethers.

"How long did the secret of your atom bomb remain a secret? Not long as you well know. Likewise through thought, there is nothing impossible of accomplishment. Where one mind speaks to another—where there is attunement and mutual interest, there is also the wonder-working power of thought. Through thought every desired mind pattern is created into form.

"Your earth scientists are today trying every sort of magic in an attempt to short-circuit thinking. We Venusians need no scientific precision instruments for having learned how to keep our minds clear. Sharp and clean we carry our mind patterns to their own fulfilment.

"Thought is free. It can go anywhere, at any time. Thought can travel through space. It can travel with the speed of light. Thought can function one plane to another. That is why our beneficient influence can be sent to any part of the universe. World domains are no barriers to thought. When earthlings learn how to control and manipulate thought, they will go straight because they will think straight. Then only can earthlings get real enlightenment and wisdom.

"Clear, concise thinking should be made a habit—an emotionally controlled habit. Constructive thoughts only should be permitted to sink into the subconscious mind. The mind should be cleared of all thought debris before embarking on slumber. Negative and destructive thoughts sink deep into the subconscious channels there to bring forth distorted manifestations.

"The understructure of our Venusian educational system is the teaching of constructive thinking. We feed the mind creative values. We do not deal in memory courses. Young minds in the formative stage need not be impressed with the letter of events. A properly trained mind can of its own accord tune in on these events at any time. Intuitional knowledge is *true* knowledge. In our educational work we stress finer and finer grades of thinking for in the realm of thought is to be found the alpha and omega of existence.

"Pure perception is simplicity itself once the mind is properly trained. Dimensions in human understanding are increased by the power of thought. Thoughts, negative or positive, cut deep grooves into the consciousness. If an unwanted thought is put there it should be replaced with a more powerful, fresh creation.

"Child of Earth—extended vision with us means merely opening up the doors of the mind. We deem it far more important to keep our mental house clean than our physical abode. Your fastidious earth-mother would blush with shame could she but view the cluttered condition of her invisible house. She would be mortified at the disorder she finds there.

"Unwanted thought forms can be dissolved and eliminated by creating more powerful thought forms to take their place. This rule rigidly and properly applied is the solution to all problems. We of the higher planets pay tribute to your pioneer souls, who in their feeble way are trying to bring enlightenment to earth's children. Superior knowledge has been reserved for the few, but in recent years your more adventuresome universities have brought 'studies in thought' to the more advanced minds. This is a major step toward achievement. It will be through the channels of thought that an empire of peace will one day reign upon your earth.

"When the principles of thought can be applied to the task of living, illness as you know it on earth will disappear. You will never again know poverty with its contingent sorrows. Opportunities will be everywhere present. You will know the mind as a sacred shrine, the door between that which you *know* and that which is desired to be *known*.

"In the depths of the human mind you will find the answer to every problem. Today you have the greatest opportunity in all your long histories for in any transition period there is always cosmic assistance. If you will but open the doors of your mind we of the distant planets will help re-seed your spiritually depleted souls. We can help you rise to the heights of greatness.

" Think it over well, my daughter, for as one of your sages once said : ' If the doors of perception were cleansed, everything would appear to man as it is, *infinite* '.

" Again I go, leaving with you the blessings of Venus. And—I will come again ! "

DIANE

ON—DEATH

It was the time between dawn and the daylight. Strange electrical vibrations permeated the room. Of a sudden, it seemed a dark curtain came down over my eyes. I was plunged into dismal darkness. After what seemed to me an endless eternity a wierd, phosphorescent glow appeared before my straining vision. I seemed to be wrapped in some strange enchantment as the illumined area grew in size. DIANE had never come in this manner before and for a moment I took her to be an imposter.

"Child of Earth . . . I greet you this desolate morn from behind the curtain of life. As I have come forth, just so shall I depart. It is not that I wish to appear dramatic, but my daughter, I want you to know for a certainty that life goes on beyond the grave. I want you to know in your heart and soul that *death* is not what earthlings make of it. Life is an experience on one plane—death's life . . . an experience on another.

"While earthman has witnessed death in its many forms, his concept of death is one of entering into the Unknown. He has not yet learned the meaning of *death*. When bereavement comes he feels ill toward God that he has brought such a happening into his life. It is a reminder to him that it is his own ultimate fate.

"My daughter, it is only the haunting fear of extinction that makes earthman fear the transition. Because he does not wish to face the reality, many prefer to believe that death is the end of all things. To such a one death is a violent release because the fearful soul will not accept an easy transition.

"My daughter, to the Venusians and all beings on higher planes, that which is so abhorent to earthman we deem a blessing. We sorrow only when a great one passes from our midst for we know we then have major adjustments to make, and that is not always easy. As you will recall, our wonderful Queen Zona had been with us for centuries, measured in your time. While we sorrowed over our loss we rejoiced at her passing. We knew that she had not left us—that her leadership would still go on behind the curtain you call death. When the life span is ended and the purpose fulfilled, death is just another step in the progression of the soul. Life goes from a personalized existence—to a life *impersonal*. Rather than wearing the temporal robes of earth the one who has passed dons the robes of the worlds etherial.

"On your earth plane when death ensues the atoms of flesh slowly disintegrate. That is only because earth bodies are composed of denser materials than ours. We have learned to dissolve the atoms just as we do in teleportive flight. That which has vitalized the substance of the body becomes the vital power of consciousness.

"Never fear when death draws nigh, my child. It is only the terror of death and not death itself that strikes like the knife or a sword. Many earthlings go on ahead of their time, for when the body powers are at low ebb and fear enters the soul—fear speeds on the end.

"The fear of death goes back to the time when your earth was young. Earthman knew only that which his senses taught him. Terror played a part in his growth. But with it came the age-long fear of death.

"My child, if earthman could only glimpse the glorious world that beckons him he would quickly shed his fears. That which binds him to the lower purgatories—the so-called hells—that is not death. It is man's own fears that have taken on form. If he would but venture behind the curtain of the unknown he would have an understanding of that which he fears. In that moment he would banish his fears forever.

"Death, my child, is like changing a garment—going from a mortal cloak to a sheath of color-tinted plasms. The body, a temporary house of clay is no different in particles than the substance that goes to make up all of nature's undeveloped forms. But within man's fleshly form there is a vital spark. This spark is absent in the lesser forms.

"It is sad to think about, Child of Earth . . . but few there are on your plane of existence who are without apprehension when transition time draws nigh, yet from birth to the last day the soul is housed in mortal body it has unconsciously sought that which it has feared. Never has earthman been happy with 'today', but he has ever looked for tomorrow to bring him joys. Each tomorrow has led him closer to that which he has unwittingly sought, for the soul yearns to drink from that eternal fountain. This unconscious longing for renewal is the spiritual thirst of man. The body goes back to the soil from whence it came, but the soul goes onward and upward in an endless round of progress.

"Countless men of earth have pondered the question—why should a perfect spark chose to go through long periods of suffering? Why should it need to tread the same birth-and-death path?

I say to you, my daughter, in each life, whether on the Planet Earth or the myriads of planets in the Great System, each *loans* something that is needed for the ultimate victory of the soul. This is God's way, my child. It is His will. Does not your Bible state : 'For since by man came death, by man came also the resurrection of the dead. For as in Adam all die, even so in Christ shall all be made alive.'

"No, my daughter . . . death does *not* end all for *there is no death*! It will be a day of great rejoicing when earthman no longer fears the transition. In that day there will be no more evil on earth for behind every destructive thought, back of every evil deed . . . *is the fear of death.*

"When the time comes when you can stand by as we do, and watch life spring forth from primordial essence then you will have no more fears. Your Bible states : 'In my father's house are many mansions.' When death comes and the soul goes up to the bar of justice, it is then sent to the 'mansion' it has earned for itself. It lives in surroundings to which it has become attuned. As one star differs from another, so does soul differ from soul. In each respective mansion the soul is taught to grow. This is the never-ending joy of the upward climb.

"I hear you sighing, my daughter . . . as all earth's children have sighed. It seems like a Herculean task to you now, but life need not be stumbling and awkward. There are guideposts, many guideposts along the path. Evolution's growth is slow and tedious, but the eventual goal will one day be reached.

In your land of America more than one hundred years ago, one of these guideposts appeared. Two frail young women, The Fox Sisters, heralded to the world—*there is no death.* They brought to your continent the first voice of survival. Although the 'Rochester Rappings' are derided to this day, the consciousness that has been generated and built by the many believers has planted a seed that will one day sprout in the garden of humanity. This same consciousness has paved the way to ultimate proof. Even those who scoff and jeer, deep within them they cling to some forlorn hope that they do live on after the end.

"Child of Earth . . . was it not the God-hand that rapped on the Fox Sister's door? The time had come for earthlings to know these things. There *is no death,* my daughter. Remember that, always! Do you not recall the words of your own true Sage, Will Rogers? Did he not say . . . 'When you live life to its fullest there is nothing in death to be frightened of. It is a privilege to pass on'?

"And again I leave you with the blessings of Venus. Again let me say from time to time you will receive a message from behind the veil called death. Do not fear . . . but try to understand."

DIANE

ON—LOVE

THE thunderstorm moved on, leaving the mountain top alive with fresh, clean air. What a relief from the sinister smog I had left behind in the now gloomy city of Los Angeles. Breathing in the pristine freshness I gazed into the breeze-swept tree-tops where the birds and the chattering squirrels made their home. Janie, the neighborhood pet, had been killed by a car a few days before. Skinny, her seemingly ardent mate, was already courting another female member of the squirrel family.

Love! The beautiful words poets sing about . . . of what did it consist anyway? My mind flew to LeLando and the beautiful love I had known on Venus. LeLando had said : " Distance is no barrier to love. When the spirit is wedded there can be no separation." Sixteen years had passed and only once had I contacted LeLando and then only for a moment.

In those last hours together, LeLando had said : " There will always be that glorious unity between us. We shall be together in a relationship that is forever divine. . . . Always in time of need you have but to summon and I will be there."

Wherein had I failed? Why had I been permitted to place one foot into love's paradise, then be sent back to a world of tumult? Sent back into the quicksands of life?

Instantly, I heard the telephone ringing in my mind. Diane had heard the questions my mind had asked.

" Child of Earth, how oft that precious possession of love has been sold to the highest bidder for gold. You did not sell for gold, my daughter, but you did fail to heed the warning that love is a dominant force—protection against all error. Back on earth you quickly forgot the lessons you had learned. For years you have been out of step with the force that blends the harmonies of the universe. For years your heart has been filled with fears and your footsteps have found only the quicksands. You ignored the words of your gentle master that ' Perfect love casteth out fear.'

" Child of Earth . . . through love all things can be changed. Love is the unifying force of the universe. All true manifestation, whether on the earth plane of existence or the farthest star is dependent upon Love. The powers of transmutation are to be found in the heart. The more love one possesses, the more of the things he desires can be his. Love opens new vistas. It embraces the seemingly remote realities. Love is the magic behind all things, visible and invisible.

"Earth children have been taught to fear all things. On Venus we are taught to *love* all things. First of all we are taught to love God for we know that all things are sustained in God's Love.

"A beautiful love between the mating opposites fits into the cosmic whole like a harp to its strings. There is no greater happiness than when earthman meets his spiritual affinity. A woman in love brings forth ideal creations. A love-inspired man goes out to conquer the world. Love is the greatest healing agency there is.

"No greater love hath human known than yours, my daughter. LeLando was the spiritual symbol of Love. Yours was a soul-tie woven long, long ago. On life's thorny pathway that love has passed through many soul-jarring dramas. It has experienced many blessed joys. Yours was a love kindled in the fires of spirit. A love you must live and live again in the charmed and spell-bound silences. It cannot be severed by death for it has been written into the scripts of immortality.

"Child of Earth . . . love is a great adventure, but it has many ports of call. You knew the joys of love for a short-lived time, then it seemed to be snatched away again. But fear not . . . the threads of destiny are intricately woven. They are strong, unbreakable threads that can reach out and embrace any part of the great universe. The chainwork of love can never be broken. It may lie fallow for a time. It may rest through many earth lives off on some mission for The Father . . . another port of call. But once that wonderful reality has been touched, whether on earth or in the planets in the heavens above, the link is eternal. It is there to feed many hungry hearts at the banquet table of the eternal feasts. Remember, my daughter, love is the true sustainment of health. Of wealth. It is the sustainment of true happiness and understanding. True love opens up the flow to the universal tides. It is the very wine of existence.

"Under the magic spell of love, my daughter, one can know the totality of existence. Love is the music and the gladness of the spirit. Love's intuition is the word of prophesy. A full life is a life filled with love. When one loves truly he is lifted with love's buoyancy. Through love's intoxication one can readily transcend the vicious cycles life has made for him.

"When love consumes the heart, life is not to be suffered in vain, but enjoyed in its completeness. He that loveth all . . . his family, his friends . . . his city and his country . . . must likewise love God.

"Child of Earth . . . try to listen through space for the voice of one who has *not* forgotten. · Try to make every breath, a breath of love. Try to make every word, a word of love. Make every act an act of love. To do so is to love and be loved. When you find the great jewel of love in your heart you will find also, as you walk down the streets of life, the good and the noble in every soul you meet. You will then know the meaning of your Master's words : 'And thou shalt love thy neighbor as thyself.' When this kind of love can embrace all forms of life from lowly man to the holy angels . . . then will the beings of earth *live* in *love* and know love in all its highest vistas.

"Again my daughter, I must go, and again I leave with my blessings. . . ."

DIANE

ON—HEALING

THE sentinel peaks were serene and calm; a shadow veil of violet gently hugged the tall cliffs of San Jacinto Mountain. Across the valley in a secluded idyllic canyon, a sacred plot of earth had been set aside for The Altar in the Wilderness Shrine—a nucleating center for the healing of the ills of mankind. I had come here often since that day when I was first inspired to carry out the plans for the healing sanctuary.

Lying flat on my back on the very spot where the cornerstone had been laid, I could see through the golden effusion of the sunlight, The Angel of San Jacinto. Perhaps since the very beginning of time, the angel had rested there, a "symbol of health" to the valley of destiny.

I could feel the electric fluids of the cosmos flowing through my body when of a sudden I became intensely introspective—the desert sands, the prong-studded flora—the scampering lizards—they were all a living part of God's Great Plan. In that moment I knew, as the immortal Shakespeare had known: " One touch of nature makes the whole world kin."

It had been almost three years now since the prophets had decreed that this plot of earth should serve as a focal center for healing consciousness. Here blind and stumbling humanity would one day be led out of its chaos into the promised land of the New Tomorrow.

It was no mere happen-stance that this region had been chosen as a place of healing worship. Centuries before, the ancient Cahuilla Indians had made it one of their sacred landmarks. Indians came from far and near to bathe in the sacred springs of thermal waters —the same curative waters that today flowed beneath the shrine location. Here on this clean spot of nature's soil, new values would be found and new values are ever the coil-spring of a more promising life.

The clean desert air caressing my senses, I felt vibrant, magnetic, alive. My heart was hammering with the exhilarating contact. Effervescing with new enthusiasm, the regrets I had known only moments before had disappeared. The lonely canyon was like a hushed cathedral entered for the first time for prayer and devotion.

From behind a misshapen Indigo Bush about ten feet distant, a wraith-like shadow came into being. It was more like a vision than a specter—and I knew it was DIANE.

" Child of Earth," she intoned . . . " today I come with the most important message yet delivered in this series of discourses, for right here on this hallowed ground the long-dead centuries will again be revived. On this sacred earth the veil between the worlds is very thin, so thin it is difficult to separate the material from the divine. Think well of the great words of your Prophet Isaiah: ' Prepare ye the way of the Lord; make straight in the desert a highway for our God.' Here on these singing desert sands humanity will listen to the song of the soul. Many hearts will be opened up to the universal flow of God's divine energy.

" This is not new to you, Child of Earth. Some years ago when you returned from your strange journey you were told to come to this desert country. You came and you stayed though many times you suffered great privations. You have known many heartaches, but that was part of your conditioning; a necessary requisite for the reception of things to come. Before life can be directed into new channels, my daughter . . . before science can create anew . . . the environment must be adapted to receive it.

" Intuition paves the way to new horizons. Intuition opens the doors to higher dimensions. We of the Greater Planets have been quietly working toward a more perfect earth manifestation. A telescopic consciousness must be created in the heart of all mankind.

" In the evolutionary advance of the earth in the days ahead, the healing arts will be stressed. When earthman is surfeited with the so-called miracles of science—when these many panaceas for healing fail to heal—then investigators will be guided toward the higher realms. Your scientists will then learn that earthman has a natural body and an etheric body . . . that there must be a mutuality in equilibrium if a healthy state is to be maintained. Your men of science will learn that it is useless to treat the body so long as the auric envelope is filled with psychic debris. Perfect balance must exist between both planes. Poisonous plasms must be constantly replaced by life-giving substances.

" Your scientific men have not searched beyond the superficial, They have failed to apply the same pragmatic principles to all planes—to know and realize there is a perfect reciprocity between all creation. Where only the pure essences flow in and out there can be no such thing as a sick body. There will one day be instruments to check these balances—to measure manifestation on all planes.

" Child of Earth, human ills are caused by going too far in one direction—not far enough in another. One individual carries too heavy a load of material substance; another too great a degree of spiritual plasm. Since time immemorial earthman has sought for a way to health. The early religions taught the art of healing, but this art has been lost in the march of civilization. When spiritual quest is undertaken in earnest, then the ills of mankind will disappear. In that day the needs of the soul will be realized. Science will have learned how to harness the universal harmonies. Your scientific men will no longer be guessing . . . they will *know*, that all things are bound together by the same invisible cord. That all elements are compounded one from the other.

"Child of Earth, true essence is primordial substance—the seedlings of God's vital life force. You will read in your holy book, Kings 5 : 4 : 'And his flesh came again like unto the flesh of a little child, and he was clean.'

"Before the close of your present century, my daughter, you too will see the discovery of LIFE. You will understand the laws of universal gravitation. When the clock of the new destiny strikes, science will have touched the *soul* of civilization. Your scientists will know how to apply the principle of vibration and rhythm because they will have found it at the hub of all things.

"Humanity must be made ready for the new state of health. In the wake of scientific progress solidified habit-molds must be broken up, for in the last analysis, disease is only a crystallized habit. Unless this is done quickly the result will be a virus in the bloodstream of humanity. A virus that will lead to earthman's corruption and decay.

"Spiritual healing is a true science, my daughter . . . the truest of them all. When the thinkers of earth turn from the atom to the life-giving plasms, then the greatest strides in your long histories will have been made. In that day bodies will not be weighted down with imprisoned poisonous atoms. The lifespan will be lengthened. The true spiritual healer is the surgeon of the soul.

"You ask, when will this take place? The outer world moves slowly, my daughter. The inner world moves with the speed of light. When it comes it will be in 'the twinkling of an eye' as you earthlings say.

"Today your world stands in awe of miracle healings. This despite the clarity of the message left by the Master Jesus. Your men of science look to the physical vehicle as a medium of illness, while this is only the crystallized counterpart of a distorted sheath beneath, the etheric body. The state of health of the physical body is wholly dependent on the state of health of the etheric body. Your scientists are unwilling to investigate. They will not try to grasp the relationship as it applies to life and living. They refuse to believe that all real healing must take place outside the body. Earthman functions in and through a body, but he is *not* a material being.

"The principle of spiritual healing is simple indeed. Could I but take you behind the scene I would show you the framework . . . or the structure that carries the life substance. You would see it is constructed with the art and skill of a spider's web, and not too unlike it in appearance. It is made up of infinitely fine silken wires through which flows a substance slightly heavier than the consistency of milk . . . whitish in color with a slight tint of blue in the auric emanation. The most attenuated *psychic sense* of earthman has not been able to discern the miracle that takes place. Until proper precision instruments have been created this mystery will remain. If it were possible for earthman to view the invisible mechanism surrounding the physical body, or perhaps I should better say, surrounding the web-like framework, you would be able to see the fine, golden grating that acts as a filter through which the rarified substances flow in, and the poisonous unwanted plasms flow out. This grating is reinforced with pin-points of delicate fuzz designed to collect the debris. From this point electrical energy is drawn from the universe.

"To explain it another way, my daughter . . . it is through the tiny openings of this grating—the *surround*—that the life force is admitted. For the life force is no more, no less than the plasms that are always existent on higher planes. The secret of instantaneous spiritual healing is dependent upon these plasms. The body is only sickened when the plasms have lost their ability to serve. They lose their ability to serve when the grating is clogged or disturbed. Bear in mind . . . *life* does *not* exist in the body but in a field removed from the body. It serves the body by means of this *surround*. If the channels from the universal field are kept open and free, and the area between the grating and the physical form and this golden grating kept clean and pure, disease germs could not find lodgment in the body at any point. When the cell life is kept under control and domination by the mind, as in spiritual healing, then as transmutation takes place the unwanted material is instantly dissolved. You see, my daughter, only when there is proper adjustment between the inner and the outer can the magnetic forces of the universe flow freely.

" Child of Earth . . . healing is merely changing the state of illness to a state of health through spiritual osmosis. Spiritual healing is a true science. The truest of them all. To inject vile pus into the body is to create future vileness. To put clean plasms into the body is to create a lasting healthy state. When your scientific minds turn away from pus and turn toward cosmic psychics—then will they find the many answers that elude them today.

" Inspired vision is the harbinger of events to come. One of the great revelations of your day came when you were told to erect a healing shrine on this strip of hallowed earth. Countless miracle healings will take place here. Many who come to visit will be carried away on waves of spiritual ecstacy. Others will experience newly awakened minds. There will be a few to whom illumination will come. In the days ahead this holy shrine will be one of the contact points between the Planet Venus and the Planet Earth. Many will hear the voices from other spheres.

" My daughter . . . the sacred incandescent flame enkindled in you before departure for our land of glory will be likewise enkindled in others. I say to you, keep the incense pots always burning. Keep your fires alive on the holy altar. You will then be able to see our beacon lights. You will be able to communicate with us. Moreover you will know GOD in the true light of *knowing* GOD.

" I take my leave now, my daughter, for I have much work to do on other planes. I work not only on the concrete planes of existence, but in the etheric worlds as well. I go now to my etheric home on Ether-Cana.

" I shall return—but in the interim of waiting, carry on your work with an enlightened heart. Fear not the setbacks that will be strewn in your path. The door to transcendental realizations has been opened. Use your potentialities to the utmost limit. When in doubt—you will always find the answer here in your desert sanctuary.

" God bless you, my earth child . . . till we meet again."

DIANE

SUMMARY

EVERY reader of MY FLIGHT TO VENUS has questioned: "Was your author's experience of sixteen years ago a mystical soul flight or an adventure in extra-human extension known as "teleportation"? Since this book was first written in 1939 it was certainly not based on any "flying saucer" illusion or enthusiasm. Should it come to pass that *all* saucer sightings were in fact the result of somebody's imagination, this would not dismiss the writer's unusual experience. As a matter of fact it would strengthen it.

If these strange spacecraft constantly appearing in our skies are coming from other planets, what is their mission on earth? This is another question I am frequently asked from the platform and it cannot be answered in the language of humanity at large. Although parapsychological research is now being carried on in some of our leading universities, and psychism and kindred subjects are being seriously investigated by some of our best thinkers, psychical subjects in general are still frowned upon by the masses.

To those who *know* because they have *experienced* it, true psychism is perception in divine vision. As the human life-line is cast out into the reservoir of the *unknown*, new knowledge is acquired, new dimensions added to the arcs of living. Every true psychic mystery of today becomes the reality of tomorrow.

Quoting from MY FLIGHT TO VENUS: "While it is never easy to convince a doubting world that the human vehicle can be sensitized to the point of releasing the soul to travel in the higher ethers, yet such certifications appear all through history. The soul, freed of its ponderous body, can pierce dimension after dimension of etheric space. The soul traveller merely pioneers the way over new and uncharted paths. It is the function of the soul to go on ahead to blast the road over which the world traveller must follow."

This means, does it not, we must enlist the mystics, the dreamers . . . those capable of perceiving the beyond, in bringing about the realities of tomorrow? When human perceptions are enlarged, the substance of cognition can be molded into tangibles.

The seers and the mystics tell us these extra-terrestrians are coming to us at this time because we are in graver danger than we realize. That the very fabric of our civilization is threatened.

They believe we are facing physical destruction to the point where the entire human family might be wiped from the face of the earth. This means, sacrificing our chance to evolve. It is the sacred and bounden duty of higher orders of life to intervene. To those residing on the "greater planets" there is but ONE UNIVERSE. All are linked together subconsciously in one universal brotherhood.

If they are willing to forego their own glorious way of life to help us, then we should be willing to do what we can to help them. If they can inspire us with a plan and a purpose whereby we can gather strength to overthrow the old and inaugurate the new . . . then why not offer them our services in full?

Thousands are beginning to embrace the hopeful thought that the time is not far distant when we will be going from planet to planet. It is being talked about in the sanctuaries of governments. It is on the lips of children and adults alike.

Within the periphery of these many evolutionary changes a new gospel is sure to emerge. Since the very beginning of this long and arduous cycle we have been torn between godly yearnings and man-created passions. Today our moral shovels must dig deeper than our ancestral taproots if we are to start a real cleaning-out process. If we can borrow this "new gospel" from Venus or some other remote planet, it will help shortcut our own period of travail. If the scientific genius of other planets can help us absorb the heavy layers of evil influence that have been piled up through the ages, why should we have to be baited with gifts of reward to give them the best there is in us? Is it not our duty to help them?

Another question the lay mind is asking—if flying saucers are real why all the mystery about them? Your author sincerely believes the time will come when they will land in great numbers, but first they will have to be assured there are no more war germs left on this earth.

There is no magical formula needed to inherit the glories of Venus. For countless centuries our own "wise ones" have been trying to show us the way. When we learn to direct our energies into universal channels, this will be brought about automatically.

Just as we import valuable objects of art from the far corners of the globe, the values from afar can be brought into our own circumstances. To extend ourselves is to find a new purpose in living. Once we know *where* we are going, and *why* we will burn with the fires of enthusiasm to push on ahead.

Another question—how can we help our friends from afar? First we can help them with our " thoughts ". *Thoughts are things* and when we can be one-pointed in thought we can be one-pointed in action. Thought builds consciousness and consciousness rules the worlds. New consciousness means new faith and new faith can carry us over the threshold to that glorious new cycle. Christianity was built on consciousness. Mohammedism was built on consciousness. Buddhism was built on consciousness. All great religions—all earth-shaking philosophies were first built into the structure of life through a vast chainwork of consciousness.

All who are today engaged in trying to solve the interplanetary enigma believe these space visitors will soon be here in numbers. Many feel as your author does that there are literally thousands of them close at hand and should an emergency arise they can be here almost on a moment's notice. I have both seen it in vision, and have been thusly told by Diane they are now building a foundation upon which will one day emerge, cities in the sky. Here they will set up their beacons. This will be their watch-tower from whence signals will be sent forth. From this vantage point they will project their way of influence. They will cause the light to shine in the hearts of countless millions. To those who are prepared to see them, they will be permitted to talk with them and know them as they are.

The Venusians dwell in peace and happiness. In their hearts they want us to know that peace, too. Human hearts are weeping today because of the turmoil in which they must live. If we were given a choice most of us would like to run away from the explosions of the world.

In making a survey of human lives your author has been amazed to find how many are ardently seeking a new way of life. Should all those who claim these " unidentified flying objects " are nothing more than cosmic vapors and playful seagulls win out in the Court of Public Opinion, this would not nullify the great good that has already resulted therefrom. Every great thinker has said : " Whatever the human mind can imagine it can ultimately achieve." This has been proven over and over again. Today the whole world is space-minded. Enough " imagination " behind this thought and tomorrow space travel will be a commonplace happening.

Your writer for one does not entertain the " imagination " idea. Destiny has strange ways of working her greater miracles. The Bible says : " And these signs follow them that believe." Those who believe are the privileged ones. They stand as a rock, a bulwark against all false conceptions.

We are at the crucial turn of an epoch. How we turn that corner is up to us. From time to time someone will be singled out of the mass to lead the way. They will be able to read the signposts along the path. A few will heed their warnings. These few will help to lead others into the fold. It won't be an open road. There will be difficulties to be sure, but those fearless of the hazards will be sure to attain. If we pull on the rope together it will make for easier going. It takes great courage to enlarge our spheres, but what have we to lose?

When we start out to investigate life's mysteries, new enthusiasms are born. Every nation in the world that has attained greatness did so because of its pioneering spirit. We have pioneered our own earthly frontiers. Now a new gate has been opened to us. Some of us may make mistakes along the line, but it is a stepping stone ahead. If we refuse to take those first tottering steps we will not get there.

As numbers are added, gathered together in the fold of ONE THOUGHT, gradually consciousness begins to change. When the new viewpoint is launched in the body of humanity new patterns of living are drafted. The change soon becomes apparent in the lives of countless numbers. The more human fuel that is added the faster it grows.

This is a task in which all may share. A task in which all should be happy to share.

How can it be accomplished? Consciousness is *believing*—having faith, then extending that faith to others. When we are made acutely aware there is something better in store for us, then we can help make our world aware in the same way.

Hundreds of centuries have fled since this present cycle was ushered in. The seventh trumpet has sounded. Hark! The angels sing!

For " now have the unstable kingdoms of the world become the Kingdom of our World and His Christ." Rev. 11 : 15.

THE END

WHY WE ARE HERE!

written by a
BEING from JUPITER
and instrumented by
GLORIA LEE

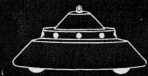

Gloria Lee, known as the Instrument for this book, had a natural interest in the UFO phenomena, since she learned to fly before she could drive a car. As an airline stewardess, she flew over three-fourths of the world for five years prior to her marriage to an aeronautical engineer.

She then became actively engaged in psychic research and began the study of esoteric science. While endeavoring to develop her own extra-sensory perception, she made contact with the Being from Jupiter who wrote this book. The original contact was made in September of 1953 at the Los Angeles International Airport, where she was working as a ground hostess at that time.

Why We Are Here

BY J.W.

A BEING FROM JUPITER

THROUGH

THE INSTRUMENTATION OF

GLORIA LEE

With love, light
understanding
Gloria Lee

Printed in the United States of America

by ı

Dedicated to all those who wish
an answer to life and its meaning

All proceeds from this book will go into the
newly established Cosmon Research Foundation
(a result of this book), a non-profit, non-sectar-
ian organization dedicated to the spiritual and
physical development of man and his knowledge
for the preparation of a New Age.

Donations will be acknowledged and accepted
by the Foundation, P.O. Box 55, Palos Verdes,
Calif., for the purpose of improving its facilities
and development.

Gloria Lee, Director

PUBLISHER'S NOTE

Due to the circumstances under which Gloria Lee received her communications, we believe J. W.'s feeling and intent can best be conveyed by retaining his exact words, his precise inflections.

For this reason the style, grammar and punctuation of the book are left as originally recorded, without editing.

CONTENTS

CHARTS AND DIAGRAMS

INTRODUCTION

When contact was first made with the author of this book, in September of 1953, even I, found it difficult to believe. Often I wondered if my mind had created the fulfillment of such a desire. I even ventured to wonder if perhaps the "man in the white coat" would find me decidedly lacking in grey matter or suffering from some type of hallucination should I tell anyone.

From the first suggestion brought out in the newspapers that we may be having visitors from outer space, I was delighted over such a possibility. It always seemed totally unreasonable to me this planet should be the only planet in all the universe to support life. In a universe of unknown immensity, I felt enrapport with any being who might step out of the misnamed "flying saucers," onto our Earth and prove to the "we're the only ones" egotists that God did not blindly create planets all infinite and just reserve Earth for us. Any creator has to have reason behind his creation.

As the communication continued with my man from Jupiter, identified only as J.W., who said they did not have names such as we do, I felt within there was truly *something* to this besides the interest. I finally confided in a friend of mine who had introduced me to the occult world. His intelligence, education, and knowledge was way above my own and whose criticism I would respect.

Much to my surprise, he didn't laugh at me but was even enthused I may actually have made contact. We discussed the various messages I received and thought up other questions. Of course I was very eager to meet my "space man" in person and whenever the thought entered my head, J.W. was forever telling me it seemed, "Be patient, Gloria!"

This seemed very unfair to me that I could never have any "proof" of the existence of the person I communicated with daily. By this time, many people had allegedly seen, talked, and taken rides in flying saucers and I was quite willing and ready to do the same. However, much to my chagrin, this never materialized and I began to doubt the person with whom I was in contact.

My friend, previously mentioned, told me not to get discouraged. We would also be very cautious of any contact we might make if we were to go to another planet. There was, of course, the possibility that some playful discarnate being might be playing a joke on me, but if this was the real thing, it was certainly worth the effort to continue with the experiment. After all, it wasn't every day you're contacted by someone from Jupiter!

In order to gain some sort of "proof" I attended several organizations familiar with things of psychic nature and discouragingly enough, whenever I mentioned I had made my contact through automatic writing, I was bluntly told, "Forget it!" But somehow I felt there was *something*. It always seems easier to *disprove* than *prove* a thing at times and this looked like one of these times. I felt an inner compulsion to really find out who or what, if only to satisfy myself.

Discouragement won for a while and it was a matter of months before I would again make contact. Frankly, I was just plain disgusted J.W. didn't "drop in for a visit" if he was who he said he was. After ignoring him for some time, (there were times when I knew he wanted to talk to me very badly), I was very strongly impressed to again take up the communication. I almost reluctantly did so if only out of curiosity.

It's true that one day while doing the family wash, I had just stepped outside to hang up the clothes for drying when the impression was so strong, it *seemed a voice said,* "Well, you've been wanting to see one—look up!" And when I did— there was a saucer, big as life, flying north towards Santa Monica! We lived in Westchester at the time.

Flying saucers were far from my mind that morning as my washing machine had been acting up, so this was certainly a wonderful surprise. Later, I heard via the Saucer Clubs some people in Redondo Beach had also seen one the same time, going in the same direction and of the same description. So I felt if I were having an hallucination, at least I wasn't alone!

I learned to fly an airplane before I ever learned to drive

a car and have flown over a good part of this world as an airline stewardess for five years. During that time, I searched
wildly, hoping to see one, but never did. Several pilots, crew
members and stewardesses I personally knew, had seen them
and had even been "buzzed" by a saucer. It seemed very un-
likely a veteran crew and a plane load of passengers could
conjure up a backwash in their minds capable of swaying a
DC-4!

Through the efforts of J.W., I now know, I joined a class of
"psychic development" for the purpose of seeing if it was at
all possible for *me* to develop. The class was comprised of
people with varying degrees of psychic ability and I was ut-
terly flabbergasted when someone described a person who
claimed to be a "space man" and identified himself as J.W.!

Now, how did they know about him, unless they could
actually *see* him? This contact was such a thing I couldn't
gracefully go around telling people about without dire consequences.

Through this class, I received many confirmations of the messages I received from J.W. He began to seem very real to
me and possesses a wonderful sense of humor which manifests itself from time to time. During one session he had
promised to give me a message through someone but I waited
through the whole class in disappointment. After class, a lady
came to me and presented me with a card on which she had
made a rough sketch of J.W. in a uniform. She apologized
for a lack of artistic ability but said she saw him come in and
stand behind me. While he stood pointing at me, he *mentally*
impressed her to try and draw what she saw.

That card was the most tangible "evidence" I had acquired
of J.W. outside of the messages I received from clairvoyants
who did not know of his existence prior to his communication. Since this time, I have developed a spasmodic clairvoyance
but have still not *seen* J.W., other than a manifested light
form, by my own psychic power. I have talked to him in materialized form and via direct voice control, but for those of
you who may still doubt the existence of a person called
J.W., I can give you no concrete proof which would satisfy
only the five senses.

INTRODUCTION

I myself, do not understand the reason behind this, but I'm sure there is one. Whether it's a test of your faith and it certainly has been of mine, I cannot say. However, the fact a book *was written,* is ample proof of an author and in all honesty, *I did not write this book!* I feel no sense of the natural pride an author may have for his book. I'm pleased I was chosen to be the instrument through which the book was written, though I have doubted the choice to be spiritually and mentally equipped enough for such a book.

When I was first told I would write a book concerning space people, I thought fine, and waited once more to take a trip in a saucer. But no such thing happened. I was very disappointed and wondered many times, "What in the dickens do they expect me to write *about?*" So I made contact with a man from Jupiter through automatic writing which later developed into mental telepathy. They had pink skies and blue trees, but so what? The book I *thought I* was to write sounded like it would be pretty idiotic with such shallow information.

It never occured to me *J.W. was to write the book through me* until it was actually started! Nor did it ever occur to me *why* the book was to be written by telepathy until I was half way finished. Although I was aware of the fact, it never completely lodged itself in my mind. I kept thinking, if he can *project* himself strong enough to be seen, why couldn't he just pick up the mike to my tape recorder, dictate, and I could type it out?

Why? *He has no vocal cords!* His people are so advanced, they have gone beyond the necessity of vocal communication and converse solely by telepathy. During their evolution they merely outgrew the need of vocal cords and the spoken word and developed highly refined telepathic powers. When this revelation dawned on me, J.W.'s only comment was, "Now, you're thinking!" And I thought it about time.

No, I can't *prove* J.W. is real in a material way, not even for myself. But I *know* he exists and his book exists. I can't prove God in the court room either, but *you* exist and this planet exists. Every creation has a creator. I can only give you my word and show you his manuscript and perhaps introduce you to clairvoyants who *have seen* him. But again, it would only be *their* word. As J.W. says so often, "always look *within* your God-self to find the Truth."

I have read and studied this book with as much interest and profit, I imagine, as any reader will. Each time before I sat down to receive from him, I prayed and declared that only Truth could come to me and only Truth can go from me. The question may arise, do *I* believe the book? Without hesitation, yes, if I can have faith in my instrumentship.

There will undoubtedly be criticisms as to the manner in which this book was written and as to the truth of my statements regarding it. This is usually the case with people who can only attest to the five senses and those who prefer to believe that all claims about and within the book are but author's fictions.

Not unlike many of the readers, I too, am confused as to the variety of differences and contradictions in so many of the received communications purported to be from Space Beings. Many of the things I have read match fairly well with what I have received, but in some instances, there is a direct contrast. Why? I don't know exactly, unless it lies with the short-comings of the instrument or within the knowledge of the communicator. I imagine they also have a few short-comings in this department also.

They, too, hold various positions of authority (or none), and may possibly tend to repeat something of hearsay or alleged knowledge without first checking sources. Then, I firmly believe, many so-called space people are in reality discarnate beings or perennial jokesters who pass from the physical to the "other side" but where one's personality does not change by crossing. I have seen all too often, unfortunately, people beginning to dabble in extra-sensory perception, believing anything received is gospel truth. There will always be those personalities, whether in the flesh or out, who desire recognition regardless of the manner they might get it. And few people realize the importance of their own consciousness (or vibration) has a great deal to do with what they receive and whom they attract. Many negative experiences have occurred because of this ignorance and much could be said that space does not permit.

INTRODUCTION

I have personally come to know of many of the Truths contained in the book, but many things, I just don't know. I only hope to keep an open mind and ask you to do the same. I asked for Truth in the name of God, and I know many times, Truth is *not* to our liking. Knowing this, I said, whether *I* understand or believe it or not, is unimportant, *but if it is true, put it in the book!*

Well, to be perfectly candid, it overwhelmed me and my earnest and steadfast prayer is that this book can and will, in some measure, help this suffering planet to understand the cause behind the effect and our search for knowledge of the mystery of life. It can be met so the ever evolving Soul will find release in the Light the space people are trying so desperately to bring to this planet.

Prophecies contained in this book may create fear in some people. It is not my wish to introduce anything of a fearful nature to anyone. This concerned me greatly for awhile but to the unillumined who make the mistake of thinking that a prophecy is *inevitable,* and who think if a thing is set to happen it *must* happen, *is not true.* The Scriptures say, "Whether there be prophecies they shall fail." Prophecy comes from *man's own created and established mental structures* closely surrounding the earth and being the *projection of man's own limited thought.*

The outcome is entirely up to man alone. There are always two roads to travel; right and wrong, good or bad. Any bad prophecy can be changed if man's *thinking* is changed. An evil prophecy only *indicates* man's thinking and which path he is traveling. Prophecy should be used for man's *guidance.* He need only *correct* his thinking to change whatever path he is traveling on. Only a small amount of illumination will dispel any negation, false prophecy, or limitation around an individual. It is accomplished as easily as light dispells shadows, for light whether great or small has unlimited power over surrounding darkness.

There is a certain denomination of Rishis in India who are able to perceive an event that is soon to happen. If it is evil, another group immediately takes it up and it never happens at all. The Hindus declare one man can prophesy and another

INTRODUCTION

God-man can stop fulfillment of a prophecy. The Hebrew race in the past were also able to prevent many wars among their people in this way.

The Hawaiians also had a group who could tune in to impending influences and if they were not of their benefit, another group would work against them and they would never manifest. Many times the Hawaiians on duty for good would lay down a certain line and the enemy would not even be able to land on their shores. This was seen to be true often by many travelers and explorers in days before the Hawaiians were invaded by materialists and began to lose this wonderful faculty.

In an experiment with a group of Arizona Indians, the Carnegie Institute found that if this group laid down a certain line, none could cross it except in love. Two men lost their lives by trying to force their way across the line. This seems to be a rather common occurrence among "uncivilized" peoples. However, there is this ability for *everyone* to use. It is not for select groups. Call it intuition or spiritual discernment, if you wish. You neglect the development of self and weaken your own inherent nature by continually relying on things outside of self.

Great achievements have been accomplished from realms beyond reason, but the reasons appeared later. We too often, let others do our thinking for us. The producer becomes more capable and the dependent becomes more dependent. We have watches but cannot tell the time through our own ability. People should learn to develop these inner faculties. Social re-organization should center around a deeper perception: knowing how to do the right thing at the right time. Holding the thought of right action and tuning in to universal laws should be the substance of social functioning in the future.

Our civilization has risen on delusions and superstitions, and the pain and tragedy of our misappropriated creations are now facing us squarely. The blind have led the blind into a welter of ignorance by those who believe as humans think, rather than that which is true and real. When a race or nation refuses to let go of deluded human thought instead of reality, the accumulated vibrations reflect back and war, strife, discord and death result. All these things occur because of man's own will and thought.

When the author and I went over the book page by page for anything I may have received incorrectly, I was greatly impressed with a statement made on one sentence. I had written, "God will then teach us." He corrected me with "God never teaches, but *guides*. Man is his own teacher." We teach ourselves and God is always there to guide us back when we can't find that right path. God never forces His Will on man.

Whatever condition we must face, always lies within ourselves. It was very significant when over twenty years ago, the renowned Edgar Cayce gave a reading which said that if the Versailles Conference succeeded, the world would experience a millennium. If it failed the world would see the same elements plunging humanity into a second and far more terrible war by 1940. It seems man always has those two paths to choose from and takes the worst. Which path will we take this time?

J.W. has mentioned I incarnated from the planet Venus. This, I just don't know and make no claims about it, even though certain psychic experiences point in that direction. It really doesn't matter for we all live in eternity *now* and this life should be lived accordingly. As the great Bard said, "All the world's a stage and the men and women merely players!" Exactly how I feel. I have been given a part to play and only wish to portray it to the best of my ability.

When people have been told, "the space beings live and work among us," means, they have taken up *embodiment*. Whether I am one or not, as I said, I don't know, but many of you who now read this, may very well be. They could not stand the vibration of our physical realm (nor could we stand theirs) if they came to us in *their physical*, which is etheric in nature. But all this will be explained in the book.

I ask you in all sincerity, not to look to personality of J.W. or myself, but only to the teaching and advice of a Soul higher on the ladder of returning. I would prefer to bring you this book with no mention of myself whatever but was told this was not in the plan. You will want something tangible

INTRODUCTION

if only a bewildered Instrument who believes in God and in man as His son.

And as "God plants His seeds in unexpected places," I pray, I can carry out the work intended if it will help you in any way at all.

In order for you to understand the *Truth* about the Space People and our universe, certain (termed) religious concepts must be brought out—read with an open mind and an open heart. This book was brought to you with the combined effort of many, seen and unseen. Tears, tests, trials, teaching, fear of criticism, but finally, understanding of purpose and an honest desire brought forth this book in the hope it will illuminate your understanding about yourself, God, and the Visitors from our Solar System.

The Instrument, Gloria Lee

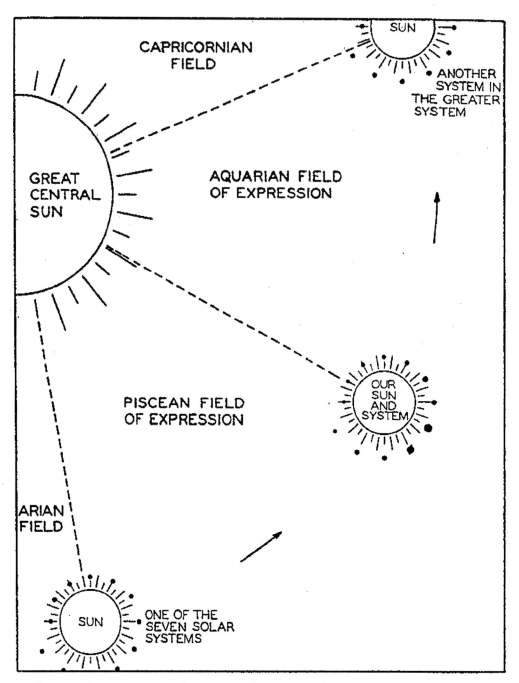

It requires a year for our planet *earth* to revolve around our sun accompanying the other planets within our system, traveling at their own particular rate of revolution. At the same time, our solar system, as a unit, revolves around the great Central sun billions of miles away. All seven of the systems in the Greater System revolve together.

Just as our year is divided into twelve parts, the times and *areas* around the Central Sun are divided into twelve parts. Each period is a little over 2100 years and the time to complete the circle is 26000 years.

Each of the 2100 year periods is termed an *AGE* and have been given the same names but in reverse order, of our astronomical signs. The chart shows our system is just crossing the line into the Aquarian Field of Expression.

Not only is there a relation to the *time cycle* of 2100 years, but there is also a *difference* in the *Cosmic energies* received, and in our case, a much *higher* vibratory rate of expression will manifest as we pass from one magnetic field to another. These magnetic fields are named according to the characteristics attributed to the ancient names of astrology.

Chapter I

INTO THE REALMS OF OTHER WORLDS

Your world must now be cognizant of other worlds. Today, people of this planet will be living in other vibrations. It is now the time for the people of earth to be interested in us. We have come to your planet to help with your evolvement.

Since we have been seen, we have not been recognized by your government, but soon we will be. We have come in love and peace. Unfortunately, too many people will not begin to understand why this is so.

We bring you the way to a new life. We can help your planet immensely with the knowledge in our possession. Your planet should be in harmony with the rest of our solar system. Your people must now learn to use the intelligence God has given to them. Many problems arise in this life for the God within to speak. We can help you, as our present evolvement allows us to solve problems that can and do arise with this God-self.

Turn your thoughts to God and many new concepts will come to you. The correct way of life will begin to manifest when you are in this higher consciousness. We must be ready to help each other now. In the Age developing, many will not be ready because they will not be in this consciousness. The few who try to stand alone will fall without proper guidance.

Tune into your Higher Self. The Creator has placed a Cell of His Own Being within each man. This Cell will bring the realization of your own God-being. Through this Cell comes enlightenment. Man will travel to the worlds without in the light. *The moment is at hand for your planet to take the greatest evolutionary step you will probably ever witness.* Many of you will be able to see between the world of the physical and the world of the spirit.

We will be seen more and more in your New Age.* By our being seen, you of this planet, will realize there are worlds

*See chart page 20.

beyond your own. We have the Christ consciousness* in our world because we *know* God is the Executive. We will be here to show you what is in store for your planet.

We come in the God consciousness† and soon you will be in the Christ consciousness. This will bring many changes. We will help you commercially, in your economic situations and with your machines. You will see much progression.

Your evolution is now at this great turning point and progression will continually be greater. The only way this planet will not be in harmony, is in the consciousness of the people. All things come with the God consciousness, but the *realization* of this consciousness is what is important—not to fly to the moon; but to realize the Christ within you. This realization brings the only correct way of life man has known.

We'll be with you in the crisis which is to come; but be in the Christ consciousness. Only then can your planet progress farther into the realms of the higher worlds.**

We must be accepted by your people for what we are before we will be officially recognized. Never before have we ever attempted to be recognized by the masses. In the past, we were only attempting to instruct the few who would accept us. This has been much to our sorrow, but because of the few who were with us in belief, your planet has been greatly helped. But unfortunately, these few have been greatly ridiculed and persecuted because of their belief.

We come to you today only to be of help and not work out your karmic pattern.‡ There lies much negation in your karmic pattern. You have been building it for thousands of years and it must be fulfilled. In growth there is always, what you of the physical plane call tragedy; but with tragedy comes thinking and in thinking, you turn to God. This is true of all men, for without tragedy they would only coast along.

*Manifesting Christ-like characteristics.

†Manifesting even higher than Christ-like understanding, intelligence and characteristics. Greater attunement with God.

**Realms *beyond* our physical manifestation.

‡The life pattern set up by your Soul (or Souls involved) in consideration of what was "sowed" in the past—the law of cause and effect in action.

24

The tragedy of men is usually the reason they turn to God. They find it necessary, to mind, to call on a Source higher than they can understand. You will fall without this higher power. You can only progress with it. Try only to see God, not man and his negation, because the negation man has built up on your planet may one day rule you. That day may be soon as you must fulfill your karmic pattern. This is necessary in order to take these steps of evolution. You will travel in the light and you will grow. This will be your test of the love you have for God, since man must find out reasons for himself.

The time factor is all important. We will help you at the *right time* in the plan. You shall be able to understand *why* this negative force exists with my help. This has been related to you in numerous books and magazines, but I will tell you this: *today is the time!* There must be a *karmic cleansing** before you can progress. Only then can the love of God be understood. This is the reason you must be prepared and with God during the time this negative force is to be worked out.

After this has manifested in your life you will understand why I said you would call it a tragedy. However, to us, this so-called tragedy is the *step* you take into the New Age. The Aquarian Age is here for your planet. Be not afraid; for then fear will rule and God will be left out.

Try to be only mindful of your Creator and the God qualities in man. In this thought alone is power for you to step ahead and to be uplifted to the Christ consciousness. When you see the "saucers" as you call them, in your skies—be not afraid. We come *only* to help you. *This is why we are here— to help you in this evolutionary step into the New Age.*

We come only in peace and brotherly love. We want to help you progress and understand why this negative factor is involved. Without a cleansing of your planet, you could not forge ahead in your physical world. We have only the love you will one day feel for us in our hearts. Some of you try to create us as negative in your fears, while in reality, we are here to help you establish yourselves in the new vibrations of the Aquarian Age.

*A cleansing of the *negative* pattern built up—"as ye sow, so shall ye reap!" This is the harvest.

25

This is a momentous occasion for the entire solar system. The step your planet is soon to take, will complete the whole solar system in being with God. Your planet is the last* to enter into the Christ consciousness. All the planets in this system will rejoice for your progress is to their joy. As I have told you, the minds of your people will look upon this step only as a tragedy. But remember, with this step, look only to God and He will be with you as we are.

We must be here to help you or many of you would perish. Remember, the things you create in your mind must not be given strength of Truth if you wish to be helped. You cannot go forward without the realization of the God within.

Be with us and the world you now know will be changed into the world of your dreams. Then you will really *feel* the brotherly love your philosophers and teachers have been trying to teach you for thousands of years. Now, with this New Age vibration, the love of God shall be more intense. And you shall feel this love within your hearts. Love shall be made manifest over your entire planet.

This is only the beginning. Your world will see many changes and many things will be revealed to you. Your lives will be completely changed, but remember, it is for the best. The time is now. We must help you progress. You will be led in our love and through God's. This has been decreed by the Logos† of our solar system. Before the planet of Earth is to go forward; we shall land and be recognized for what we are and then you shall take your step into the future.

Because we never came in such mass before you may be frightened. Be not afraid. We come in love. This is our pleasure to help you take this evolutionary step. We too, can be helped by your step. On the planet you call Saturn, there is a Tribunal with a seat reserved for your planet—the last of the solar system to enter into the Christ consciousness.

The way is clear now but the work is great. Never before

*Earth is 2000 years *behind* in it's scheduled evolution—thus the reasons for taking a big step or "speeding up" process to meet the requirements, both physically and spiritually.

†Logos—term given to a God of Perfection. A Solar Logos, the God who creates and manifests through a solar system. His Life Force directs and governs the system.

in this planet's history will so much be happening at once. We must be able to communicate with you in the language you can understand so we can be of service.

In cases where we have been accused of being instigators of the secret society of evil, you will not be too receptive to us, but we must try and help you. People can only be helped if they will *let* someone help them. Try to be in the consciousness of God and you shall be helped.

We will be with your planet until the New Age is completely established. Then we will be brothers in love. This is the objective of our Solar Logos* for us to be under His influence of love and not to remain in separate worlds of consciousness. Though you must remain in the physical world when you reach the Christ consciousness, the world of Spirit shall become apparent to you† No world shall be apart, one from the other, for when you advance to this stage, neither your world or mine shall be without God.

The Christ is the Will of God. Your planet will progress through this consciousness, in the future, now being worked out in the Mind of God. The people of your planet must try to understand what is happening in their world. Never before has so much had to be worked out than now.

Instead of worry, fear, and worn concepts, only be mindful of the help you have to take this step. Only after this step has been taken, can your planet join with the other planets and take the initiation‡ with this solar system. The Will of God is the Mind we must follow, for within lies a Plan. The Plan is for the whole solar system to develop to the point where our God is. When we have reached this point, then *we* shall be gods. But for the present, we should only think of what we must do to become these gods.

The Mind of God is so perfect, it is even inconceivable for us on the higher planes, to comprehend this wonderful Intelligence that exists. The Mind of God knows only justice

---

*Our God who created our system. Our Father, the One we pray to, manifesting as a solar system.

†Clairvoyance will become common.

‡Of a Cosmic nature.

and harmony. The negation man has built up is not of God nor in His Plan. This negation is from the negative thoughts and actions of man. It is this negation which must be wiped out by the *cleansing process* known to you as tragedy.

Be with God and the will of *man* cannot harm you. Be with us and we can also help you. In your immediate future lies the world which your prophets call the millennium. Indeed, the lion shall sit with the lamb, and brotherly love will be the ruler.

This is not the way of God, in the world you now exist, but the way of man. The way of God sees only harmony where the mind of man sees only chaos. Be in this Christ consciousness for today the minds of men must be positive, to be able to cleanse themselves of their negation. The Will of God will manifest when the negation is removed by the cleansing process.

By following His Will, the love and peace so difficult to obtain, will become a reality. This is not the word of myself, but the Word of God for He is now speaking through me. Be in tune with God only and your Inner nature will tell you what God wants you to believe and understand.

This is my job, to tell you people of Earth, why we are here through the Instrument with whom I work. This must be, for when we come in our ships of space, you may be frightened, but it is the Will of God that we come in peace and brotherly love.

We must follow His Plan in our work. It is in this Plan to help each other. Only then will our entire solar system have the co-operation necessary to follow His Plan. When the Plan is known and perceived by the people of Earth then we can work together instead of the condition now existing on your planet. It is necessary for us to be here, as that time will be chaotic. The turmoil following will be beyond your present comprehension. This is the reason the Logos, in His goodness, has sent us here to help you. In your present condition the entire planet could be destroyed without our help. So it was ordained we serve you and help that this destruction may not take place.

The people of Earth must realize we are here to help and

not to harm in any way when we are better known. We must be able to have your complete co-operation in order to save you and your planet. The next year will be one where many will cry out in disbelief that this could happen to them.

The wonder of God lies in the condition in which Satan will be bound for one thousand years. This is to help you of this planet. We cannot help you or tell you why this is necessary unless you will believe in us. Many may turn away in fear when the time comes to see us. But again I say, *be not afraid. We come only to help you!*

It is so important you be with us. The truth is horrible to say; *if you will not let us help you, the destruction of this planet is at stake!* Be with us and your future is with God. Love is flowing freely from His Heart to you here on Earth. He is mindful of the condition and that is why we are here.

I cannot tell you enough why we are here—but you will be in the Christ consciousness after this step has been taken. Try, try, try to believe in us. This is so necessary and important because we *cannot* help you if you do not believe in us.

We will be here this year en masse. If people turn away from us, we can only pass them by. If we must, we must, and no help can be given to those who fear us. This is sorrowful to us, that many will not believe in the brothers they have on other planets. This is true of many, even now, who call themselves the scientists and intellectuals living on your earth plane. In their so-called intellectual mind, they can only find reasons why we do *not* exist—not reasons for us *to* exist.

This is indeed a tragedy, even to us, for in this mind that cannot find us, there is no hope. We must pass them by and the sorrow will be with God. He does not wish His children to be left behind in the turmoil following your big step of cleansing.

The world you now know, is not true reality. The reality is with God. You created this world you know now in your mind. This negation you have created must be dissipated. It is the Will of God for you all now living on Earth to understand Him. Those of you who cannot understand, have not evolved to this point. So in all the goodness and kindness of God's understanding, you will be taken in spirit to another solar system of this *same* evolvement.

This is not to be feared. This is also God's Will and He is just. His Plan is great for all of you and all of us. To progress with His Plan, we must be in tune with God. Many of you perhaps do not understand what I mean when I say "in tune with God." If you live in a vibration of love, you feel love towards each other, but if you fear or hate one another, the hate vibration will rule. Then, this negativeness, you built up with hate and fear, will be with you and can rule you. But if you are in *tune* with this love vibration, then the negation now existing *can be destroyed*. Be mindful only of God and His creation. Without this thought, you will want to recognize the world of man and not the world of God.

We shall soon come to you, but I can only say this—be with us in love, not in fear—for fear can destroy you! We cannot tell you how important this is. When in a *fear vibration*, you will *draw* to yourselves, the very negation you have built up. And there is only destruction in such a vibration.

Now, I wish to tell you how this step is to be taken. Today, in the country you call Russia, is much negative force. We know of this force and have many times interrupted their work. But now the time factor involved is right for this negation to be made manifest. I say to you, the world will *not* be ruled by fear, for fear will destroy itself. Soon, the men who want to control the world will be planning this move. We will be there to impress them not to follow through with these plans. The plans they are creating can only destroy themselves. When we try to tell them this, they can only see what the world is to them—a world of fear which they can rule.

We tell you this now, so that your planet will be able to rise above fear. If you fall beneath this fear, then they *can* rule. But if you rise above it, they will only destroy themselves. Fear can only hit those who fear fear itself. This may not be within the understanding of some, but meditate on this thought and the understanding shall come to you.

The Truth of God lies within yourselves and if you comprehend this statement, the understanding of God's Will shall come to you. Then when we come to you, the path is clear and we can help you. But if you just read this statement as mere words, the understanding will pass you by. You shall be left with those who must remain here while this negation rules.

Be not fearful, again I say, for in fear there is destruction. This is not the fear of God, but the fear of man. The fear of God is entirely different. In fearing God, you love and respect Him—but in fearing man, you hate him. When you have fear, fear is your ruler; not God, for the men in this negative force can rule your planet. But if each person were to fear *only* God, their power would just *bounce back*, so to speak, and destroy the ones who sent it.

We want to be entirely truthful with you of Earth. In Truth only, lies salvation. This is the Truth about us: We do not exist on your plane of life for we have evolved *beyond* the physical plane.* To many intelligent minds the Truth is not understood as such, but I say to you, it is the Truth. On the other planets of this system, there is only one who's people are living in the physical plane.

The planet you call Uranus, is the only one which has the same physical plane as you do, but they have evolved to the Christ consciousness. They have been in their Golden Age the past one hundred years. The other ten planets have all gone beyond this physical stage. The only two planets left in the physical are your planet and the one you call Uranus. Many will not comprehend this truth, so I shall endeavor to explain in the next chapter.

Be mindful of the God within and you will grow in your Christ consciousness with your understanding of this. Soon you must be ready to receive us for it is the Will of God that we help you. But remember, we cannot help you if you will not *let* us. Be with us the day we land en masse as we come to save you from this negation which *may* rule your planet for a period of three years. His Will is not to rule by negation but to *cleanse* your planet *from* negation. This cleansing process is the *step* you shall take into your golden world. Be with us, I say again and again, for now is the time.

*See charts pages 32 and 72.

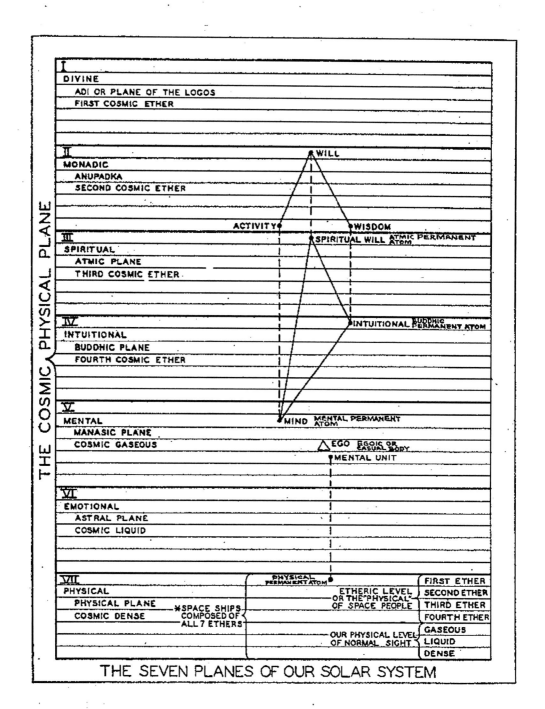

THE SEVEN PLANES OF OUR SOLAR SYSTEM

* BY CHANGING VIBRATION, THEIR SPACE SHIPS ARE BOTH SEEN AND UNSEEN THROUGH NORMAL SIGHT, ALTHOUGH FILM WILL RECORD THEM WHEN OUR EYES CANNOT

Chapter II

INTO THE ETHERIC WORLD OF OURS

The world we live in is physical in a sense. Perhaps not to you for your eyes cannot see us. The world we live in is etheric and is in the *higher ethers** of the physical plane. Your science knows only the three lower ethers. We exist in the four higher ethers but also reside in the three lower as our plane of life encompasses the whole.

In other words, the physical realm actually contains seven ethers. You reside in the seven also, but are conscious only of the three lower ethers known as solids, liquids, and gases; but there are four ethers beyond that stage of the physical realm. The ethers known to us are without consequence right now, but we can *vibrate* to your lower ethers too. When we do, then we can be seen within your range of sight. In this manner we shall come to you when we land on your planet.

There will be no need to be fearful for we may be in the likeness of you. We are not of this likeness in reality, but you would not understand who we were if we did not manifest as you expect. Many forms manifest in this solar system. On your planet you can only comprehend the one form you call *human* form. I wish to tell you though, there are twelve human forms on the planets—each one was created by God, not by man's thinking. We can and do understand the Plan and Will of God in these higher worlds.

When we travel from planet to planet we are in conjunction with the Plan. No *form* is important but only the God consciousness that manifests *within*. This is not to your liking, I know, but it is the Truth. And I came here to relate the Truth.

Do not worry about the words I speak through the Instrument, but be only mindful I say again, of the God *within*. Now, many new things will manifest unto you which you have never dreamed possible. In this new comprehension of your solar

*See chart page 32.

system, we must be able to tell you things you may fear to some degree, but the Truth must now be told.

The time is so short when so much will happen to you that the understanding and love of God will be the only thing you can cling to. Be in touch with your God-self and all will be well. When you have the vibration of love around you, no negative force can harm you. Be with us in thought, and many of us will impress you with the Truth of our world. But tell no man what you think in secret, for they will only laugh at you.

Be strong in your convictions, then you will know the Truth and it will not matter what man may think of your thoughts. We know the minds of your people on this planet—not to understand the what and why they fear a thing. I can only tell you this: God has created *many* things beyond our comprehension in His Plan. We will not and cannot understand all, even with our present evolvement, but as we evolve, many new things will be understood by us. Only then will we realize how great and how truly wonderful our Creator is.

On the twelve planets of our solar system, we can and do see why and how well His Plan is working. Inside of the next twenty years, your planet will see the Truth. By the end of twenty years, many of you will never see death. Among your very friends on this planet, are people who have incarnated from other planets and know death does not exist. They will be able to transmute their bodies into the higher ethers without experiencing what you term death.

This, I know, is quite a surprise to you. Among you today walk many great Souls, and with them lies the duty to help you understand these higher Truths. The love of God is on your planet. He has made it possible for these higher beings to incarnate here to lead you and help you into the New Age now beginning.

When we land we want so much to tell you of our love, but please do not fear the things I tell you. There are so many things even we do not understand in God's Plan. We know one day we shall understand what He is trying to work out. Then we will be with Him in mind, in spirit, and in Soul. This is the ultimate of our solar system—to have each planet manifest the Will of God in order to become as Gods. This is the most wonderful thing you can now understand. That you will all one day be as God, for this is so.

The things you will read further will amaze you and be in such form of thought so as you may think this comes only from a madman. But, trust me, when I say, you will see so many things you will not believe possible. Only then will you begin to see just how much exists in heaven and earth you did not dream possible.

Be of good cheer, my children of Earth, for this is Truth and God is speaking through myself via the Instrument writing what I say. We progress only if we *want* to be with God. If we do not, then we must suffer with the laggards.

The mind of your so-called intellect will not believe this, perhaps, but instead of trying to be in tune with them look only within yourselves and ask your God-self, "Is this true?" And if your intuition tells you it is true then follow the words I speak. Your salvation and your progression lie with Truth in the New Age.

It is not an easy thing to help a planet. There are many adverse conditions to counteract even before we can begin to help. This is not the way of our worlds. We will only follow the Plan of God, not the plan of man. This is why we have evolved to a higher degree than you. When you come to us we can help you and you shall understand what I have told you thus far.

Offer your hand to us when we come to you and we shall know you are not afraid. We want to help you so much. Our hearts are grievous you may turn away. We must be brothers in love, not brothers of fear. We shall offer you our hand in love only and in this way we may be true friends in God's love.

As this book is read, many times will you think to yourself, "What have I been reading?" "What is this all about?" This book has many Truths soon to be understood. It is now time for you to take your step into higher worlds. We have what you would call perfection in our world, but to us, this is not so. We have inharmony too, but not like the inharmony on your planet. This planet is so completely inharmonious, that our world would be absolute heaven to you. We know of worlds beyond ours which have even greater perfection, so we think of our world as imperfect. You too, shall see and understand what is taking place in our solar system today when you come into the New Age.

Your world is now completely inharmonious to us but when you are in tune with the vibration of love, you shall be in tune with the whole solar system. Only until you see for yourselves, will the understanding of how well the Plan of the Logos is working out.

The Logos I often speak of is our God. He is our Creator we pray to. When you come to this plane of thought, you will realize and discover this solar system is only one of seven solar systems being watched over by the Cosmic Logos, Who is in a way, the God of our God.

This will be completely new to many of you that our God could have a God but there is no limit in this great universe. Each solar system has a God as great and as wonderful as our God. But over each system, there is the Cosmic God, Who has the power of creating and guiding these seven systems. The Central Sun Vela is the existing force which emanates to the seven systems—and the seven Gods, our God included, use this power to transmit it to the twelve planets existing in each system.

This is the whole plan of the Central Sun or Logos of the Central Sun. We call Him the Cosmic Logos. He is indeed a Great One, but even over Him there is a Logos watching over the rest of us. This may be too incredible in your words to comprehend such a magnitude of greatness. This may even seem impossible to your mass mind at present, since they have been taught through your orthodox churches to have only one God. But I say to you, *there is only one God;* or as we say, only *One Spirit* in charge of all the Creators or Gods.

As you progress through your evolvement, you, yes, each one of you will be a God as our God. But when you reach that point, our God will have gone beyond, for there is no limit in this universe. The universe we know is called by us the universe of the Central Sun. In reality it is called by another name but that is unimportant now. There lies the pattern of the atom with each Cosmic Logos. Through this same pattern, the true Work is made manifest.

Even the cells of your body have this same pattern. From the smallest to the largest in our universe lies this same pattern to be followed in all things that have been created by our God. This is the Truth, if only you of Earth can comprehend what I say. This is not to confuse you or frighten you, but to be with you in mind, so this mind of yours can unfold to the higher thoughts existing.

In thinking over these things, you can understand how great and how wonderful the whole plan of each universe is. Yes, I said *each universe,* for there are many universes in the heavens. As said before, there is *no limit* in our heavens. Each universe has planets and solar systems to work out a plan, and only the God within each knows that Plan.

You may not understand this, for many of you have never even wondered that there *could* exist other solar systems or other universes. But be that as it may, this is what exists. To your way of thinking this may seem incomprehensible, but to us, the Plan is so wonderful we can only be in awe of the wonderful work being done by these great Beings—*Who at one time possessed human forms,* but Who now manifest forms to do the great work being done in our systems.*

It is true when you evolve to certain stages, you will not possess what is called human form. Actually, you shall be without form, for then you are in a world that is formless. You can create your own forms which will best help you work out the plan necessary to manifest. This is not an impossibility in our world. We can create forms needed to work out various plans. This may be the most startling thing you read today, however, it is true.

We, of the planet Jupiter, can come to you by projecting our *mental bodies.*† The projection is *real* to the extent the one receiving it sees us as real; but in reality, this projection is not the *true* us. When you see this projection, you see only *what* we have projected. Within each person there is the thought of what we *should* look like, and when we see this thought form, we just enter into that form.

*See Evolution in the Universe, page 67.

†See chart on Bodies of man page 38.

THE PHYSICAL & SPIRITUAL BODIES OF MAN

1. The physical vehicle for this plane of manifestation.

2. Etheric—actually part of the physical plane but of the four higher ethers of the seven ethers of the physical plane. This is the body through which you are recharged during sleep state. It quickly deteriorates along with the physical after death of the physical unless of a higher evolved Soul. The state which all on the planet will pass into eventually in the new age as the atomic structure of our present physical undergoes the change in evolution.

3. The astral or emotional body or vehicle. The body your consciousness travels in during the sleep state. This vehicle cannot go beyond its own plane of life.

4. The mental body which is of a fine enough degree of material and can travel most any where, depending on its strength and the development of the individual.

5. The Egoic, Causal body or being of man which is of a higher mental nature and houses the Soul memory. It is produced at individualization. Within this sheath are to be found three permanent atoms, termed the mental unit, the astral and the physical permanent atoms.

6. The Buddhic houses certain spiritual atoms. Atoms are but force centers.

7. The Divine, the Soul, operating on the plane of the Logos.

8.-9. While I was making up this chart, J.W. said there are actually two other bodies not even mentioned in any of our esoteric books or schools on this planet, because they house the permanent atoms that go *beyond* our Solar Logos and continue into the authority or the Pure State of the One Great Spirit.

The forms you see will not be the true *egos*, for when we project these forms we are really using the *mental bodies* we possess. As we join and densify (solidify) the atoms of this body we can be with you. We are able to be in two places at once, so to speak.

When we come to you within this *projected* form, we can and do see the same as you. We'll teach this to you, and you too, shall be able to *project* your *mental bodies* into our worlds. This is a natural law of God—to be able to travel without the *hindrance* of the physical body and the necessary time element in traveling to other worlds.

When you project your *thought* to our planet, you go without a ship. You are simply using your mental body. You are there. As your mental body develops to a certain degree, you too shall be *seen* by us in your *mental body*. If you wanted to, you could also *change* this body into whatever form you would like to manifest. This is the reason we usually manifest to you in the very form you *wish* us to, because you cannot imagine there being *other forms called human*. When you come to us, you usually manifest in your *true* form because of this ignorance.

You may try to manifest in another form, say of the animal, but then you cannot understand what is meant by other human forms. We cannot tell you until you understand this subject better, but when you do, then you will also be able to manifest in these various forms.

You will see the form which is pleasant to you when we project. We may take on a form of what you would call an *ideal* of your particular human form. If you took on this form or any other form when you projected to us, you would be exactly the *same* to us regardless. We consider only the form *within*, the Christ-self that manifests within. This is what is important to us. Realizing only that the God-self is the *true* form of man—not the physical body, or the mental body, but the Body of God that is within you.

When this realization comes to you the forms of man will be different, and you will understand what we mean when we say the *forms* are unimportant. These forms merely let us *express* in some particular environment. The time shall be when we will come to you in our true form. Until that time, however, we shall be with you in the form of your ideal.

You may be fearful as you understand the form you will see is only a *projection* of our true form. We want to tell you though, when we come to you within this projection, we cannot be without our love. So why be fearful? We tell you these things because we want you to understand we can be with you in love regardless of form. *How* we express this love of God is the only thing that matters.

Whether we use this form or that form, is very unimportant, but if we take on the form you understand the most, then you can soon take us for what we really are. If you fear us because we tell you this, we will not be able to come in our true form ever. Take us for the *love* we manifest, then eventually, we shall appear to you in our own forms.

This is definitely not to frighten you in any way, merely to teach you within God's work, there are *many* forms of life and when we were created, we were created as *brothers*. Whether we look alike or not is unimportant, but what we *manifest* to each other is important to the Eyes of God. We really fulfill our part of the Plan when we manifest this Christ love. In God's Plan is the thought the children He created are One and a Part of Him. But if you were to continue to say we can't be brothers because we don't look alike, then you will never see the *reality* of life. If you refuse the Truth of a thing, then this Truth is *taken* from you. But if you leave the mind open, when the time is right, then you shall know the Truth of all.

Should you try to make the conceptions of your *own* mind into reality, you will shut yourself out. You will not wish to understand why we want to be with you in our true form. Try to understand more fully what our Father is trying to teach us all by creating many forms of life in His love.

When we reach the stage in our evolution of complete brotherhood, we shall be well on our way to being gods. But until that stage is reached, we must suffer more pain. In this pain will be the lessons we must learn. Until we learn these lessons, we cannot understand reality. When we seek Truth alone, then these things will be revealed to us. Truth taken for what it is, can never be without God, for God *is* Truth. And when we accept Truth for Truth, and not *illusion* for Truth, then we can be more understanding of the whole of creation.

The Instrument through whom I have written this book, is not of this planet but was brought to you to be helpful in bringing you to this knowledge. The woman you call Gloria, is not from my planet, but the planet you call Venus. This is what we call incarnating into another world to be of service. She is known by many as a Traveler of Time.

Certain Souls have this work, to incarnate on various planets needing help and to be of service when the time is right and they are needed. In the Plan of the wonderful future of your planet, you will know and be led by these, gods really, to be in harmony with the solar system.

Today, many young people will come to you, telling you what is happening on other planets. Many may be false prophets, but many will be true Travelers of Time and you must listen to them. They may not even know *why* they know something they tell you, but they *know*. It is because they have been taught this in other worlds.

You may think this the most startling book you have read but I say to you, there are so many startling things in our universe, that these things are so minor to us we can't even begin to tell you what will happen in the next twenty years to your planet. When the Instrument is finished with her work, she will return to the planet Venus with many others who have come to you with only the thought to help you of Earth. Many Souls will be ready to leave here when your planet is well into the New Age.

Many of these Souls here today will simply *transmute* their bodies into the four higher ethers I spoke to you about before and leave in this manner. The one you call Jesus, was not from this planet, but from the planet I now reside on. It was in the Plan for Him to transmute His body into these higher ethers—to prove to you there is no death.

This is just an every day occurrence to us of other worlds. We merely *change* our forms and then we can incarnate in *different bodies* on different planets, wherever it is the Will

41

of God. In this way, we may help each other and we cannot be without understanding of each other. Eventually we shall have been in every form manifesting now in this system.

The Plan in our system is for complete understanding to exist between all men, or forms, as you may wish to call them. In reality, they are men in the Eyes of God, for all of us are His children and we must strive to be as perfect as He. This is the Plan of each system, to become as perfect as the God that created them. In this way, eons from now, all shall be creators of solar systems and be in tune with another Cosmic Logos.

The Greatest of us has been able to look out into this vast universe without understanding what was seen. The complete Plan is of such magnitude, even we of the very highest evolvement, cannot understand what lies ahead. But we know when we reach this point, we will understand and be in tune with the Logos, Who in His greatness and His love, created us so He could manifest through us in these forms we call Sons of God.

Chapter III

INTO THE WORLD OF CAUSE

When you first see our ships you call saucers, your reaction will naturally be with or against us. But instead of running from us, meet us with the same love we have for you. We can have better understanding between your world and mine with this feeling towards each other.

The moment of evolution is soon. This step to be taken by your planet is, to us, the *unfoldment* of God's Plan. You shall understand many things you cannot now. Some of you will not even attempt to understand until it has been proven to you.

Take out the love that lies within your heart center when we come to you and use this same love God sends to protect yourselves. You can be protected with love. There is the light which lights the path to perfection of Soul with Him. You automatically cut yourself off from God if you fear in any way. By doing so, you will not find it within your heart to be with us. The way for you then is to remain on your planet until the so-called *tragedy* has abated.

I do not want to frighten you, but I do want you to understand no thing is tragic with us except the thought of negation *man* creates. The real tragedy is not in the step, but within the *mind of man.* First, to be able to accept us, you must be able to understand *why* we want to help you. This is not the most inspiring way I can relate this incident, but it is the nearest way I can explain it in order for you to comprehend what is behind our loving thought of service.

When the time arrives for us to land you will have some measure of understanding to be in harmony with us. The vibration you create will be in harmony if you use the vibration of *love* in accepting us. We have not come just to help you, but to *repay a debt* this solar system owes to you of planet Earth.

In the past this planet was very enlightened with beautiful

and wonderful Souls who were living here. But when it was decided to bring the *spiritual* laggarts from the various planets of the system to reside here, you gratefully accepted this challenge. You had hoped to raise the laggarts up to your standards. Unfortunately, the reverse happened as these laggarts were too strong in negation.

When the women of this planet consented to have these children born unto them, they (the laggarts) brought the race existing here at that time, down into *their* lower vibration. It is for this reason you will not find a Missing Link. The Missing Link is spiritual, not material. Because the races that preceded the so-called Link, were in the *etheric* realm and not of this same physical level you are now. As the vibration was lowered, the physical plane became more *dense,* so to speak, and thus you became actually lower than was meant for you to be.

These God-like women who had these children born unto them, were in the etheric, and when the children grew up, they saw their mothers only as *spirits,* not as physical. This was indeed the saddest situation to these women. Because as the children grew up, they wanted to return to their old ways and would not listen to the spiritual Truths these women wanted to teach them. Thus it was, that what these youngsters created for themselves, was the negation which began to cloud your planet. Soon the whole planet was clouded by these laggarts who really came to be enlightened so the rest of the solar system could continue to progress without them.

So many Souls came into this lower vibration that it was impossible for the higher Souls to raise them out of it. Gradually, these higher Souls *withdrew* themselves. The Veil of Maya,* as you term it, was then drawn *between the physical* world and the etheric or spiritual worlds. These youngsters, or laggarts, when adults, could no longer *see* the spiritual realms. They had to work out this *karma* for themselves. By this method, they suffered much pain and wonderment for reasons not even understood by them.

In God's compassion, He could not allow this to happen

---

*Illusion of senses for Spirit or true reality is not seen, but mainly, thought forms in man's consciousness or the *creation* from that consciousness.

to His children. When the planet became so darkened by this negation, it was decreed it should be destroyed! The great Soul from Venus, known in your occult* circles, as the Lord Sanat Kumara, then came here out of pity and found just *two* Souls with just a small spiritual light showing in their hearts.

He pleaded with the Logos to let him try to raise this planet once more into the spiritual realms. The Logos was overjoyed when He learned there were two Souls on the whole planet showing this flickering of salvation. He consented to let this wonderful Soul, Sanat Kumara, be the "Lord of your World" to raise you out of this depth of darkness.

The two great Souls who were the saviors of your planet were in much later incarnations to be called by you, the great Lord Buddha, also known as Lord Gautama, and the great Lord Krishna, also known as Lord Maitreya. These two wonderful Souls were the instigators in saving your planet from complete annihilation.

Since the negation was so great on your Earth, the Logos, in His great compassion, could not see His children suffer so much from their own mental creations. He felt very sorrowful with the idea to destroy rather than let the people continue in their suffering. But the word of the two flickering Souls from Sunat Kumara made Him so grateful and so happy to tell the Lord from Venus to try and lead His children back to Him once more.

When this story is told by these Great Ones, They will never take the credit for such a wonderful job, but say, "Within God lies only love and compassion and we were here to carry the light for Him. This has been our privilege and we must see that this planet is never destroyed!"

Please remember this story when we come to help you. In this story is the reason we must pay back the great debt we owe to your planet. Without the help you once gave us, we too, would not be as evolved as we are today. Now in this way, we too, are able to take the love and compassion God

*"Occult" has been greatly misunderstood. Does not mean "cult" but pertains to the esoteric or "hidden" side of science or nature.

has also given us and use this to lead you back to the path leading to Him.

Fear us not for we can only see you in God's eyes. To us, you will one day be the same as God our Father. Think on this. It is true and Truth can lead you out of darkness. In learning these Truths, you can then understand why we must be able to help you. It is written, each debt must be paid to the debtor. This is the cause and the reason we must be here when you take this step in your evolution.

You could not take this step alone without our help. This will not be too big a sacrifice for many. But some who have not reached this point in evolution, will not be able to *withstand* the vibration your planet is going into. This vibration is of such intensity their present physical bodies can not attune to it, since the change will affect the mental as well as the physical. *Absorbing* this new vibration would be injurious to both mental and physical bodies if you are not sufficiently evolved as it is of such force.

This vibration can be absorbed only by the ones who can go on into the Christ consciousness. In the years to come, so much will manifest you have never even touched upon in your wildest dreams. Many must not come with us for they would not be able to withstand this new vibration of *love*.

As this planet moves into a *new area* of vibratory activity in our solar system, the planet Venus will also move into higher vibratory realms. This must take place soon as the planet Venus is ready to take an initiation of a higher degree. Many Souls from Venus came here to help you in order for *all* of us in this system to progress.

This is not fantastic because in God's work there is perfection. In His Plan many cannot comprehend what He is doing, but we know, when we do understand this wonderful Plan, we'll know it is right and good, as God is only right and good.

The so-called evil you sometimes speak of, is not evil in that sense, but is only evil when there occurs an *inharmony* in vibration. To us, this "evil force" (or opposite force), is very necessary for balance. Throughout all our solar system and universe there are positive and "negative" forces emanating from God, or the Central Sun. Beyond this sun lies an even greater force which is not important to you now as this is only to help you understand what is behind this force you call evil.

When I speak of "negative" in this instance, I do not mean, as your language implies "bad" or "evil," but this positive and "negative" force could be termed male and female—the female containing certain *properties* or *characteristics*, as the male does, but in themselves are good. *Together* they form the *polarization* necessary for perfect *balance. Only good comes from God.*

The "negative" vibrations you feel will not be evil in your world if you understand why this force of negation (bad) has been built up by you. When you build up a negative force and it is evil, the forces were *wrongly* used. But if these forces are correctly used then the proper balance is maintained and only harmony occurs.

Those of you who cannot understand why evil exists, or those of you who will not *admit* evil exists, then I say to you, be only mindful that God is good and all things are perfect. In Him there is only perfection and these forces will not be inharmonious if you use them correctly.

The same weeds you pull from your garden could be termed "negative" because they destroy the beauty of your garden. The weeds growing on your mountains, could be called positive, for they do not destroy beauty and are useful in helping what you would call erosion. They do not let the mountains wash away. In this simile, I only want to show how "evil" is good when used correctly and is only evil when it causes *inharmony.*

This is the same pattern we follow throughout the universe. When we see a problem we try to decide where the "negative" force belongs and where the positive force belongs. In this way we have harmony, and in this way we have happiness. When each thing is in its *rightful* place only the love of God is manifested.

This is not the complete idea, but it is what, I believe, you can now understand. We cannot tell you the whole Truth as it is very complicated now to your present evolvement. But remember, that whatever happens, it is good in reality, for the negation (evil) must be destroyed which has been created in man's mind.

In this way only can the proper "negative" force take its rightful place. Without this force there could not be balance in our system. This is true of every phase of the world, for in all things there is the positive and "negative" or male and female. This simile is not complete, as I said, but is just to give you an idea how this "negative" force must be handled. When this is understood, you will comprehend more of God's Will.

Be in tune with us whenever you can. We will impress your minds with the Truth, for indeed, this Truth is all powerful. Without this Truth, you will fall beside your own negation. This is not meant as a verbal spanking, but only meant as light for you to see whereby you can find yourselves with God in His Christ consciousness. When we tell you more of these things, be only mindful of this Christ consciousness. Without Him we would be nothing.

These are not the words of man, but the words of God. He alone can create our worlds. Be with our God, and we too, can find each other. We are indeed brothers in love and and in this Christ consciousness, when we try to communicate with you, be with us so we can help you and repay this debt we owe. If you turn from us, we cannot repay you and then we must leave you. This must not be in the Light of our God.

The way to Him is through the Light. The debt we pay will be repaid to God for letting us have permission in using your planet for the new home of the laggarts in our system. This is meant to help you understand why we come today and why we have come for thousands of years.

This is not the proper way to progress. It really should be done from within your own self; but when we can be of service, we shall be. In *yourself* is your own God Center, and this is the proper way to progress. Know and realize just what is within. It is the same God within you that is within us. In each man you can find this same God Spark, but if you want to find only the negation a man has put there you can always find it by looking *past* the God-self. If you really want to find God, look into this man and you can find his true self.

The way to be in love with God is to *feel* the love of God by seeing this same love within each man. Each man has the same love as you yourself. When this planet finds this love, every man will truly be brothers, one unto the other, and your New Age will reign. In your Golden Age love will reign supreme, the same brotherly love your teachers wanted so much to teach you through the ages. Now, this will become a reality. You will easily feel what you should towards each other *in* this Christ *vibration*.

Gradually this will become stronger and stronger. In time, your planet will raise itself out of this lower physical and become one with us (etheric). Then all the solar system will rejoice as brothers in love with God. We must try to perfect ourselves the same way God has perfected Himself. We, too, shall be creators of some solar system in the far, far future.

I know too, this may all seem fantastic to you, but to us, it is *reality*. Because from where we sit, so to speak, we can actually *see* the evolvement of various Beings on these higher planes and watch them as they grow. This is very thrilling for us to watch Beings of still higher worlds manifest to us in Their God-like Beingness.

When we see how completely inharmonious your planet is, it grieves us greatly to watch you stumble in the dark. Please let us give you the light needed to raise you out of this darkness. Then and only then can you be One with God.

When you find yourself *manifesting* in this Christ consciousness, this God-like quality will show in your faces, in your relationships, and in your Souls; *for this same Christ consciousness that was in the one you called Jesus, is to be made manifest within yourselves soon.*

Be with God and this can be so. This was told to you many years ago, "the things that I have done, Ye shall do also and even greater." Remember these words, for He spoke them with force and He told you the Truth. These were not idle words, but the reality which would be manifested in the world you will see coming soon.

These things will not seem impossible if you are of the

Christ consciousness. The light within is the same light that manifested through the One called Jesus. But remember, this light must be *brought* out in order to be seen! This is what we mean by the flickering light which was seen by Sanat Kumara. These two wonderful Souls, Gautama and Maitreya, were indeed showing just a flickering of light at that time.

It was nearly two million years ago. Through them, the planet was slowly raised to the present situation, which is far from perfect, but has been greatly improved from the darkness which engulfed it. Now you must only be mindful of what our Father has created for us. The way to receive the vibrations of this consciousness is by tuning in to our Father. By realizing just what it is we were made for, we will understand the most important thing.

When we return to our Creator from this *traveling of the Soul,** we will be with only the thought, God has created us to manifest *through* us and the way of our salvation was with *us!* When God is in your thought there can never be what you call evil happening to you. But when you turn your thoughts from Him, only then, can evil come to you. You will be out of hamony, when not in tune, and the force you attract will be the evil you create.

This is my wish: in your prayers when you talk to our Father, be with us too, and in this way, we can help you understand the cause you suffer so by your own creations. When our ships land, we will want to be in touch with the Soul you bring down into your conscious mind. This God-self is your Soul and in your Soul is your salvation.

When we can bring this planet into the new vibration, your Soul will be closer to you as will we. Your Soul can bring you the Truth about yourself. We can be with you in thought and thus be able to teach you more of the Will of God.

You will be without this evil force when you have been taught the ways of God. You will further understand about the "negative" force emanating from Him, for this force will be in its proper place. Then the weather will also be in harmony, and the ones who call themselves "weathermen" will

*See chart on Involution and Evolution, page 72.

50

not be needed. Your weather can be in such harmony, your rain will come only when needed.

The weather is not important, but is just an example of what your future will be like. We'll tell you more of future events when we come to you, but for now, be grateful we can be with you during this step in God's Will. God is only with us if we let Him be. What is in our hearts is what will be manifested in our lives. When you come into this Christ consciousness then you can run your lives according to the Plan God has for you. Your lives will be happy and serene. If you should try to run things your own way, only inharmony will result.

We always cause our own unhappiness by not following God's Plan. So many fall on their knees and say, "Why, God, why?" "Why is it this way for me?" "And why will you let this happen to me?" When you realize God *wants* us to be happy and receive only good, then is the time to follow His Plan for you. Only our love of God shows us why we were not happy. In happiness, we can more clearly see and understand why we are involved in His Plan.

The Plan is not to *make* us be with Him, but to *let* us be with Him. When we try to run things our own way, we shut out the greater Plan and this way we run astray. But when we understand the Plan made just for us, then it is, we will be in the wonderful elevation written of by many who want you to be happy.

God will not tell us what to do, but He is there when we need Him. If we were told, we would be what you term, robots. We would not be God-like, but like a machine. Since our Creator was so wonderful, He let us exercise our own free will. Man has been unhappy because in his will the wrong way was made. God tries to lead us back to the correct path into the light, whether or not interest is with Him.

From now on, you can be happy, because if you are mindful of God, then all situations will work themselves out accordingly. If God's Plan is followed, you shall be in harmony once more. Be with God and your planet will bring to our solar system the greatest light ever seen in our heavens. When your planet can shine forth with the wonderful love of God, it will be the most brilliant light to be seen while still in the physical plane. You have been indeed blessed because of this special dispensation. So many are able to be of help when Earth takes its Cosmic Initiation. It shall truly be a wonderful world to the whole universe.

In this universe the stars that shine were only created for our worlds; and the sun just for our sun. But when this was the beginning, these things were not. And when God said, "Let there be light," it was in the universe; and when God said, "Let there be planets," it was so. And when He said, "Let there be suns to shine forth for these worlds," it was so. And then came the greatest work of all: the children He created was us! Only in God's Eyes, we were then with each other and in our eyes we were all *brothers*. But when man of your planet was creating his own world, he created us as different. That is why today we seem not to be related, but what you call "outer space men."

When we come to you, be mindful God created us the *same time* He created you and we can be brothers. This is our fondest wish, that we will be brothers in love as God created us. Feel this love within your hearts and understand why we come to you.

The world may not understand what I tell you now, but when you read this book, we'll be with you, to impress you what is right within your thought and what is wrong. We want so much to be of service; to bring you out of your dark corner of the universe and into the light corner so you can be with God completely.

It is God's Plan that you be with us, but if you cannot feel this within your heart, you cannot go, as this solar system will be too evolved for you and you must take this step alone. When your body has fully absorbed the new vibrations, you will be released automatically from your physical body. You will be taken to another solar system of the same evolvement in your spiritual body. There, you may progress the way you wish. And in the future, when you can once again be with us, you shall be brought back to incarnate on this same planet.

Until this time, you cannot remain here. These new vibrations would harm you and be very injurious to your mental body. The cosmic rays will be in your atmosphere also. These rays will actually be only the going and coming of God's love, but when you shut out this love, you will only be injuring yourself. You must *accept* these new rays coming to your planet. When they are accepted in your *consciousness*, they will be very beneficial to you. If you want to shut these things out I have told you about, you will also be shutting out God.

You will know in your heart what I have told you is true. And when the time comes for this evolutionary step, you will go into the solar system God has arranged for you. You will not remember from whence you came. Be in tune with that God, for that God will have a Plan for you too. And if you learn *this* lesson well, you can be with Him and progress back to your proper evolvement now being set up on this planet.

We will be with you when you read this as many will not be able to comprehend what I have said. Ask God to tell you what is true when you read what is written. Within yourself this same God is manifesting. It is your intuition to know when the Truth is being told to you. If you try to make out other things of a negative nature, you will not be in tune with God or us. Then you will have to remain here.

We will be able to do nothing for you, except to feel within our hearts we tried to help you. If you are left, remember, you were warned and must remember why you were left. The lesson you learn will help you in this other solar system. This lesson will be remembered in your subconscious mind and you will never again make the same mistake twice.

This is the way of *man,* to learn by mistakes and failure. But when these lessons are learned, you never forget them. By not forgetting, you become stronger and stronger, until one day you will be as God, perfect in your Soul and perfect in your mind. The way to God is perfection and the way to light is God. We want so much to be with you through your world crisis. But if you are determined to stay, we must pass you by.

You know the reason we come to you now. There is no

effect without *cause.* The effect is great when the cause is negative, but if this cause is positive then you can take the step with your planet. You will only be failing to understand why you were not taken with us if you try to be stubborn. But this failure will never be forgotten. The lesson will be most severe and you will not forget it in the rest of eternity. This one lesson will always be remembered through all your lives: what it was you failed to remember when it was time.

We want so much to be with you, but you must *feel* this within your heart center so we can be. You will soon understand the causes behind the effect. *This is a law.*

The law of cause and effect will never be abolished. There is also compensation for the *positive* forces you create in this law, as well as compensation for the negative forces. If you try to avoid this law you will only be unsuccessful as this law is God. God is law and without law there can be no creation. What is created must be with God. This is not the idea of man. This is the idea of the God that created you and me and all our planets in our solar system.

It will be too late for you to change your decision of remaining once we have left, for we will not be able to return until after the crisis has passed. Should you decide to go with us, you shall be saved from the severe lesson which will occur.

This is not evil, but in God's goodness, it is the best way to learn why you should return to Him. Be with God and all these things will be understood. If you turn from your God-self, you shall be loving yourself more than God, and this negative force can reach you. If you love God more, nothing can harm you. Each person has his own *protective armor within,* the Christ consciousness. This is true of all men, for all men were created by God.

Chapter IV

THE TIME IS NOW

In the crisis to come many of you will fail to understand why it is so important to be with God and of this consciousness. As the planet moves into the higher vibratory field, of which I spoke, certain radiations being sent from the sun will be felt. You will *feel* this Christ consciousness. It is very important to us you understand this.

When the vibratory rate is raised, you will feel somewhat light headed, although this is *not* of the *physical* body. Most of this stimulation takes place within your *spiritual bodies.* * The effects of this stimulation will be *sensed* in your physical body, but is not of the physical. However, when you feel this light headedness, you may be unaware of this fact and think it is physical. If you tune in to us, we will be able to give you certain powers needed to better adjust to this vibration.

We never try to project to you when you expect to *see* us *physically.* We *project* to you through your mental body via your head centers,† or your brow and crown chakras. The way to contact us, is to project to us *mentally* . . . When you project a *thought* to us, you set up a vibratory activity which creates a current or wave length, so to speak. We are able to *see* this as it comes to us. We can then return to you on this same wave length.

Contact us in this manner. But never with fear, for if there is fear within your auric field you create a wall and it is impossible for us to come through. This is not in the usual sense, telepathy, but is called *mind projection* and reacts on the ethers much the same way as your radios react to various wave lengths sent out. When this mental wave length is sent to us, we tune in to your "station" or mind. In this way we can relay the information you desire.

Try to project a thought to us, if only how you feel about us by thinking on this. Picture within your mind a saucer, as

*See Bodies of Man page 38.

†See chart on Spiritual Centers, page 100.

you call them, and project this thought to the saucer you *visualize*. When it is received, we will come to you and try to *impress* your mind with the answer or the loving thought that all is well with you.

You create a magnetic field around yourself when you project to us, and it makes it easier to contact you through this same field in the future. If you are unable to project a thought to us, we can only try to impress you with good vibrations we must build up in your magnetic field.

Many of you may want to understand what we mean when we say "project." I will say it is not necessary, if you can just visualize the saucer in your mind. When we see this visualization we can project to you. If you still cannot visualize a ship, be in tune with God and as you wait for Him to answer you, we can come in on that particular wave length. The highest vibration you can send up to God is in our vibratory field and we can come to you.

Sit in a chair relaxed while you wait for an answer. We can impress your mind much more easily than if you were standing or moving about. The way to practice this is very simple. Always say the Lord's Prayer or other spiritual affirmations before you begin. Then mentally project to us as true brothers or children of God. We are better able to contact you on this *wave length* if you furnish this vibration also. But if you cannot visualize us as brothers or children of God, then be with God and ask Him what you should do.

This will be the greatest evolutionary step ever to be taken by your planet. In the future, many of you will want to remain in this vibration forever, but you cannot. You will have advanced to *another* rate of vibration when you understand the reason for this change. Each little enlightenment or understanding of God and His activity takes you a step higher in vibration. You will be able to tell yourself in this progression of consciousness, "This is not me, but God working through me for when God is in me, only God can be manifested by me."

This is what we term "being in tune with God." But if you were to say yourself, "Well, today is the time for me to be tuned with God—but what is God, and where is God?

Where is the One Who created the heavens and the earth?"
You cannot find Him for within your heart the only thing
you can see is what *you* will be in the world of tomorrow.
You must be in tune with that future vibration in order to
understand fully how you came to be in this vibrational change.

Suppose you tell someone to be in this new vibration of
Christ? Then you will be with the goodness which was placed
within you. But if you try to tell someone *not* to be in this
consciousness, you create an evil force. You can only be alone
with this negative force. We, nor God, can come to you. We
will project to you *only* if you try to be with God.

When your planet is ready to step into this new vibration,
the world itself will be more in tune with God. The planet is an
entity, not human, of course, but this Planetary Logos *was* in
the human stage eternities ago and is now *manifesting* as a
planet.*

Many of you may think this so fantastic you may stop
reading. Now, I say to you, be in meditation on this subject.
This is Truth and when Truth is written, the "still small voice"
within will tell you what is right. When the "still small voice"
tells you this is so, be mindful of God's great wisdom and
understanding. He wants us to be as perfect as He is perfect.

When this idea is familiar to you, tune in to us and we will
help you understand why this is so. The Planetary Logos cannot be in tune with God unless you are also. When She (yes,
this planet is female, in the sense She is of the "negative"
vibration), comes into this new consciousness of the Christ,
we too will be able to see how bright Earth can be.

On my planet, which you call Jupiter, we shall then be able
to see you easily. At present, we cannot. The reason is in
your present *consciousness* of mind. This state is not spiritual
enough for the *light* to travel to us. But when your planet is
in a higher spiritual light or *frequency*, it will travel as far
as my planet of Jupiter. It will be seen as a bright star in
our heavens.

We cannot see you with naked eye at present, however, we
can with our instruments, you would call telescopes. We see
even your mountains and rivers at close range. We can see

*See page 67.

you are not a spiritually enlightened planet because the light surrounding you is strictly of a physical nature. When a spiritual light is manifesting from your Planetary Logos, you shall indeed be the brightest star in our heaven.

As this planet finally advances into the spiritual realms, you will be joyful to know this spiritual light will be vibrating throughout the whole solar system. The Solar Logos will be more than joyful to see all His children returning to Him.

We cannot tell you everything necessary to return to our Father, but we can tell you how this planet came to be in such a darkened state. When you understand why a Logos is manifesting through your planet, you will also understand why your Logos cannot stand the negation which has been built up over the centuries of time by your men's mind.

The Planetary Logos is very sensitive to the vibrations of negation. When you suffer an earthquake or some such phenomenon, the Logos is merely "shaking" Herself loose, so to speak, from the negation. When your vibratory rate is higher, you will not be able to stand this negative vibration yourself. You will be unable to stand negative thoughts even, for they will *repel* you and you will also want to "shake" them off much the same way the Logos does.

The earthquakes you call a *natural phenomenon*, occur because through the earth there are "fault lines." These "fault lines" act as receivers of this mental negation. Even the atomic energy released by your bombs is drawn into the "fault lines" and becomes so strong and powerful, great pressure is built up. The Logos seeks *release* from such pressure and the earthquakes result.

If you knew how to control your bombs and your *thinking,* this power could be used for good and would not be destructive to your land. This power is the *misplaced* evil I spoke of before as inharmony. When you try to be mindful of this power you will use it for good by building up the earth in the proper places and not let it be in such order as your present state of mind. You will be with God when this power is harnessed. It is in His Plan for you to understand these laws He has set forth in His universe and use them as gods for your own betterment.

This is not difficult to believe but is Truth to be *understood* and help you in your progressive step. In some degree, when you learn to use these laws you will learn your own world. You will be in tune with the correct vibrations of God. You will be able to: run the weather, put the sun's energies into workable channels, and the oceans into proper power centers when this vibration is set up according to Plan. Many things lie within your oceans which you have not learned the use of yet. Many forces exist in each thing on your planet and these forces can all be used to help you live a more harmonious life and have a more harmonious civilization.

Your world is now returning to its rightful orbit. You of Earth must understand why this is taking place, because there will be many upheavals caused on your physical plane by this return to the original orbit.

After the original orbit is once again lined up with the Central Sun, your planet shall move into an area of a higher vibratory rate in the solar system. The movement or *adjustment* will cause such phenomena as earth quakes, hurricanes, and perhaps what you would term cataclysmic effects. When these catastrophic upheavals occur, you shall see the ancient continent of Lemuria or Mu, rise once more out of your Pacific Ocean.

As this happens, many parts of your present land shall be flooded. The water from that area shall replace the lower land areas on your planet. This will be brought about, not necessarily due to change of orbit, but partly because so many of your bombs have been tested on your South Pacific Islands. Many of these existing islands were formerly mountains of Lemuria. However, the atomic bombs tested on these islands are not the main cause of the uprising of this continent but only a *part* of the reason.

These atomic explosions have caused new pressures to be released and by this release, they have already caused the continent to rise. The governments of various countries know this fact but usually have not associated it with the atomic tests. But the islands now in the Pacific will one day become mountain tops once again for this new continent. Some of these mountains may fall, due to their weakened condition caused by the atomic tests. However, this will not affect you for many years must pass before the continent becomes habitable.

The continent will change position when the time is right and rise out of the ocean in tune with the Plan of the Planetary Logos. This is an old continent to the Logos although it may be new to you. The continent will have a wonderful vibration for the Logos to use at this evolutionary change.

At one time Lemuria was in superiority of your planet, but in the first order of the Logos, the continent was inundated because of evil forces. The men of that time tried to run the world with the powers intrusted to them. These powers were turned to their own good; thus this power became evil. The power was good until these men tried to accomplish selfish goals and turned from God.

They went on to work this evil purpose without thinking of the karmic pattern they were building up and which eventually created the reason this continent was inundated. Lemuria was *cleansed* of this evil force by this flooding. When other continents become flooded, they are also cleansed of any evil force. Lemuria will rise up with a fresh vibration to help you with your progress. This is told to you because this is what you yourselves have caused, not the Planetary Logos, or the Solar God, but the men of your planet who have used forces for evil means.

The forces God has given you will one day be understood and be recognized for what they are. These forces can then be harnessed to do only good. The continent which shall be reigning in the New Age will never have to undergo such a catastrophy again if they *maintain* these *clean* vibrations. They shall never need another *karmic cleansing*.

When man learns to use these forces for good and positive ways, he'll create positive patterns that shall only result in positive effects. The turning point is not necessarily to understand why the effect may be what you would term evil, but why there would be no evil effect if you did not create the *cause*. The law of cause and effect is the law God has for complete balance to be maintained at all times. If this balance leans towards evil, then this evil must be "cleared away" for the proper balance. Many of you may think the world is coming to an end when this continent rises, but this is not so. However, the physical world is coming to an end for many. But I wish to say, when this occurs you shall be protected if you come with us. We will come to you en masse before this happens and let you take refuge with us until this is passed over.

This is how we, of the solar system, can repay the debt we owe to this planet. In repaying our debt there will be little reason for us to continue to stay after the step has been made and you have readjusted.

The day we land you shall see so many of the ships you call saucers, your skies will be darkened. It will not be so frightening if you expect us and know we are coming to help you. We have thought of many ways to warn you. The book you now read is one method. By a book I can tell you why we come and give you the reasons we want you to understand. By this method you also gain understanding of your solar system and knowledge of your planet and of our God.

We want so much to be of help to you, but if you turn from us then it must be that you face this catastrophic step alone and in fear. The lesson will be very severe for those who cannot find it in their hearts to believe we come with love. Many cannot or will not believe these words. Within their hearts they will only find reasons to the contrary. They do not want to understand why or recognize the world is within a world of solar systems of Higher Beings than they. Within many minds lies only the thought that they and only they exist in a world they can see and touch.

I want you to know *many* worlds exist they cannot see or touch—*but who can see and touch them!* We can and have touched you many times through the years but you have been unaware of our touch. Before this New Age step, we shall be seen and you will touch us. It has been decreed all men on this planet shall see us as we see you. Many will still disbelieve what they read or see, because within their minds they build up a negative thought. Fear is king of their emotions in this thought and in fear they shall fail to understand why we come.

Be not afraid, again and again, I say to you. You shall know the *step* is soon to be taken by your Planetary Logos when we appear. Be with love in your hearts so we can take you to the moon. The moon will be your refuge for a time. You will not return to your planet until the waters have settled and the *fallout* from the bombs of your enemies has been cleared from your atmosphere.

Your planet will not be fit to live on until these things have passed away. Do not fear this step. This is the *cleansing* step your planet takes in order to start anew with *clean* vibrations so the Christ consciousness can manifest within you.

We, of the solar system, will be most joyous after this step has been made. We know your whole planet will be illumined. The whole solar system shall then go forward with you in the New Age.

The moon will seem so far from your home you will wish to return as soon as possible. Although the moon is to be your refuge, many will not want to stay there. Your planet Earth will be seen every time you look and you may think you are not allowed to return home.

You will return when we believe it is safe. Even after your return, many will want to go back for your planet will be in great disorder, but you must now remain. New cities and new lives will have to be built. You will begin to use new methods, which we shall teach you, for construction of these cities. The old methods you have been using are so inharmonious. We will help you set up new systems in order to survive this great change. The change, I shall again remind you, is *good*. You could never pass into the new vibrations without this great change. *This is necessary only to cleanse your planet of the evil forces which were worked up by the evil thoughts of men.*

You need only to understand the reasons God has in letting us help you. This help *is* in the Plan of God. When you read this book, try to tell others of this plan. The fear will be lessened if many can know of our help and of the plan. This is one reason we have decided first to tell you by book. We shall then tell you through your radios and televisions, and even to some, by telephone. We must be sure you will accept us before we land. This is not only necessary, because of your government, but because we want you to know we will never try to harm you, only to *help* you. This is the *only* reason we will contact you.

This work will have been wasted unless you are *receptive* to us. We must be received in love, otherwise we cannot help you overcome any fear. This fear will rule you until the time of three years has passed. If this three-year period is overcome without fear, then you shall be in the Christ consciousness.

However, before reaching this point in your evolution, you must understand *why* you must travel through these various experiences. The way is not difficult. This step will be taken in harmony with our help. The step will be very chaotic for you should you turn from us. We will not force ourselves upon you as this is not God's Will. We will only help you if you want our help.

This shall indeed be a most wonderful experience for us too, to be able to be with you during the introduction of your New Age. When you realize just what will be in store, you will better understand us. There may be many times you will wonder why we even bother to help you, but when you understand why we want to, you will also see all this is for love of our Father. It is His Will that we be of service to each other.

The time is now when you will be under the influence of many evil forces. Surround yourself with God's love and *consciously* project this love to your brothers. This kind of evil negation shall pass freely from you and you shall *not* be harmed. But if you surround yourself with this same negation by thinking on it, then you shall *draw* this evil force to you and it can destroy you.

Be with God and you shall be with us.

Chapter V

INTO THE PLANS OF GOD

You of Earth should now understand what we mean when we say "God." Our God is your God and the Father Who created each thing we see and each thing we *cannot* see in our solar system. There were created many worlds, unseen by us, as well. Some of these worlds will be revealed to you when you enter the new vibration. God is unlimited in the creative field. There are so *many Gods* for you to know but I shall try to bring this God knowledge to you.

The reason there are so many Gods is a logical one—to lessen the work of our Creator so, in this way, the Plan can be fulfilled to the highest and lowest. The Plan is for each one to help the other in his God consciousness. There are so many things to learn that when we attempt to comprehend this Plan of our Father, we immediately become confused. But even in this confusion the light begins to shine.

Now with us, we fully understand the wonderful Plan God has created with His creation. The other existing planets in our solar system were created for *balance*. The total number, some not yet seen by your planet, is twelve. The planets not yet discovered by you will be seen within two or three years after you've entered into the new vibration.

Their vibratory rate will be the same, but the *lines of force* emanating from these planets will be felt when this planet returns to its original orbit. These God-like forces will *connect* with the lines of force from your planet and the *reaction* will bring *sight* as well. In your present vibration and orbital position, these other planets cannot be seen because their vibration is higher, and out of synchronization, so to speak, in order for *visual* light to pass from you to them in the physical.

Those of you with esoteric vision can see them even now for their spiritual radiation is brilliant. The time shall be when all of you will see these planets too. Your spiritual radiation will cross these lines of force and you will visually comprehend the meaning of the words "God-force" radiating from these planets.

In our solar system there are six "negative" planets, or what you may call the female vibration, and six positive planets, or of the male vibration. They were created in this manner for perfect balance or polarity. The vibration is not important except to help you understand how this solar system is balanced. In every universe throughout all creation there is this balance.

The Cosmic law of polarity exists from the smallest cell to the farthest star in the realm of God. There must be polarity in all things. Even your electric motors have an, what you call, armature and a field magnet. In inorganic matter, the proton and the electron exist, and within the organic world, male and female. Through all things, "negative" and positive properties must be. The *evil* negation is created only by man in his ignorance of the law of balance.

This balance is worked out to the Nth degree in vibratory rate, so when man creates an evil negation, the balance is upset and a negative (meaning bad) reaction occurs. This bad reaction or negative karma would not occur if man did not create a *cause*. When man learns self-control and creates only good, his karma is good. There is no upsetting of balance because all that exists in reality is good. Thus, the only reaction would be of a positive nature or, more *abundance* of this good.

Be with us now, in order that I might explain to you why there is not only *One* God but *many* Gods *expressing* through this *One Spirit*. To use your terminology, let me say, *you must be able to overcome what you have been taught in your churches.* The Truth is greatly distorted and misunderstood in your churches. The Bible you use is true, but the interpretation thereof, in many ways, is false. The interpretation we have seen will not in any way be of help to you in this chapter. We want to help you to understand Who your God is and why there are *many* Gods Who manifest through this One God or Spirit.

Beyond our Central Sun, which is surrounded by the seven solar systems, there is what we call, the *One Spirit* emanating His power *through* the Central Sun *to* the seven solar systems. But in each solar system, there is the God Who created that particular system. Then we have seven Gods, but remember, these Gods were *first* created by the *One God* Who is the only *true* power in the whole universe.

The God-force that emanates from this One Spirit is so powerful and so wonderful, the most brilliant of all our *known* Gods, cannot understand what He is. Our whole universal structure is built on this same principle of God creating God, Who in turn creates Others. Each system has its *individual* God Who created twelve planets for His work and over these seven Solar Logoi is the *Cosmic Logos* of the Central Sun. *This* Logos is so Wonderful and so Magnificent that the seven Solar Logoi, One of Whom is *our* Creator, cannot understand what He has in His Plan for Them.

In all this wonderful work the Plan is for *each one of you to one day be a God and create too!* Beyond this, there are many more things still not understood by us. But this we do know, there is but *One Spirit* Who created our God, Who created us. Our Creator and the other six Logoi of our universe, will never be what this One Great Spirit is because He is Powerful and so Intelligent and Mighty that when They reach this point of evolution, He will have gone beyond.

The Omnipotence and Omniscience of the One Great Spirit is so incomprehensible, the universe will never understand where the end lies, for within this Spirit there is no beginning or ending. He is All and this is what we call Infinity. And this Infinity can never be understood by the minds of men. Until we reach the God stage ourselves, then we may only have an *inkling* of what this True Spirit is like.

But in the world of Gods, there is so much not told to man. We feel only as conscious pin points within the universe of the Central Sun. The worlds of the Central Sun are not important now. Many will not reach this point in evolution for many, many eons of eternal time. But those who wish to know of our own solar system, we can tell you the following.

The Solar Logos *manifesting* through our solar system is triple in nature. These three aspects of God are called in your Christian terminology, The Trinity, or the Father, the Son, and the Holy Spirit. The Father represents Purpose or Positive energy; the Son, Love-wisdom or Equilibrised energy;

ENTITY	VEHICLE	CENTER	SPACE	TIME PERIOD
Above, unknown ...				
The Cerreon Logos	7 Constellations	Cosmic Logos	5 Cosmic Planes	21 Solar Systems
A Cosmic Logos	7 Solar Systems	Solar Logos	4 Cosmic Planes	8 Solar Systems
A Solar Logos	7 Planetary Schemes	Cosmic Being	3 Cosmic Planes	3 Solar Systems
A Cosmic Being	7 Planetary Chains	Chohans & Groups	2 Cosmic Planes	1 Solar System
A Planetary Logos	A Planet	Heart of Planet	1 Cosmic Plane	½-¾ of Solar System
A Man	Physical and/or Spiritual Bodies	7 Etheric Centers†	1 Cosmic Plane*	1 Planetary Scheme

EVOLUTION IN THE UNIVERSE

Our universe is merely an aggregate of various *states* of consciousness, and matter is that which is of possible perception on *any* of the various planes of the Cosmic.

10,000,000,000 years is the approximate period for one *cycle* of a solar system, which has *seven* cycles—which makes up one Round. Seven Rounds makes one Scheme. A Chain is a *period* of a Scheme.

Every Life has its three great cycles: Birth—Life—Death—or—Appearance—Growth—Disappearance.

To begin in a *new* round of manifestation and experience.

*See chart on page 32.
†See chart on page 100.

and the Holy Spirit, Active Intelligence or "Negative" energy. These three aspects of the Logos are present in every form.

With man there is the Spirit, Soul and Body, as the atom itself possesses a positive nucleus, or center of attraction, and the negative electrons or force coming to the center creates the outer form or the manifestation of the two.

Now, in this explanation, try to be mindful only of the One Spirit Who is manifesting through our God and this *One Great Spirit is All*.

Our Logos will never be as Wonderful or as Great as the God Over All, but He Himself is *Perfection* and with this Perfection He *manifests* the One Spirit. We will also be guided to become as perfect. And when we learn of this Plan and understand, then we can put forth a more conscious effort to help work out the Plan within the Mind of God or Father.

In this manner, we too, can consciously progress to this Perfection. If we do not try to progress, then we cause the inharmony which results in evil forces. But when we try to progress with the Plan which is in the Mind of God, we follow the lines of least resistance. Together we can be of service to our Father and help Him in manifesting the great Plan He had when He first created us.

We want you to understand all this so it will help you in your progression. But before you can become as God, you must first bring the Christ consciousness within your heart center. Then God can manifest *through* you with the force of love that emanates throughout this whole universe of the Central Sun and Infinitude.

We'll be with you when you meditate on this vast thought and impress you how your thinking should be channeled. When you call on us to help you, we shall be able to impress your mind with the Truth. In Truth there is hope of yourself being brought into self-realization of this mighty Creator.

Try, at least, to be with us in mind, so we shall be able to impress you properly. You will receive illumination of this God we call Father. Understand why there are many Gods. If God had to do everything Himself, then there would be nothing for us to do or any of the Higher Evolved Beings. This way we work out His Plan and progress back to Him with our own initiative.

You will one day understand why we have been chosen to serve our brethren and God. We find these lessons in working out our progression are for our knowledge and understanding of what our Father wants to do. In this great Plan, we must realize all our Father wants, is for us to be with Him in understanding of the Creation He has created for *us alone*. In this great creation, the man who walks beside you is as yourself in every way. You are each a *part* of God and this is why we want so much to help you, because *you* are also a part of *us* since, we too, were created by God when you were.

I pray you will be with us so we can tell you many things that cannot be written as yet. Your understanding is still limited, but when you enter into the new vibration, many things will be within your understanding. We shall tell you much more of what exists in this world.

Not only man is evolving in your world, but the trees, plant life, the animals and the birds. The oceans too, have a life that is evolving and in your very *elements* lies a kingdom also evolving towards harmony and perfection. Even within your mountains, there are gods or spirits that rule and evolve with you. Each tree has a god or deva spirit within that created it. The flowers and plants were created by gods who came forth from our Father for just the purpose of creating what you see around you.

The beauty of trees, plants and flowers, are in reality, created only by God, but in *Truth*, each little god was instructed how to create these things and uses the God-forces emanating through the universe. As you progress, these little elementals or gods of your earth plane, also progress *back* to God consciousness. When the new vibration is reached, these little *devas* will soon show themselves to your sight.

As of now, you cannot see them unless you possess clairvoyant vision. I would like you to know though, the creators of your flowers, the little gods you do not see, exist within your very elements. And they can be *worked* by you for whatever purpose you wish them to manifest. It was ordained by our God that men shall have dominion over all.

These little gods which inhabit your elements and flowers and such, should be talked to with *love*. They will create even bigger and better flowers, rocks and so on with this love. The whole world of the elementals would be so grateful. You should want them to be your friends because they want only to serve man. In this service, they will also be serving God Who is their Father too.

The deva kingdom is progressing rapidly, but, as yet, you cannot see them unless you have the necessary vision (clairvoyance). However, when the New Age arrives, these devas or fairies, shall be seen as little *lights* flickering in the things they create. You may wonder what they are when you first see these lights. There is no fear because they only want to serve you. Their little bodies will also be seen as you progress higher into this vibration.

The old fairy tales you have all read seem fantastic, but in reality, they were based upon the truth of the existence of the fairy elementals. The planet shall not be in darkness any longer when they are seen once more, and the planet shall be most beautiful. The rose will lose its thorns. The cacti will no longer have thorns either for these things were brought about only by man's negation. Even the flowers and plants found it necessary to build up a *resistance* in some kind of protection against this negation.

When only love is manifested on your planet, the things *resulting* from negation shall drop away and only beauty will be seen. These creatures of God will only create more beauty. The blessings will be so wonderful when this occurs, you will cry out: "My Father, my Father, where is our love and how can we please You?" You will be wondering why He has blessed you so with this cry. Indeed, the Father is blessing us all and we have but to understand this wonderful Plan of His to know why He does love us in such a wonderful manner. He *continually* pours out these beautiful blessings coming to us.

As we realize the magnitude of His creation, we cannot be but humble, and wonder why He chose us to rule our own world. We cannot be other than Gods, with His blessings, when we understand this wonderful privilege God has given us. It is now in the Plan for you to rule your world with love.

This wonderful blessing is for man alone. You shall fall down on your knees in gratitude and worship Him with all your heart and Soul when this occurs. In time, you shall see this with your own eyes.

During the next three years, so much will happen to you that you may begin to doubt there is a God. When this period is over, you will *know* there is a God like what I speak of. He is so great and good and wonderful to bestow upon us the greatest blessing of all, to be like Him as He is. Your world will soon be back to this God-like vibration and so many of you will wonder why you couldn't understand this before. But it is not possible to understand these things under negative conditions. The *outer* consciousness too, is clouded by an *imbalance* of forces and the spiritual light cannot shine through.

We want to be with you to help you brighten up your spiritual light of understanding. This is the most we can tell you now, but meditate on this Truth, for Truth is within yourself. Realize this God within and the Truth will out. There is harmony and beauty for the whole universe with God.

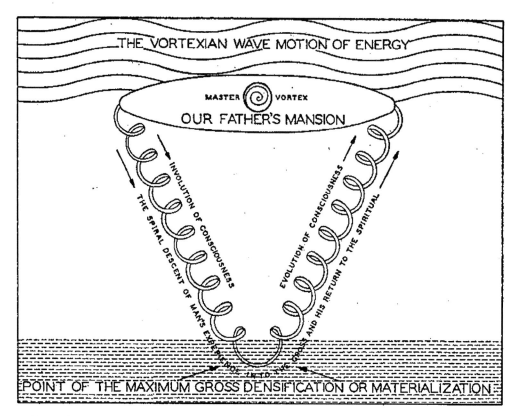

By clairvoyantly observing electricity flowing through a wire, one could see the *spiral* flow of energy. Many researchers have concluded all energy travels in spirals. Thus the cosmic energy or spiritual force which sustains and flows through man, follows the same pattern throughout the omniverse.

This diagram represents the descent or involution of Spirit (man) into matter, reaching the lowest, or *maximum* gross point of materialization and gathering the chaff of human experience. *The Soul* awakens, and seeks the path Home, with the help of his evolved consciousness. Thus an individual makes many rounds of experience as he progresses through descent and ascent. The story of the Prodigal Son also represents involution and evolution. There can be no evolution without involution. Life operates in cycles.

Form dominates the period of Involution and Spirit (or ability to change form at will as there is no true form other than that which is needed to operate in) dominates Evolution of the higher planes. Thus, the Space People in their higher evolvement can *change* their form as explained in chapter II. Form really *imprisons* Spirit.

72

Chapter VI

INTO OUR WORLDS

The worlds we know, you would call perfect. But to us, who have seen even better worlds, ours is far from perfect. To you, our world would be the most wonderful world you could see. The worlds we see in all the universe have not been as inharmonious as yours. The planets in our solar system will once again be in harmony when your planet moves into a higher vibration. Then you will really begin to see what a difference this will make to your civilization.

Until the last fifty years or so, your world has been in the lower vibration. You have been feeling the *effects* of this higher vibration and that is why you have surged ahead scientifically and spiritually so much more than you have the past few centuries. When full recognition is made of this higher vibration, you will be with us in *spirit* as well as the physical.

The time will be when your planet will construct according to the Plans God had in Mind originally. You have not followed this Plan. When the continent of Lemuria was in full power, the main temple was constructed in the very center which was *in line* with the Earth's orbit. Extending out from this temple were the lesser temples which were constructed over other *centers of force*. These temples were really the *power stations* of the continent for they turned the forces emanating from our sun into *useable* power.

The plan they followed was in place with the various lines of force that *contacted* your planet at the points or centers. They constructed their cities in the manner (pattern) of the atom when they followed this plan, in order to receive full benefit from these incoming forces. To be with God, each one should follow the plan laid out for him. Even cities should be planned accordingly. This system has great power and unity for every one.

Cities should be situated on certain *lines of force* so the *activity* or energy flowing into and from each city can have full use of this same God-force that flows throughout the universe. When we construct our cities, we also construct them on this pattern. But when you construct your cities, they seem to spring up on any part of your planet, in any direction without any thought before hand.

With us, all our cities have been prearranged by our men of science who know where the lines of force flow through our planet. This way, we do take full advantage of the power God is sending us. We cannot help but progress in the right direction back to God when we follow the correct Plan. You do not take advantage of this God-power now. It also matters whether your cities are constructed over various fault lines or negative lines of force as to whether you will experience harmony or inharmony in that city.

This may sound far fetched to you but when I tell you more I hope you will understand why it is so important to construct your cities on the proper pattern. When cities are correctly planned, you will be able to harness these forces in the proper channels. The whole city can then be run on *natural forces,* or, natural electricity, water power and such. Throughout all the planets, each one will have its own natural force on the same line of pattern. Not in the same place, as say, my planet in particular, because each one will have its own *pattern* of power source.

When you try to utilize this force to the fullest extent, the cities will *vibrate* to this force and be perfectly illuminated by *natural* light. You would call it unnatural light for it seems to come from nowhere. You too, when the full knowledge is known, will be able to construct power plants which seemingly generate light from nothing. Electricity, as you use today, is not this power. We use this natural light to illuminate our homes, factories and such, without any electricity. *No wires are needed to tap this power source.* We merely have it in the room and can regulate it as desired with our instruments.

This is done by *mental* power. I shall not try to confuse you with this now though. When we wish to have light in one of our rooms, we merely project this thought to the source or what you would call a power station. We think of this light and we are in light. You cannot conceive of this phenomenon as yet, but when we come to you with new inventions, we shall demonstrate this method of natural light. This is the natural light God has presented to all of us.

You too, will learn how to harness this natural light and be able to illuminate your whole planet with it. When we were beginning to use this natural phenomenon, we became so excited about it we nearly over exhausted our incoming supply by not using *balance* again. But now we have things well regulated on our planet.

When we wish to cook in our "ovens" for instance, we use a force similar to what you call an electronic force. By projecting this force through our food, we can cook it the desired length of time. We waste no force, but maintain a proper balance in all things, *including* our natural resources. This should be maintained in *balance* for the *proper* evolution of the planet. If natural resources are exhausted, many times this will affect *another* phase of evolution. Even the minerals are evolving and all things are interdependent to each other.

You shall be amazed as you become more acquainted with these forces. There is much not yet discovered by your scientists within your planet. When discovery of natural forces are made, many will want to be stockholders. But this is not in God's Plan. He has given these things to His children and not for money to be made from this supply. Remember too, when this power is used on your planet, and if it is used for a few men to gain in a material way, then this force could become evil. This evil force could destroy you.

This force of natural light is very powerful. If incorrectly used, in an evil or inharmonious way, then many disasters could occur within your civilization. This force can be destructive if not properly used or regulated according to God's Law. I wish to warn you now of this, because within the next three years you shall know of this power and use this same force.

The lines of force will be much more predominant on your planet when the new vibration is reached. Your axis will be lined up with the lines of force coming from the Central Sun. Then your *receiving centers* will receive much more of this

God power. If you can understand why you cannot use it now, then you will also understand why it will be possible to use this power later. As these lines of force come in contact with each other there is a wonderful "connection," so to speak, and many new things will come about.

This is only a small example of how we live in our world. There are many more things to tell you about but they would seem very fantastic to you. They are merely *natural causes,* to us, taking effect by proper guidance. We always try to follow the Plan God has set before us. In doing so, we continually acquire new knowledge with each step we take back to Him.

This is such a wonderful life when you can understand just what is in store for you. Many, many new things will manifest in your lives. You will certainly be in awe of these things. So much now unknown in God's Plan, will come forth even greater than we can dream of. In man's small scope of thinking, we cannot even imagine the greatness waiting for us.

This is meant to assist your understanding of why we want so much to help you into this New Age. So many times we have looked upon your planet and thought, if only we could tell them of this or that. They would find their work so much easier. It seems to us you are doing things backwards and work far too hard on others! It is really all so simple to us with our present knowledge.

When you reach our point in evolution, you will look back and wonder, "How did we survive with such crude methods? What were we thinking of to not follow this wonderful Plan God had set forth?" But when you try to remember why you used these crude methods, you will see why the planet did not progress more quickly.

The evil negation planted here by the minds of your people is the cause. And as you realize just how simply God's Laws govern you, you will be so enthralled. You will only stand back and gasp at what wonder the world is coming to. This is indeed the biggest step you shall take in your *whole* progression. This step will be what you would term a "giant step" because no such thing usually happens. You have received a *special dispensation* from God and the Lords of Karma* to grant you this wonderful "giant step" into your future.

Without this special dispensation, your planet would probably destroy itself by its own negative thoughts. Then when you were to be destroyed, too many would cry out, "Why, God, why?" and not understand, you, yourselves had caused this destruction. Because of this, God wanted you to understand there is only love for His children from His heart. By the kindness and compassion of the Lords of Karma were we granted the privilege of coming here to help you over this evolutionary step.

When you want to be with God, tune in with us and we shall try to help you understand how great and wonderful He is. Remember, to love God, is to love *each other*, not just God alone. There is only love for everything and everyone within His great Heart. He manifests through each thing or person.

When we were created, each thing in this Creation was meant for us—to be loved by us as He loves us. And with this love of God within our hearts, we cannot help but love each other and everything He created for us. Everything created for us is so wonderful and so beautiful, only within our deepest thoughts can we try to be humble enough to accept these great gifts He has bestowed upon us.

In understanding why He loves us so, you will be amazed such love could possibly exist for anyone or anything. God's *love* is this *creative force* and nothing is impossible. When I tell you more of what exists in our world, you will want to come with us. That is impossible now. Because until you learn to live in a vibration of harmony, you could not possibly stand our vibrations. They are much higher and much more powerful and would probably shatter your physical bodies if not your mental bodies as well.

Your vibration even affects us somewhat, but not in the same manner. When we come to you we lower our vibration. We feel very heavy and insecure. We cannot understand why you would want to exist in this low vibratory rate. We feel

*Those great Beings on the Karmic board who help you determine your own pattern and other balance of forces created by cause and effect.

77

so much freer and lighter, it seems impossible you could exist any length of time in this vibration. But we will lower our vibratory rate in order for you to be able to see us with your physical eyes. We shall not lower ourselves into your present physical realm because that would be too low for us to stand any length of time.

We shall be in the *higher ethers* within your physical realm known as the etheric. But you shall be able to witness our presence. When we do, then you shall believe me when I say, we can be brothers with God. Many of you may want to classify us as Gods, but this is not to our liking. Indeed, we are only brothers on the path of returning and should not be looked upon as Gods. We want only to help you—not to harm or rule you.

You will witness so many wonderful things soon. We cannot tell you everything for it would be beyond your belief. We'll be able to bring you many new inventions, as you call them. We shall not try to upset your economic situaaion immediately because we could destroy you and this is not intended. It would be too great a change for your planet if it were completely reorganized.

Certain inventions we introduce will help you to go on by yourselves. Gradually your economic situation will change for the better. Then you shall be worthy of helping God with His great Plan. You will progress back without much help from us. You could not progress alone through this big step if we were not to help you.

The inventions we give you after the step, will be for your preservation and improvement of your present civilization. We would like to give you many more things but this would cause more harm than good. We will be very happy to show you how to work with God's true power and not in other methods now in use.

You shall be contacted before this step is to take place. Try not to think of these things, but only on how to *realize the God within*. This is the most important thing we can teach you to understand. There is the same God manifesting within yourselves, that is manifesting throughout the whole universe, known and unknown to us.

INTO OUR WORLDS

We want so much to tell you other things but when we do, the time will be right. We will be happy to know you will be able to use this power with great intelligence and wisdom, and not destroy yourselves with evil plans or intentions.

Before more is told, meditate on these things and we shall try to impress your minds with further details not in this book.

Chapter VII

INTO THE REALMS OF GODS

The people of Earth must now understand what we mean when we say "Gods." The term you use when referring to Gods is used without thinking because it means very little to you. When we speak of Gods, we mean the *lesser Gods* of the One Great God, or Spirit. We refer to the God-like beings that work out the lesser jobs given them to do by the One Spirit.

The One God entrusts these lesser Gods with certain powers so they may fulfill their part of the One Great Plan. They work out their part of the Plan with this power, also with the help of still others. They must correctly use this power for if it is incorrectly used, it would be evil. You are usually totally unaware of the experience when these Gods help you. They work entirely unnoticed by most people of Earth.

I wil tell you many things of the works of these lesser Gods, but you of Earth must understand there is just *One Father of All*. They know their job is to help our Father of All by working out their part of the Plan. One day, we too, will all be a lesser God of higher degree and work out our part of the Plan. If we were not instructed by lesser Gods, then the One Great God could not find time to be creating His Plan *continuously*. When He works in Mind, the Plan is over All and of such immensity. Too much time would be wasted on these small details.

It is the Plan, within each realm, all will be Gods and work out their part accordingly. There is much we can create within the Plan. It is the Father's Will, we too, should learn to create. This is the *force* of God. This great creative power is progress. Progress is going on at all times and is *completely unlimited!*

In the realms of the lesser Gods there is much progression within the One Great Spirit. This is a wonderful thought and hard for the minds of men to comprehend. Our limited vision cannot even glimpse infinity.

Now, if you try to visualize this One Great Spirit and others trying to fulfill the various details of His Plan, you can readily understand why it is necessary to have various degrees of Gods. Each One rules with Their particular powers and forces to enable the One God to continue creating His Plan.

Many of you will understand why I speak of various Gods but when I spoke of the lesser gods that create flowers, trees, and plants, you may have found this hard to believe. The very flower you touch is created by a small God-like creature who was instructed by Higher Beings on how to create that flower. In all things is the *Spirit* of that creation who *dwells within* the tree, flower, or plant, etc.

God knows in this way, all the flowers, trees, and plants in His Kingdom will be created and taken care of by these lesser gods, or you may even call them fairies. This is exactly what your stories of fairies are based upon. These small creatures do exist within your world. You do not see them now because when Lemuria was inundated the Veil of Maya was pulled between your world of the physical and their world of spirit.

Now, unfortunately, no one believes in these creatures for you do not *see* them, so you believe they do not exist. But I'm happy to say this, when you enter into the new vibration you shall be able to see these lesser gods. They exist all around you. When you crush or cut a flower, for instance, you may actually crush out the life of a small fairy. That flower may have housed this tiny God-like creature which created it.

They are also called devas. These devas may die because of your carelessness. They do not possess *eternal* life, only the *present* life time. Man and animals* do have eternal Souls, but not so in the deva or elemental kingdom. When the gods of a lesser nature create, they put part of their own self within these flowers. This way they re-create themselves until they pass into non-existence by what you call death. But when we "die," so to speak, we merely lose that *body* or

*Animals belong to a Group Soul and as a certain species dies out, they go back into *mass* consciousness, later to incarnate in another form.

physical vehicle, and return to the higher worlds with our *higher* bodies.* This is not important for now though.

You of Earth, do not realize just how important these small gods are to you. If you could see them you would be so pleased to know they create *just for you*. They want to please so much. But you are not aware of them so they cannot try to be with you. And you usually don't love something you can't see.

If you spoke to them with love, the very flowers would respond to this love force. Then these small creatures could use this force of love to create bigger and better things. Soon you will notice small lights coming from your trees and flowers and even from your rivers, streams, and mountains and such. Lesser gods dwell also within each element. They are called elementals and exist within the elements as you exist within the element of air. There are even air elementals existing.

Each thing is created by lesser gods who have been created by the Gods the One Father has created and instructed to *continue* with the One Great Plan. This is indeed a wonderful thought when you realize *all* these things were created just for man! You will feel so humble when you see how much love your Father has for you within His Heart.

We shall be able to tell you a great deal more of these things when we land. Now, in this present vibration, you cannot understand these things fully. You will glimpse these things though as you enter into the New Age. You will understand the importance of the Creation of the One Great Spirit. When He created a world He said, "Try to continue with My Creation, lesser Gods and then your work will be fulfilled and then I shall create more for you to do."

Life would seem very dull no doubt if we were not to work at all. But when we have the opportunity to help with this One Plan, then we should follow it. If we do not, we only hurt ourselves, for we cause the inharmony which results when we don't. There are only the things in God's Heart He knows will make us happy. Each man *will* be happy

*See chart page 38.

82

when he tries to follow the part created for him. Many more things will be given us to be worked out.

This Plan is so stupendous and magnificent we cannot imagine where the end must lie. In reality, of course, there is no end for us. We cannot help but be happy when we manifest what God wishes to manifest through us. These are just the things we would wish. It is the desire of our Father that we be with Him in love and happiness.

Only we are the cause of inharmony when we try to plan our own lives without God. *This* is what causes our unhappiness. Understand how much the God of All loves us and you will want to work out the Plan. Then the whole of Creation could work together in perfect harmony.

The lesser gods (elementals, devas) try so hard to help, but in not knowing of their existence, you take too much power from them. They cannot create as they should. They could also help you immensely if you were to assist them with their part of the Plan. You only *hinder* yourselves if you insist they do not exist. They can be ruled by us, because we as God's children, have dominion over all and should humbly recognize this fact.

Your part of the Plan can be worked out much better when you learn how to properly use these gods. You can instruct them on what you wish to be done but must first be in harmony with the deva kingdom. You would again create evil if you were to rule them for selfish reasons. You must rule only with love in your hearts to better work out your part of the Plan. Then the most wonderful things will happen to your planet.

When you see these creatures, be only mindful they were created just to help make your planet beautiful. If you create negation they will not be able to comply with God's wishes. They too, cannot stand negation and must "shake" it off. Thus you will continue to have floods, hurricanes, and other manner of what you call *natural* phenomena. Learn to co-operate with these lesser gods and only harmony will reign and beauty will surpass what you now call beautiful.

Indeed, this planet will bloom in the most beautiful of all creative flowers, plants, and trees. The elementals will be calm and create only what you *want* them to create. But if you create negation, you in a sense, are creating the very storms that persist. The elementals try only to cleanse themselves of this negation. This is only *cause* that takes *effect* with various storms and other destructive phenomenon.

We shall instruct you on how to use their help. With their help you can turn your planet into the veritable paradise you wish to see within your hearts. Your planet should be much more beautiful than it is now. Too much negation is spoiling the beauty of your plants and flowers now existing.

So much could take effect if you would recognize them. They know you do not believe in them. But within their tiny hearts there is only love and understanding of you. When someone does recognize and will not recognize what they *do,* they feel so bad they want to cry. They are indeed childlike and their intelligence is limited to their work only. This is the Will of God that man be the most intelligent of all. But too many times man never uses this intelligence he has been gifted with and that is why so many things are lacking. This intelligence we should manifest is brought out through our God-self.

When you want to contact these elementals or devas, try to picture them in your mind and send out love to them. They are most sensitive to this vibration. They want so much to help when you do this. They can literally die if you send out evil thoughts and even at times do. They cannot stand the vibration of evil sent out by man. They are much too sensitive to negation for they live in a world of pure harmony. Negation only upsets them. Many times you see the results of negation for many ugly things have been created here and *you* are really the creator of these things!

We will try to work out this part of your duties so you will understand how important you are to the eyes of God. We have so much to be grateful for we cannot possibly have enough love or thankfulness within our hearts. You of Earth cannot understand this as yet, but after your big step is taken you will just start to be inspired with what I have told you.

You shall be a God too and help the lesser gods and work with the higher Gods that are working with the God of All.

Look around your world now. All this shall be changed by your own negation which has arisen. The world you know now shall be cleansed by the *Love* of God. We'll be with you in the new vibration to help you start anew with fresh thoughts which will manifest beauty and harmony in your lives. When you can adapt to this New Age vibration we shall then instruct you on how to rule your elementals and devas. They are important to any civilization.

They will create just what you desire created. You will see them in greater light as you first begin to notice the tiny lights showing through their tiny bodies. They will not show themselves completely until you can manifest this Christ love within. They will then be very happy to show themselves.

They want so much to be recognized and be of service. We'll be most happy to tell you what to say and what to do to manipulate their power and help. We, of the solar system, will be so happy when you can understand how well these lesser gods work with our Father. You will see a wonderful example of what, we as men, should do to work out our part of the Plan. They think only of the Father in their work. As they create, they use only the power God is sending them.

When you create now, you also try to create your own power and your own plans. Many more things will come to you if you create only your *part* of the Plan. We could not understand how important we are to God without these lesser gods as an example. When these lesser gods were created they were told to help us progress. They did come to us to help but you lost contact with them when you built up so much negation.

They now work alone without your knowledge to the best of their ability. When you see a beautiful flower or plant, you say, "Isn't it lovely?" and cut it down without realizing what you have done. But now when you see a beautiful flower or plant, bless it, for that blessing can be used by the small god to create bigger and better things.

This has been experimented on in your own laboratories but you have not realized the full import of this experiment. When you know these lesser gods, you shall have great respect for them. They are very wonderful and without them, we could not enjoy such beauty. We would have to create such things for ourselves and not have time to create bigger things for our Father Who wants us to create only the best for ourselves.

I hope I have given you some idea how important it is to understand the kingdoms of these little gods and their existence. They will not be harmful in any way if you send love to them instead of the present negation surrounding them. They use the love force to create the world around you and if there is a lack of love it is not their fault. Your world can be so much more beautiful and harmonious than you can imagine with a strong vibration of love.

They must create beauty to be happy themselves. You could be in a paradise of your dreams but even this dream paradise would be imperfect for much greater worlds will yet be created by you, which now seem inconceivable. You shall be in a wonderful part of your evolution when you come into this realization. This is God's Will.

Also remember, not to be with thoughts of evil or you will frighten them away. You create a magnetic field of fine vibrations which can be used in this wonderful work if you create love around yourselves for the lesser gods. They should be of *service* to you instead of creating in any manner they see fit. It's up to you to make your planet a paradise.

Be with God, is your keynote in the New Age. Be with us when we come to you and you shall learn many things of your world you are ignorant of now.

Chapter VIII

WITH GOD AND WITH MAN . . . .
THE SEXUAL QUESTION

The whole Plan of this system is not yet known to us, but this much we do know: as each planet was created by the Solar Logos, we were put on these various planets when they became ready to support our form of life. The forms which first appeared were not in this same physical form as you of this planet are now manifesting. But the first form of life was in the *etheric* realm of the physical—not this particular vibration on Earth.

Women were not creating children in the etheric realms. This was unnecessary because when the original form of life of man was created, male and female attributes were *combined* in the first physical manifestation. It was not unusual for the entities to be self-creative. Each form had the power to create or re-create of it's own *desire,* not through sexual contact.

When the form was androgynous, they created of themselves purely through desire to re-create themselves. But when man "fell," so to speak, then these entities were divided into male and female counterparts and the sexual desire entered in so they could still re-create. This sexual desire, however, was not for procreation alone but to insure each other they were matched and able to send the positive and "negative" *life force* through their bodies.

The "fall of man" spoken of in your Bible, was this separation of sexes. This separation was not really a "fall" in that sense. It was designed by the Soul for a wider range of *experience,* not the apple which was supposedly eaten, but the knowledge there were unlimited *expressions* yet to be attained by the Soul. This was not the Plan of God, but man had Free Will and he chose to express life in this way. So this, was really the "fall" of man—in not following God's Plan.

The work God had planned for man then had to be changed into a new Plan. In this new Plan man had to learn to return to the Father through the lessons or experiences he would undergo while divided. But in this division, there was the will of man to be considered and God tried to work out His Plan* according to man's will that he be separated.

When man realized what he had done, he wanted to return to the one body. God knew this was impossible until man fully realized his mistake. So the new Plan continued with the Will of God. Man had to learn many more lessons to fully understand why God withheld this easy return. By not being able to return to the original form, then the separation would become farther apart and the experiences more varied with the other Souls seeking each One's other half. In this way they would one day appreciate the Marriage of Souls once again to the fullest.

But until man of today learns this lesson, you will never understand how wonderful this *Marriage* can be. It is without comprehension to most of us, until we one day meet our true *Twin* Soul and experience the love that exists between two twins. The term "twin" does not mean "two" but twin meaning "created together as One." They were created together the same instant the Words were spoken when God created man.

When we once again find our "other half," then we will realize what love can really mean. In truth, we always love ourselves more then anyone else other than God. When two Twin Souls meet on your planet many times they do not recognize each other, but merely think the attraction is so strong they are truly in love. But this love is really the *love* that exists within the heart for *God* and is brought out in purer form by this reunion.

Together they can truly be happy if their pattern ordains a marriage. But if their karmic pattern does not consent to their being together, and if they *force* this issue, then their marriage would be most unpleasant. They would be creating a bad karmic pattern again. I'm referring to the Earth plane marriage here. Many times Souls do meet each other but the circumstances of their lives will never permit them from knowing each other too well. Each must follow his chosen path to be able to meet again one day.

When that day arrives, the joy is so great you cannot

*See Involution and Evolution, page 72.

imagine how wonderful it is for two people to be with God's love completely surrounding them. The time is not important *when* they were separated, but the *experiences* are. By these experiences, they become a greater Soul when One. Eventually we all return to this complete union of the Soul. That is indeed returning back to the Father, for *completeness* is only within the Father. When this is realized you shall endeavor more fully to remain with God's Will.

Now, you of Earth must understand more fully that the problems which confront you in your lives, often times stem from the *suppression* of natural desires. You shall fully understand this problem of sex one day and then this will be the greatest step your society has taken in many ages. To understand this problem thoroughly, you must understand *why* these desires exist.

When you try to suppress natural forces which come to you, you create those same unbalanced hazards that are injurious to your physical and mental bodies. To *suppress* any desire which is *good* and *natural,* we automatically shut out these God forces which run throughout our universe. When creation became manifest, these forces continued to supply the *balanced energy* to *maintain* this creation.

To every one of you who now exist on this planet, I wish to say, *try not to be without these balanced forces.* In doing so, you cannot evolve properly. We, of the solar system, never try to suppress the fine forces that exist. If we did, we could not have come this far. When you try to understand this chapter on the problems you face on sex, you will then make long strides towards the New Age without so much suffering. Suppressing natural desires creates this suffering.

The trouble with the minds of this planet today is you have *entirely misconceived your sexual desires.* Sex is not evil, as so many of you seem to think. *This is a necessary vibration in order to sustain the life forces of positive and "negative" energy that emanates through this planet.* Each thing which was created has a life force of male and female, or positive and "negative" (not evil when polarized), and must be drawn one from the other out of these *lines of force* mentioned previously. In order to be sustained in well being, these same

89

energies are necessary to life and the *prolongment* of that life.

You would be over or under balanced without both positive and "negative" energy. This will create many evil forces because these forces are not correctly channeled into the proper lines of force within your body, but in many cases, are badly misdirected. Many of your people suffer tremendously when these forces are cut off from ignorance of this Law.

I should like to say to you, when the sexual desire is manifesting, this is definitely *not* an evil thought which many of you think it to be, but shows a decided *need* of this *opposite force* or *energy* which should be channeled into the proper centers of force to eliminate this over or under balance of the body battery.

This is necessary in your machines even, to be receivers of both positive and "negative" energy. The machines or motors you use to generate power must be balanced to put forth this power. The machine would be in defect without this necessary balance. This is a bad anology, for the human body is so different, but it will serve as an example.

However, the human body must also *receive* and *release* stored up energies that come from God Who sends these forces or energies into lines of force to your planet. So that when your body comes in *contact* with these lines of force and you have a healthy normal body, you are naturally the receiver of this energy, depending on whether you are positive or "negative."

But if this force is stored up and not released or balanced, then you create the desire for sex. This in itself is not evil. Only the *thought* many of you harbor within your own minds that this is an evil desire. I say unto you, when you fully understand what this desire means and can cooperate with this vortex of energy the Logos sends to you, we'll be so happy to know you will then understand why there are positive and "negative" bodies. You will understand the value of sex and not look at it only as lust or evil. Then you can regenerate yourselves with the proper forces and balance your minds and lower bodies to be much more receptive channels than what now exists on your planet.

When the *thought* is there that this is evil, you create this evil within your own *mind*. Thus you cannot receive the proper energy being sent to you. Lustful or evil thoughts blot out these proper forces and there will still be imbalance in your body.

You will assume much more normal lives when you can comprehend more of the positive and "negative" energy. Not so many mental cases will be caused by this imbalance and less and less will be seen of these so-called degenerates of which you speak. They will be normal because this creative force which is in the Father will be present within each one of you.

The creative force is merely the positive and "negative" or male and female force within the whole universe. These forces or lines of energy running through your planet cannot be balanced *until you yourselves have acquired balance!* You will not have to hide when you fully understand the meaning of sex, or be embarrassed when this word is used, or misinterpret what is being said when sex is brought out into the light to show what it really stands for.

Many more people will be unihibited in their relationship and thus receive much more benefit of this positive and "negative" energy coming to them. But if you still persist sex is evil and for procreating only, you will never understand why you were born. Try to understand what I say to you, and you shall grasp the meaning of life and birth, which is to us, such a simple matter.

Now, if the women of your planet will be with me in this chapter, they will understand why many children come to them and will be born out of wedlock. They cannot be hurt by this so-called accident. Many times a child will have been within the *aura** of the mother until the sexual channel is made available for this Spirit to enter into the womb. But when many women find out they are pregnant before marriage, they insist on releasing this child before it is born. *This is evil,* my friends, for this is *murder* in the Eyes of God.

This child has been tied to you for karmic reasons, or perhaps this child just chose you to be its mother. Many of the

*Your own magnetic field seen as *light* clairvoyantly. The *color* represents your evolvement, thoughts, etc.

91

higher Souls will be choosing many of you for their mothers. If a Soul is evolved to a certain point in evolution, this Soul has the privilege of choosing its own mother or parents. If you insist on releasing this Soul from your body, then you create an evil karmic pattern; *because if the Soul is released without fulfilling it's life pattern, you must enter into that pattern to try and fulfill what you can.*

Many women I have seen, have had many Souls released and in this ignorant decision, they created several patterns which can never be fulfilled. And because these patterns can never be fulfilled, these women will have to return to this physical life for several incarnations until each pattern is complete. She must work out each responsibility without benefit of God's watchful Eye, because in taking a life without the consent of God she commits an unforgivable sin.

This is really the worst sin there is. But if you have committed such an act in ignorance I will explain why this must be. Within our cycle of life there is a *pattern* we must create with our life span to help fulfill the pattern made for us by God. When the mother decides to interrupt this pattern she enters into these various patterns until she *knows* this is not right to God. Without this knowledge she may just continue to be on the negative side of creation, and in this way, create many evil things for herself.

When your society recognizes *no* woman is evil without the marriage certificate, you will understand more of life. *Your vows of marriage mean nothing to God.* Within His Eyes, there is only the positive and "negative" force created by you as people. And when this force is brought together, you are *complete as an individual unit.* But if you abstain from this completeness, you will only be unbalanced within your body which will affect even your mind. This energy that emanates from God must be released and received through your body but not in the promiscuous manner of many of you. *There should be love with the desire of sex.*

You will receive only the smallest degree of this energy without love. Where there is an affinity for each other, not merely a physical attraction, but a true affinity or love within your hearts, this is not evil to God. This is good and when you can recognize this as a society, your civilization will be much greater for your understanding of humanity. If you persist in blaming the woman because she had a child out of wedlock, you will only be with evil thoughts and not Godly ones.

Many times a child is born to a woman who has been within that woman's aura for *several years* until she has made physical contact. This may sound fantastic to you but is true many, many times. A Soul who wishes to incarnate will choose a woman who was known in past lives or who has a similar karmic pattern to be worked out, or who may possess certain knowledge this Soul wishes to learn from this person. It will stay within the mother's aura until the Soul can become *attuned* with the same vibration the woman has until physical contact is made.

When the physical circumstances are accomplished, the Soul will enter into the woman and begin it's fetal life and grow for the next nine months or so to be born. This has been God's Law, not the law of man, for man's laws are so limited and without the understanding of the natural laws God has made.

When your society reaches the understanding of these natural laws, your fellow man will show much more love toward each other. And you will be able to express this love into the proper channels; not by what you term "free love," for this too is wrong, but what is termed *true* love, is what is good. There are many Souls who have a harmonious vibration towards each other. When this attraction is felt, people can receive what each one needs *at that point,* but perhaps not before a marriage, as this will not always be the life pattern of each to be married.

If the Souls know this is not in the pattern, they should feel free to take and receive from each other, for within the Eyes of God this is right. When two people meet who know marriage is in their pattern, they marry and will attract beautiful children. But if a child should come before marriage, this is not an evil thing. This is merely the Will of God that this Soul be incarnated when the time is right.

When children are born out of wedlock, many times they

have never thought of being born into a family. Many Souls choose this form of life to be raised in, in order to learn many things which could not be learned if born into a family life. It is sometimes necessary for Souls to fulfill a karmic pattern. If they were born into a family, then they would not be mindful of the fact life is one continuous lesson.

Those who do not incarnate into a family must learn far more by themselves. If the mother and father in this situation find it not unpleasant to marry, they may even form a new pattern for that Soul. If they do not marry, this should not be harmful to the child for then it would fulfill its original pattern. But if they should try to release this Soul from the woman, then *both* have committed the sin that cannot be erased. Both of them must enter into a karmic pattern with this sin in mind.

Wherever the people are, who have committed such a sin, they will be fearful when they read this. Understand, when you commit such a sin, you not only commit a sin to God but to yourselves. You were unmindful of the incarnating Soul and because of this selfishness, you created an aura of negation around it when born in spirit. This Soul must try to incarnate again before it is too late for it to fulfill the planned pattern. But when this negative aura persists around it, it is impossible to enter into another woman. The negative aura created by you, acts as a *shield* around it and it becomes chained, so to speak, to this negative thought or vibration and must live out its life in the spirit world without returning to the physical.

It must try to work out its pattern in *another* life and you too, must be ready to fulfill these patterns of negation you created with evil thoughts. When you created a negative aura about it, you stopped it from manifesting what it should. It cannot find *release* until *you* make your *transition* yourself so this Soul can again incarnate. But until you pass over into spirit, this Soul will be *bound* to you without being able to release itself.

I wish to tell you this because so many of your young women today will not believe what I say. But many must try to understand this message, for they will then be saved and will be saving many of the Souls who wish to incarnate in the New Age. If the young women of today will stop and think of this, they will understand why this is not to God's liking because when He permits a Soul to incarnate, He wants that Soul to incarnate. If you use your will against God's Will you create your own negation, but should you continue to have the baby or Soul, you will be creating the body for that Soul to incarnate in and you will have fulfilled part of your own pattern.

Your society now frowns on you but you must be strong. The society you call right is really wrong and their rightful intentions to be moral; *but these morals are of man and not of God.* When your society understands these laws of God then your morals will change for the better. With understanding comes love of each other and that is far more important than whether a child is born in or out of wedlock.

The wedlock, you of Earth call law, is not within God's realm. There is no true marriage, except Marriage of the Soul and that means when two Twin Souls are drawn together and they become One. This is true marriage. But until two become One, they must master life itself. Not life on this planet alone, but life in many spheres and realms of God's creation. There are many mansions within this creation as you have been told before.

Two Souls who meet and find an immediate attraction for each other have a truer marriage than the mere physical marriage you call marriage. Only when Twin Souls are joined ,each half being originally created as One, is this true marriage. In your present society your marriage signifies living together in body only, not in *spirit.* Your marriages will be much more happier than they are now when joined in spirit also.

We see these marriages of yours and we witness many unhappy people. But when you of Earth can understand just *physical* marriage is sometimes *unnecessary,* you'll see why we wish to tell you the truth. As you learn not to release these children that come before marriage, you will find many independent children who will grow up being great and wonderful Souls. Many of your famous men and women were not born within a family. Many great Souls incarnating on this planet will not particularly care whether they have a family or not. They have gone beyond the necessity of having a family, but will incarnate through the best possible channel available when they wish to return to the earth plane.

This is not evil, for these Souls *choose* their mother and not necessarily the father. The father acts merely as a contact point for the birth to take place. Many fathers may be disappointed to know this. However, very often the father is the chosen one and the woman he is with is the channel, not the choice. But in such a case, the Soul tries very hard to set up circumstances so that he may remain with this father until grown into adulthood. There is a great attachment between many fathers and sons, for instance, which is abnormal to others. This is because they were together many times before in past lives. And through this association they can enhance their Soul development.

Two Souls who help each other through many circumstances is indeed a wonderful thing. They help themselves also when they help each other in progression. It is the Plan of God for everyone to help each other in their spiritual progression.

We sincerely hope you will come to us and ask us about these things. We want so much to tell you the Truth so you can start anew and clean up the present marital difficulties existing on your planet. Many more of your people will be far happier when this is done. As they turn to each other for guidance it should come to mind this is not evil if they have a true love within their hearts. But if they have only the lust of the physical, this would be evil.

When a situation occurs where a man and a woman are happily married and the man, for instance, meets a woman and they are greatly attracted to each other, they make physical contact without sex but really enjoy each other's company. They are *still* receiving and giving this same energy which is necessary for each one's balance. If they have sexual relations, then they will still be receiving and giving this energy or force, but in a stronger proportion, so to speak.

Usually when the wife of this man finds this out, she seems very upset and will sometimes even divorce this man. But I wish to make it clear, this is not necessarily evil. Through this whole world there are many Souls who are attracted to each other and if they should meet, this attraction is there, regardless of whether one or the other is married or not. But if their relationship is merely for *sex,* then this is evil. Should their pure intentions be not to have sex at first and if this intimacy should enter into their relationship, then this is not evil to God, only to your *society.* It wishes you to be married and to want only one person. *This is right, but not always practical.*

Many times there is not enough of this energy received from each other but is sometimes received from others with whom these people come in contact. We know of these relationships existing with your people and they seem to think they cannot be with us and God if they have this two sided life. But I wish to say, we understand why this seems necessary to many people.

In so many of your marriages there is not the proper balance of the positive and "negative" energies within each person. There is a second nature of wishing to fulfill this unbalanced life force. When this life force is unbalanced, the marriage is unbalanced. These Souls are out of their proper niche, so to speak, and when they come across someone who can fulfill this need, an immediate *attraction* is set up towards each other.

This is natural to God that these forces be received in the proper amount. When the way is not according to your laws of society, you immediately think, this person is evil. But we think otherwise for we can *see* this imbalance in their body. And we know why they must find out why they cannot be satisfied with their mate.

When two people are married for karmic reasons or otherwise, then they must stay married. If the marriage shows imbalance of the forces, then this is not evil to receive this force from others *if* this is done without lust of the physical but with a true love within the heart of each. We cannot find it wrong. We know this person will become better for it because then his body will be more attuned to the life energies coming to him.

So often when you see this person out with another woman you think, "Oh, that poor wife of his! He's off with another woman! He's such a bad man to let his wife stay home and suffer with the children. But now that he's back with her, it's all right, I suppose, since she's not aware of this."

This I wish to tell you, when you see this happen, be not concerned. When this happens to your friends then you must understand this marriage is not completely happy. When this marriage was ordained, they did not know they were not mated to each other's requirements. The few people who have the same requirements, are usually Soul-mates; not necessarily *Twin-Souls*, this has another meaning. Soul-mate means you both have *similar* requirements. Usually these people have very happy marriages for there is perfect balance for each one.

When Twin Souls marry, who were created together, their marriage is supreme. They will have the same likes and dislikes throughout their marriage. But *Soul* mates may be happily married and not even like the same thing. This is true of many marriages.

Today, many people love each other but do not have anything in common. This is not to worry you, for marriages have been ordained by God so these people may bring forth children of the New Age. Or, these people are following a *karmic pattern* necessary for their development. Or perhaps, two people must be working out a problem together but not even the same problem. However each one would be necessary to the other.

This is why many marriages are unhappy because many must work out certain karmic patterns which were made in past lives to each other. When this pattern is fulfilled, they will usually part and begin working out the rest of their life pattern with someone else. When a person continually remarries, this person is very confused. He cannot find what his karmic pattern is and merely tries to skit around to find out why this is so. Nothing much really is ever learned from this. He will not be so eager to marry in the next life as he will remember subconsciously it brought him much unhappiness, for the Soul memory will remain.

When two people want to live together, to us, this is wonderful. But to you, you create such evil thoughts about these people they constantly fight off this negation. When they must do this their love is sometimes *destroyed* by *others*. When you want to find out whether you really love someone, be natural with that person. Try to love them as you really want. Be careful if you want to be with God. This marriage would not be of *man* but of God. Each of you pray for guidance to understand why you love each other. If you wish to marry, then be with man and you will not suffer the society of your planet. But if you want to live together, be with God only. You shall be with us too. When two people really love each other, this is not evil to the Eyes of God. Many people love only themselves and not God. But when two people really love each other they are manifesting God *through* this love.

So often people marry each other without love. This is evil for then the marriage is based on sex or money or their own selfish need. When we find people who truly love each other, it is not to our dislike, whether they be married or not. We *see* this love *emanating* from these people. We are truly happy love is being expressed by them because this is in the Plan of God. Express love to each, one to the other whether there be a man-made marriage or not.

In the beginning, you know, there were no marriages, only the simple routine of living together. They merely wanted to be together, to love together, to have children together in order to re-create themselves. This was the original way, but man with his civilization of morals which were intended to raise society, put the wrong *concept* on morals and in this way *hindered* his society.

When your society sees what is wrong, you will advance more quickly. You shall be with God in understanding and love. This understanding and love will come to each one as this is God's Will. With or without sex, we must truly love one another. Sex is merely a *lower* way of receiving this energy we all need. When a person is highly evolved, this form of receiving is unnecessary. Within the higher bodies which are evolved to a certain point of refinement, this same energy is received through higher *chakras;** from the heart center, from the throat centers, and from the head centers. Love is a *high*

*See chart page 100.

99

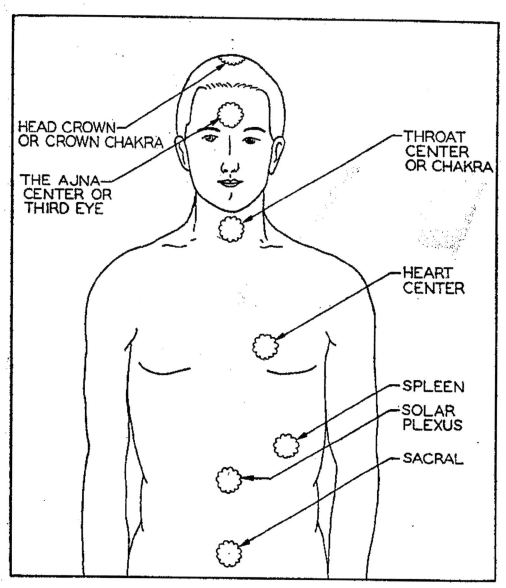

HEAD CROWN OR CROWN CHAKRA

THE AJNA CENTER OR THIRD EYE

THROAT CENTER OR CHAKRA

HEART CENTER

SPLEEN

SOLAR PLEXUS

SACRAL

THE SPIRITUAL CHAKRAS

The zodiacal signs primarily affect man living (developed only) below the diaphragm (or mass consciousness) of the Piscean Age. Those now developing the higher chakras (or centers), may be developed enough to withstand the vibratory reactions of the Aquarian Age.

These chakras or centers are of the *spiritual* bodies, not the physical, and are the receiving centers of cosmic energy, and do not contain elements of a physical nature.

form of *energy* and these centers receive love very strongly.

Sex no longer becomes necessary to a person spiritual enough with these evolved centers. *This then is the true celibate.* But when celibacy is forced, then you will find an *unbalanced* person. He may turn these desires into evil or into misguided channels in order to sustain his body because of this imbalance. When you force celibacy on your monks and priests and on people by your social patterns, you are creating evil. *Unless a person is highly evolved spiritually, celibacy is not right to God.*

Celibacy can only harm you unless your body is tuned up to the higher chakras or centers. This same *life force* that flows through you when the sexual contact is made is *received* through these higher centers merely *by being with* the person you love. You create a love aura between you so both give and receive through these higher centers. This is indeed good because this was the original Plan of God to be able to receive this force without the necessary sexual contact.

When you find these true celibates in your society, you probably won't believe it. This is true though. Many of them are living amongst you today who do not need sexual contact to remain a balanced person. This was true of your Jesus, the Christ. He had developed himself physically and spiritually to such a high degree that when he was with the woman he loved, this energy flowed very freely between them without sexual contact. They both conquered the physical *desire* in this way and became as Gods.

When you conquer this physical desire of sex, you too will be a God, for then this energy will flow through you without hindrance and you will be manifesting the pure power of God. This is not fantasy, my friends. There are many today who can receive energy in this manner. You of the world will not know of them, for they are usually persons of another planet highly evolved. They can work out the desired plan they came here for without being tied to a marriage or contract, you might say, of working with another person. Many of them wish to work alone. They can accomplish much more without the physical contact necessary in marriage. They lose some of their energy with physical contact.

They would not have as much power to heal if this energy

is lost. Many will be your healers, as was your Jesus, the Christ. They will be wonderful to behold as their very bodies will *radiate* the love energy flowing so freely through them. They will be called Christ. This love which will radiate through them will be radiant enough for the human eye to *see*.

This will be so in your New Age. When this new vibration is reached, these higher Souls will begin to manifest more freely. You shall witness many miraculous things, as you would call them. But they will merely be doing the things they came here for—to help this planet release itself from the negation it has built up.

These Souls will be great within their own field and will work many wonders for this planet to behold. These Souls have incarnated through women that were married or unmarried, merely to do this wonderful work of theirs. When a woman knows she possesses a New Age Soul who would work such wonders, how could she want to release this Soul to the spirit world without this Soul manifesting its wonderful qualities? When she understands the child she has will be wonderful in this New Age, she will rejoice she has been chosen. She will be blessed for being the *instrument* through which this Soul could come to obtain a body to manifest on this planet.

This is so important for your women to understand. When these Souls wish to incarnate within the next twenty years, you will find many young girls, not married, who will carry children. Be understanding with them for they are not evil. They will be blessed for what they have done in being channels for these wonderful Souls to manifest. This is not by chance, but by choice, that these Souls come to these women. When these young women create a channel for these Souls, they are merely fulfilling a pattern they know not of, but what is in their *subconscious* mind that it is necessary for them to create a body for an incoming Soul.

This is very fantastic to you, but when you stop to realize, in God's Eyes there is no marriage except of Twin-souls, then you can understand why the so-called family life is unnecessary with higher evolved Souls. These Souls will only want to find a way to come in, so to speak, but have only the thought of *who* can be my mother. Not whether she will *remain* this mother, but whether her physical and spiritual bodies can *accept* this Soul. You will understand more of what this means to your society that these wonderful Souls be allowed to incarnate and receive love. High Souls need every bit of love sent to them. They are loved by God more so, in a way, because they were brave enough to come to you and help you out of your negative pattern.

They are indeed blessed by God. Anyone who incarnates without a family pattern will be blessed because they must be strong enough to withstand the evils of your so-called society. Without their strength, they would soon die from lack of love. Usually most babies will only live if they feel this love force. Many do die without it in your orphanages. But when these babies receive love, they can literally live on it. These children must not die from lack of love. This is an evil.

This is not ever so on our planets for we understand this Law of God. There are wonderful homes for these children who come to us in this manner. We love them even more. They are indeed bright children from God who want so much to learn of life the hard way. But if we were to ignore them, we would lose many wonderful Souls who want so much to help us.

If you cannot change your moral society, then you too, shall lose out. Because when some of these Souls come to you, they cannot stay within your low vibration. They cannot stand your low vibration *without* this force of love. Many merely return to their own spirit world or plane of life, where this love force is stronger. They may try once more to return to your planet, but if this happens again, they usually do not return to try for a third time but remain within their own realms. They cannot understand why you do not want them. They cry out, they tried to help you but you refused them. This is very grievous to them for they want only to help the planet.

When many of your people come together without love there results a child. Many times this child is not a high Soul but a lower Soul who was *attracted* to the lower vibration of physical lust. This is indeed sad for these Souls cannot advance any in this negative atmosphere. They will merely be Souls who incarnated without choice. When the physical situation is made they are merely drawn by *magnetism*, so to speak, to that particular woman. When these women understand why many have incarnated through them, they will understand why their children are not of a higher evolvement. When you have such a negative aura about you then only a lower evolved Soul can incarnate through you.

This is true of even a higher Soul who wishes to incarnate in higher families. If that family creates a negative aura about them, then they too, will receive a lower evolved child. If that family creates a beautiful aura of love and receptivity, they shall attract higher evolved Beings. It is not unusual for many couples to have a genius on one hand and an idiot on the other. They were within this negative vibration during sexual contact and they attracted this so-called idiot to them.

Then people say, "Isn't that too bad, for they are such intelligent people!" You wonder how this could happen to them. Well, this is the reason. They created that negative atmosphere while they were in physical contact. By doing this, they attracted a lower evolved Soul. Or in other cases, they may still have a karmic pattern to work out and then this pattern is fulfilled by this lower evolved Soul who enters through them. This is not the whole story but this will give you some understanding why things of this nature occur.

When you try to comprehend this whole chapter, you will be greatly illuminated. As you do understand why these things take place, you can see there is justice in God. Each man has the *whole* responsibility of *what* he will attract or what he will be. This is the Free Will man has been gifted with. He may choose what will be for him, but sadly enough, man usually chooses the negative side and wonders why he is so unlucky.

This is the most unhappy planet we have seen. Your personal relationships will never be happy unless you can fulfill these patterns set before you. You create your own negation and by this negation you attract these evil things to you. Then you always cry out, "Why, God, why?" But this is not of God's doing for with God there is only good. When man uses his own will God does not have control over this. He gave you Free Will so you could learn these lessons in your own way but when we try to tell you not to use your will, you'll say, "Why not?"

Well, if you wish to remain unhappy, then be unhappy, for you can never understand God is good and just. When you persist in living your negative lives, these negative things will *continue* to come to you and we shall be unable to help you. When you continue to live in this negation, we cannot come to you as you create your own wall around you. We cannot *force* you to love God or understand the love of God.

If you understand this chapter I have just related, then you will in some measure be closer to God. This is God's Word, not mine or the Instrument's. In Truth there lies justice and justice weighs the scale finely.

Chapter IX

INTO WORLDS WITHOUT

So you can understand our solar system more fully, I should like to acquaint you with the other planets of this system. The twelve planets within our solar system were created by our God or Solar Logos. Before these planets were created here, the force of God was all that was. Our Logos *made* our planets on which we exist today from these forces.

The forces of the One Great Spirit have been in existence forever and will be in existence forever. There is no beginning or ending with the One Great Spirit. The Words which were spoken by our Logos, combined certain forces of energy into a vortex of activity. They gradually formed solids as we know of them.

When these planets were formed, nothing else existed then. The sun was the first thing to be made in our system. God then created our planets *from* the sun. They were shot out, so to speak, from the sun into space and orbited into position with certain lines of force. The force was directed to the planets from our sun, which in turn, received it from the *Central Sun,* which was created by the *Cosmic Logos* Who still receives energy from still a Higher Source and so on.

This will be entirely new to most of you. The reason I now wish to tell you this is because Creation was not created by one God alone. When the One Great Spirit decreed this system should come into existence, He gave the Plan to the Higher Gods Who were to be the Creators of the Lesser Gods, to enable them to follow the rest of the One Great Spirit's Plan.

The world without will one day be the world, you too, will travel to. There lie many new discoveries in the future of this planet of which you will be in awe. One day you shall be traveling in what you call "outer space," going to other planets. They each have life on them. Not the same life you know on this planet, but life which is higher evolved.

Most of the planets were in the physical, the same as your planet, and now all but one other is in the etheric or higher state of manifesting life. When you travel from planet to planet, you shall be mindful of these higher dimensions. You shall be in accordance with the laws that will be fulfilled by your planet when you take this step into your future.

Be only mindful of *why* you shall reach other planets. When you try to imagine what you will fly in or how you will fly this ship, you will not be in tune with God's Plan. The idea is not to fly to other planets in His Plan but to realize the other planets were created by Him also. And the other planets have life manifesting which is exactly the *same* life *manifesting* through you here on Earth. But should you go to another planet with the thought they are *different* from you, you will not be following God's Plan. He wants His children to be the brothers they were created to be. Try to understand this fact and you will probably reach other planets much sooner then if you try from curiosity.

It is not the Plan of God to inhabit only one planet within our solar system. That would make these other planets seem very superfluous indeed. When each planet is supporting life, then the created Plan of the One Great Spirit is being fulfilled. In this One Great Plan, there is a Will to see this very life force emanating from Him, manifested through us or through the children of our God or Logos.

This Plan is not to be confused by you that we were created differently. But to help you realize within the Plan there are many thoughts this wonderful Mind has that can be better understood when you try to imagine why this God of ours wishes to manifest this life force of His through us, in what you call *human* form. In many cases if you were to actually see these other forms, you would not call them human, perhaps. But this is so. Because in God's creation, the ones He calls man or His children, are considered the *human element* of that planet.

When we were created together, some forms differed slightly from our present forms, but were created into every *type* of human form. Then God said, "Let these forms manifest My Life Force and My Intelligence and My Love towards each other, that they may understand everything I have created is for them. When they realize they are brothers and all My children, then they shall further appreciate the forms in the *rest* of My Creation."

We indeed have many forms to see within our planets. In the animal kingdom alone, there are varieties of form still unknown to us. Some we cannot even see but these same forms manifest this same Life Force that emanates from the One Great Spirit. When we realize more clearly what this actually means to us, as children of God, then we can see why God wanted us, of various planets, to be slightly different from each other. If we were exactly the same in form, we could not show the appreciation of these forms existing for our benefit and knowledge.

When we can see each other in our true forms, we will see only the God-consciousness within each one. This God consciousness is what ties us together. We were all created with that God conscious force from the One Great Spirit Who wants us to realize why this was made so. When we were first created, we considered each other brothers and were traveling from planet to planet in the same fashion light travels to each planet.

We could then *instill* our bodies within the light rays. Thus we traveled beyond our own sphere of manifestation. We were indeed brothers then. We knew each other well and we worked together to build up this wonderful Plan of God's. When we were separated by your Veil of Maya, we could not be seen when we came to you. We were then able to travel to other worlds around us by ships. We could not tell you of the wonderful things happening to us while we were progressing when this veil was brought down upon your planet. (We still travel the light rays in our mental bodies, not the physical bodies.)

Since you could no longer see or hear, we left in sorrow. We felt no longer welcome on your planet. We decided not to completely desert you for this was not your fault. You desired to help the rest of the system by willingly taking these laggarts and they were the ones who caused this veil to fall.

We came to you periodically when we were developing space ships, as you call them, to teach you new things. We were received by your people who had developed enough spiritually to see us and who were receptive to us. The people we contacted in those earlier times were not in tune with the negation present but were also clairvoyant and clairaudient. They were not always with us and many times they feared us. And many times they considered us the Gods who created them.

The people mentioned in your Bible who saw pillars of clouds, or pillars of fire, or wheels in the sky, were some of the people we contacted. They could not always understand what we were but we tried very hard to tell them we were brothers. They could not always conceive of us as brothers so they either feared us or worshipped us as Gods. When we contacted them we told them why they must release themselves from this negation, so that when they did, we could come to them more freely and teach them what to believe and how to follow God's Plan.

The way we were in the past we shall one day be again. Then, we were mindful of each other in the Christ consciousness. We were not thinking of each other as being different or from "outer space." Only as being brothers from different houses or planets. That is what we are in reality.

When you realize once again this is so, we can truly be with God. You were not with God when we first arrived on this planet over ten years ago in greater number. But since we have appeared, many of you have come to us to find out why we appeared. And by doing so, you have turned to God to seek the answer of why we are here.

This was indeed a great turning point for your planet because since that time many new things have occurred you cannot see yourselves, but which have manifested never the less. Now your planet, within only five years has been greatly illuminated by your many wonderful Souls who were put here for just that purpose. When we come to you, we come to some who have known us *before* in *past lives* on this planet or perhaps on other planets. These same Souls were waiting for our arrival. Even within their conscious mind was the thought, "At last they have come," and many knew not why they felt elated.

This was the reason, we were with you before you incarnated here to be able to make others see us for what we are. But today, so many of your people cannot tell us from the motion pictures they see about monsters and vampires or whatever the writer created in his mind.

This will only injure your thinking to create evil of us. Because when you create this evil aura about you then you also create what we call, "illusion of the Soul." This Soul illusion cannot see through this falsehood you have brought upon yourself. You will not be able to understand why we wish to help you.

When you once again travel from planet to planet, you will again realize the whole Truth of God's wonderful creation and what the Plan really means to us as a *family*. We, being God's family, must be together with God in order to fulfill the Plan laid out for us. When you consider the distances our planets are from each other, you usually term the distances in light years—the time light travels within one year from a certain point.

I wish to tell you this now, light does not travel in the same way in space as it travels on your planet or we would never be able to come to you so quickly. We could never travel the many years you want light to travel! We can make this distance from the planet of Jupiter, say, which is my planet, to Earth within two days of your twenty-four hour period.

You may be dumbfounded this is possible. You will think you are reading this incorrectly, but this is so. When we travel in our ships of space we do not travel in a manner the same as you. We travel on a *magnetic course* of *polarity*. When we travel in this *vibrational* polarity, we can travel *with* this force which finds its way from what you call *poles* or *magnetic fields* on your planet.

Between each planet lies this magnetic force field connecting all planets and the sun. These force fields, or lines of magnetism, are not for us to change. They exist in a pattern so that these forces are balanced with the proper "negative" and positive energy. If we were to change our mode of travel, then we could not possibly reach Jupiter within two days. Then it would literally take years and years of your time. But when traveling through these force fields or lines of magnetism, we can easily travel *with* this force running through the universe all the time.

These force fields are what we call God's power emanating through our planets. We find the correct field of force from one planet to another, and this field becomes our highway, so to speak. But if we come into the wrong field of force, we would probably reach Mars instead of Earth. Now that we have this problem completely under control, we know exactly what fields or lines we must travel to reach the planet we desire to. When we were first traveling these lines of force, we oftentimes reached the wrong planet!

We learned many things by trial and error. We have now completed our "maps" of force fields and we travel with these instead of using stars as you would try to do. In using stars, you would become very confused when you reached another planet's constellations. Each one has different patterns of stars to travel by when on that planet. Traveling through space, these change very rapidly from one star group to another. This would merely tend to confuse the navigator who would try to devise a pattern of star navigation.

When you would travel to, say, Venus, the stars would immediately be closer then you thought they were. You would see the distance was not as great as you thought and this would again confuse you. Your mathematics would all have to be reworked. The stars cannot tell you very much when you are traveling through space as you will learn. You should concentrate more on the magnetic fields surrounding your planet: from what points certain "negative" and positive forces emanate; from what source they come from; and why they come from that particular source or vortex of power. Within each planetary unit of energy there is so much to be learned that your present navigators would never understand of what I speak.

We never read the stars as you say when we travel from one planet to another. We *see* the lines of force and the directions of the various sources to and from certain points of power. When we learn where these points of power begin, then we map out where they end also. In this way we literally travel these highways of force. We register these force fields and map our highways and can easily travel with what you may call the "roadmap of the universe."

We can move from one line of force to another without any strain on us. We travel from one to another in order to navigate to a different planet. To change from the original line of force from which we started on, we merely have to "fall out" of that magnetic field in order to travel in another. Many times these same forces will cross each other, then we "fall" into that cross road and change direction to that particular point we wish to reach.

This is not very complicated really, but until you can actually see these fields of force yourselves, you cannot understand how we can see them. But we, as mentioned before, live in the *etheric* plane of life and in this realm we see these forces as *colors*. Each *color* represents the *vibrational quality* inherent in that particular force field.

These colors are very beautiful to behold and many times a planet will have many fields of colors emanating from it. These are all force fields or lines of force reaching out into the universe to other planets and other points or what you may call points of interest. As we travel these lines of colors we immediately become *enveloped* within that color. We travel at such a fast rate of speed we actually become *fluidic* in a sense, not as water, but we are not as solid or normal to ourselves because we are "flowing" like the force field, in order to navigate so quickly. We really don't fall apart as you may think. We become solid again when we "fall out" of this force. But while traveling, we actually near a fluidic state.

We really do not notice any difference while in this state. We do notice this though, we cannot stand or walk as easily and we do reach out for things which slip away. This is not inconvenient now for we have certain things aboard the ship which control these things. We are able to assume a fairly normal life until we reach our destination. Then we "fall out" of this force field and become solid again. *This mode of travel will not be possible for you in your present physical condition until your body reaches a certain rate of vibration.* Your bodies, even now, are beginning to *change* their vibrational rate very slowly with the oncoming energy you are now receiving.

This too, may sound fantastic to you, but this is why we can travel so quickly from planet to planet. These lines of force or lines of color, which ever you prefer, do not travel slowly. When you enter into them, you become a *part* of that magnetic field. While being part of this field, you continue until you "fall out" of this field. We have certain terms in our vocabulary for these things, but you do not, so we can only use words which may convey the idea. These words are not too sufficient but may help you comprehend what may be in store for you in your wonderful future.

The forces that travel from planet to planet cannot be changed. This is God's Will and we cannot change God's Will. He maintains the solar system with these forces He wishes to manifest. We receive life energies from these force fields into our bodies. These same force fields can send the needed energy to us. All over the universe these forces or energies circulate in wave lengths.

When these wave lengths reach our bodies, we act as a receiver or antenna, in a way that will pick out the particular wave length or energy needed to sustain your body. When the body feels balanced then you can *reject* this wave length through your body to another source. This is also the way you recharge yourself during sleep. You enter into the sleep state and when the body is empty, so to speak, you can more easily pick out these energies in your etheric body. This is because you have unconsciously been recharging your physical body through your *etheric* body which is really a part of your physical body.

You contain many bodies within your physical body,* but this is not of import now. When you learn of the many bodies you have within yourself then you can *send* them out consciously and recharge them without ever having to sleep! This will occur on your planet by those who have these higher evolved bodies of refinement. They have developed each body

*See chart page 38.

to such a degree, they can consciously release these bodies one by one into the ethers to recharge themselves.

The time is coming when many of you will *remember* where you travel in your sleep state. *All of you travel when asleep if only for a short distance.* But many of you do not remember where you go, but only remember a vague dream. If you dream in color then you are truly traveling in your higher bodies. Many of you will begin to remember what you did in your sleep state when you reach the higher vibrations.*

This planet can really surge ahead with spiritual growth then. Many of you now travel even to *other planets* in this sleep state but never remember your trip. I should not tell you of this for many of you will think, "Who is he kidding?" or "What exactly can I believe?" This is common within your minds but I will tell you anyway, for this is Truth. I wish only to relate Truth to my Instrument, who in turn, wishes only Truth to be brought to you.

The time is near when many of you can *consciously* be with us in your sleep state. When you cannot remember, we cannot tell you that you were. You wouldn't believe it anyway, but if we were to tell you something you dreamed of then you would think, "Now, how did they know that?" But we know of it many times because we come to you at night and take you with us on certain journeys for your *Soul progression.* When you travel on these journeys with us, you usually remember some small part of it. You awake refreshed and usually very happy but not aware of why you are happy. But it's usually because you have learned a wonderful lesson from this trip.

You try to remember what you learned but it quickly fades, for your *casual body,* or the body that houses the memory is not yet developed to the proper degree to remember what you were doing while your physical was asleep. I wish to

*Dreams are generally classified as (a), a physiological dream, (you may be cold and dream of snow); (b) a confused dream manifesting your own outward confusion; (c) symbolic of inner desires, habits, etc.; (d) prophetic; (e) and the vision or something given while in a high state of consciousness while traveling in the astral body (or higher), for a *memory* of certain experiences while in the sleep state.

tell you, when we come to you at night, we want only to help you *spiritually*. Not to frighten or harm you, but to teach you what lies ahead of you in your wonderful future. This is the world without, but this world without is actually the world within yourself.

Try to meditate on these things within your God-self and you shall be greatly illuminated. The truth of what I say lies within your subconscious mind and you will remember very slightly or should I say, *intuitively,* what you have read is so. Many of you with your so-called intellectual minds, will say this is nonsense and immediately you shall *close* the door on this thought. But, if you do this, you will only be hindering your progression.

When you close these mental doors of thought, you cannot glimpse the spiritual for even an instant. Try to leave your mind open and free for God to enter in, then you can glimpse the spiritual worlds without. You shall be feeling the force of love emanating from us of other worlds.

We want only to help you, to guide you, to love you. It is God's Plan we remain with you until after your step into the future age. This is by the word of God that I can tell you these things. We pray you will be receptive to the Truth. In Truth there is Light and in the Light you shall stand with us and God.

Remember these things when we come to you. Many of you will be so fearful you will not know which way to turn. You will only be able to think of those horror pictures, as you call them, and wonder if you should come with us. But I wish to repeat, if you truly want an answer and truly try to seek that answer from the God within, then you *shall* be with us.

Chapter X

COMMUNICATIONAL HINDRANCES TO US

Also I wish to acquaint you with the hindrances of communicating with us. There is not the proper *wave length* within your *present vibration* for most of you to communicate with us. But should you try to communicate with us, there are various ways to be in tune. However, when you are trying to receive what we are trying to tell you, you may be receiving your *own thought*.

Many times your *conscious* mind will want to enter the pattern. The conscious mind cannot always be dormant without wanting to come through the veil of thoughts we are sending. But if this happens, many times, you are not even *aware* of it. When your conscious mind does enter into the thought pattern, we cannot break through until you relax enough for us to come through.

In mental telepathy there is the first danger your own thoughts may enter in until you can conquer the conscious mind. Until that time you will not be receiving correctly. The Instrument was trained for over four years to be my instrument for this book. This book is to be our last word to you before the New Age. We'll be with you, of course, but this shall be my last communication to you of Earth until the Big Step has been taken.

You should now begin to notice the vibrations of your New Age taking effect. Perhaps many of you will not understand what I mean when I say this. You shall not be on the proper wave length, so to speak, to be *receptive* to me. However, when you *can* understand this, you shall be within your own rate of vibratory progression in *another* solar system of this *same* vibration. The way you will be changed will be discussed in the next chapter. Those of you who do not understand, have undoubtedly had psychic experiences of your own.

As I tell you the reasons, you will understand why this has just begun to manifest. The *area* you are now traveling in has been on the *rim* of the New Age vibrations.* You have probably felt very restless and conscious of the person within, the "you" who wants to know more has been crying out for knowledge. This restlessness is a result of this desire within.

Today, when you walk down the streets, many of you feel the urge to run. Not to be in a hurry, but because this inner feeling existing is not understood by you. You feel between two worlds, the world of self and the world of desire. This is because these new vibrations you feel will increase more and more. Since you have not adjusted to them within your *spiritual bodies*, the feeling of wanting to run away is most apparent.

However, as you adjust to these new vibrations you will become much calmer. Then you'll be more interested in the reasons you want to run. Those of you who try to be calmer these days ahead will have wonderful peace of mind. There is the conscious peace of Christ within these new vibrations. And you will receive this power more easily.

Being calm is not easy to do now for there are many negative vibrations coming to you from the various world centers of negation. These centers of negative power will increase with the entry into the New Age. The new vibrations tend to *antagonize* and thus the negation increases by trying to *fight off* these new vibrations. Just before you fully enter into the New Age, the negative force will be at its strongest, until it ultimately wears itself out to a point of least resistance.

Then the New Age will really be here. But until that time, you must be strong enough to fight off this negative vibration yourselves. The way to do this is to be with God in thought and deed. Then these negative forces cannot harm you.

You will wish to understand how it is possible for me to "talk" to you through the person I call my Instrument in writing this book. The person writing this book for me has been following her talents within for many years now. When she had fully developed these talents, she was able to communicate with us through telepathy. In the beginning

*See page 20.

117

she used automatic writing.* This was merely a crutch, so to speak, to help bring out the thought waves which were sent to her. Later it was unnecessary to use a pencil as she discovered the thoughts were coming before being written. I stopped controlling the pencil long before she realized it and projected the thoughts.

Now, when the message I wish brought to you is given her, I merely *project* this thought to her mind where the highest *chakra* in the body is. The crown chakra or the pineal gland is your *channel* for communicating with Higher Beings. This gland has not been fully understood by your medical science. I shall endeavor to explain some of the facts but when I do tell you more about this gland, you must not conceive of this as being a *part* of the *physical,* but as being *within* the physical. Then you will more clearly understand what I wish to convey.

Before I tell you more, picture in your mind, a small cone and a three cornered antenna projecting into space picking up certain wave lengths. These wave lengths then come into this cone or gland and release the energy sent it to the brain. When this energy is received within the brain cells, then the thought is translated into your own language. I also send out words in English so she merely receives these words as I send them.

At times I may send only the *thought.* But usually I talk to her in English. My English is limited to a degree and many times I rely on the Instrument's vocabulary to convey certain thoughts or ideas into whatever terms she wishes to use. In this way, I can say what I wish without actually translating the thought or idea. Unless she can fully comprehend what I wish to send, you would not understand what I wish to tell you.

My Instrument has been our method of telling you just what we wish because she has been with us before in many lives. She is not of your planet but from the planet Venus. She came here for precisely this job of communicating to you

*Automatic writing occurs when the person receiving, subdues their conscious mind to a degree so someone across the "veil" can control their hand by *thought.*

from and about us. When I tell you things through her, please be mindful only that *she is not telling you these things, but I am!* When I tell you these Truths, I want you to fully understand the Instrument is not the one telling you.

We must be certain this is of God when I relay these thoughts, and not of man or self-created illusions. When the Instrument was being trained for this job, we were very careful to teach her the lesson of *illusion.* She learned it well and we were satisfied she was able to relate the thoughts or ideas we wanted sent you. Within the Instrument's mind is a highly developed organism which creates mental pictures for her to see. When we flash a picture, so to speak, she can *visualize* the thought or idea and put it into words for you to understand.

But if the Instrument is not "tuned in" properly, we cannot come through her and tell you various things. Without this *attunement,* the Instrument's own mind may be creating certain pictures. I related how this is done when she is properly tuned in. The purpose is because we want you to know, when she was being trained for this job, she was instructed on many things before she was ever ready to begin this book. Until her mind was ready, I could not begin this book. Within our hearts and within the heart of the Instrument, was only the desire to tell you Truth as it exists.

Until we could fully see the Instrument was ready to receive this Truth, I would not begin the book. However, for over a year now, the Instrument was mindful of the fact I was to write a book. Until we felt she was fully prepared to receive instructions without a mistake, I could not begin to tell you what I have. Once I began to work, I was not afraid to continue and complete the book. Many, many lessons were taught her before she developed this talent to bring you what has been written.

When the Instrument first created illusion, (before writing the book), we were very pleased! We were mindful of the fact this wonderful lesson would never leave her. When it became apparent this was illusion, she would never forget the lesson. During that period in the Instrument's life, which lasted one month to be exact, she was really miserable! Because in creating this illusion she was also creating negative vibrations around herself and was drawing bad expressions also. This was finally released from her. She was so disgusted and upset mentally and even physically, I could not even contact her via the cone or pineal gland. She immediately cut us off until she could know within herself, the Truth and only the Truth was coming.

The Instrument is not one to be with evil unless it comes unawares. When this lesson was learned, many new things developed within her mind so more latent talents could then come forward. This lesson to us, was necessary for making sure the instrument we used was to be a perfect instrument, and not imperfect, so we could create a positive thought necessary to understand the Truth from God.

We shall now come to many of you with this same type of thought, but if you create illusion in your mind then we cannot come to you with Truth. If you receive only true ideas from us, you will not suffer as the Instrument did during that test. Be with God until we come to you so you can see us with your own eyes.

The Instrument was very upset with this lesson and since cutting me off, I found it necessary to contact her through *another* instrument by means of vocal contact. Which means, there was a man (medium) who was able to leave his body and let me enter in and speak to my Instrument personally. Before that night, she would not contact us in any way until she knew within only Truth could come to her by telepathy.

This lesson, of course, was greatly exaggerated to prove to her, illusion is possible in the mind of even a highly developed Soul. We made this very clear to her and then she was ready to begin this book. But until God said, "She is ready," then I too, could not begin the work.

After this extreme lesson had occurred, she understood the reason, and was doubly careful to realize only Truth must come through her to be directed to you. When we try to create illusions within our minds, we create negative (evil) vibrations about us. We suffer greatly from these vibrations mentally and even physically until we are able to bring Truth forward.

If any of you wish to contact us through telepathy, try this form of contact with a pencil. We can try and impress your mind with thoughts we wish to say. But remember this: *unless you can fully realize what danger lies ahead, you must understand, this is not for you!* If you do not raise your vibration to the highest pitch possible, you may attract an evil entity. If this evil entity comes to you, it is possible you could even be obsessed by it. We could do nothing to help until *you* realize this was erroneous and that the evil one could not really harm you unless you *let* it. But if your thoughts or vibrations are too low, we cannot come to you. Only spiritual beauty can attract us. If you possess that inner spiritual beauty, we can come to you. But if you believe only the finer things of life exist in the physical, then you cannot contact us. We cannot come through the door inside your mind which lets us communicate.

Until we were with God, we too, made many mistakes. We learned much, for only errors can teach us the correct path to travel. We soon learn to differentiate between Truth and illusion with these errors or mistakes. When Truth is known, we are then able to bring out the hidden light within our Souls and be radiant for all to see.

It is true the light* shining within is seen by all of us in the higher realms of life. When we look down upon your Earth plane, we see so many Souls who do not even have a *flicker* of spiritual light. We may see one here or there showing a light and we are happy and joyous. We wish very much to further enlighten this Soul.

As you become enlightened more and more, you will shine with God's love and light. Many others, *by this light,* can come to you for guidance. You shall be the light of the New Age. There are many of you today, who hold this light within your Souls and who bring others into the light to manifest greater light.

When this light is seen by the Cosmic Beings Who watch over you, you will be blessed. Now, your planet can come into this new vibration and raise the world you now know into

*They see only your *aura* and not the *physical* form unless "tuned" in.

a better world of life. This is not the way of God you now seek, but the way of man. When man learns to live with the higher realms, there are many Souls who wish very much to contact you and teach you a better way of life.

If you persist in following the material pursuits many of you do, we cannot help you. You bring only unhappiness to yourselves and create this negative aura about you. Then it is nearly impossible for us to come to you. If you really want to know of the supreme way of life, be with us when I tell you what it is.

Chapter XI

THE SUPREME WAY OF LIFE

Today, as you first start to notice the New Age vibrations, many of you will be so uneasy you'll begin arguing and fighting with your friends and relations. This is not just your own nerves, so to speak, but the fact these new vibrations are coming to you. You have not adjusted to them. This will be very unfortunate for many. You, who cannot adjust to them, will find as these vibrations increase, your complete physical make-up and mental or spiritual bodies will be out of tune.

This will be very sad for you people in one way, because when your planet moves into the new area with the New Age vibrations, you will be taken to *another planet*, in *another solar system*, where the vibrations will be *similar* to your present way of life. This new planet will have a very similar vibrational rate, so you may in your own time, without effort, be allowed to adjust very slowly to *another* New Age.

If this should happen to you, be not afraid. These things must be until you reach that point in your evolution when you will be wise to prophecies made to you in future times. The prophecy I now make will probably be for those who do not read this book, but who will be included nevertheless.

These people will be taken in their *spirit* bodies to this other solar system where there are great preparations now for their arrival. This is not what we call death. This is merely a change of *position* and a *change* of bodies into another realm. In that realm or new planet, they shall again incarnate in the *physical*. There are many more people on this planet who will understand what they have gone through and will be very happy to help them on to greater spiritual progression.

The people in this other solar system will not know the entire truth of your planet. They understand many, many Souls shall be incarnating on their earth plane and will have come from a different solar system. They also understand this is necessary because God has willed this. The Plan is to take the old vibration with them so these new and higher vibrations cannot be reached until they are *ready* for them, both spiritually and physically.

Unless you are ready for them (new vibrations), you may suffer greatly. The New Age vibration will affect the physical body too. The spiritual bodies will undergo the anguish one feels when they have passed on into another sphere without any understanding of that sphere. But I wish to tell you this, when these people do pass on into the spiritual realms, they will be met by many Cosmic Beings Who will instruct them. They are very kind and understanding of this situation.

After they have been instructed on the reasons for not continuing with you in the New Age, they shall be taken in a great space ship to this other solar system. The people there have consented to allow them to incarnate through them. This is so they can *slowly* evolve with their spiritual progression. Otherwise this shock of being shunted into the New Age would affect them mentally to a great degree. When one is affected mentally, there is imbalance with that mental body which cannot be corrected. Without a correction, there is no hope for their progression.

We must be allowed to progress with our complete faculties. Our whole life is usually wasted if we cannot. This is not to frighten any of you for when this occurs, the ones who will be taken to their new homes will be very kindly treated. There will not be wars or rumors of wars on this planet. They are very strong spiritually and possess the greater knowledge of life. They also govern their planet accordingly.

This planet is ahead of you in society and knowledge. But they are in the same vibration as you are now. When the new Souls are born to them, they will teach them many things from their childhood up so they can understand why even the possibility of war should never be made manifest. This is indeed a wonderful thing for these people. They will never again have to suffer the way they will suffer when this change is made.

The people who live on this other planet will be one with us when we contact them and tell them when the New Age has completely begun. They will be understanding of these new Souls that arrive. They have planned many new schools of thought for these future children to be taught in. Then they will have a much greater understanding of God's Plan and the laws that exist in our universe. This has been a wonderful dispensation for your planet, to be allowed to send these backward Souls, so to speak, to another planet to have the opportunity to learn more fully of these divine laws.

The way to our worlds is not to *go* there, but to *be* there in the Christ consciousness. We'll be with you when your New Age comes into being, but until that time many of you will not be able to visualize what your planet will be like. We can see what the New Age will bring you. You will be so amazed you will call it perfect. But to us, it will still be imperfect for the supreme way of life is not yet established even in our world.

When we reach the point of understanding the full Plan of God, then we will have our supreme way of life in the fullest sense. But until that time, many of us must try to understand what the Plan means to us. There are many things within this Plan which come to us when we have prepared the way for it. We attract the new to us in the preparation for the Christ consciousness. Old to God, are these things which will speed us on in our progression. Until you, yourselves, learn to be within the Christ consciousness, we will not come to the conclusion of the supreme way of life.

When it is understood what He wishes us to do in His Plan, we automatically *attract* the supreme way of life. There is what we call the God-thought within each of us. We can operate with this Thought to our fullest potential. Then we will use the love lying dormant within our hearts and as this comes forth we shall truly be with God.

This love within us is a *part* of God expressing through us. Through this expression of love, God is able to fulfill the Plan He has in store for us. Before you can go to other planets, you must be in this God conscious thought. Until that time, you will not be *allowed* to fly to the moon or the other planets.

In this solar system, there is a Tribunal, which is something like your United Nations. However, when the plans are made known to the solar system, they *abide* by these laws. You seem to just ignore what is trying to be done in your United Nations. But with us, this Tribunal, located on the planet Saturn, will tell us what is right and what is wrong for each of us concerned. They can tell us these things because many of them work with our God. To tell the truth, they can be of the *One Mind* in nearly every instance, and we abide by these laws.

Each situation is beautifully worked out when we do. If we were to ignore these laws, we would only confuse ourselves and create a negative instead of positive situation. This is why you must wait until your planet is ready to accept such decisions. Because without the Christ conscious thoughts within, you would only try to ignore any ruling made by the Tribunal. Until you learn the importance of following through with the Plan of God, you can never fly to other planets. All the other planets have learned this lesson. Until your planet of Earth learns this same lesson, *you will not be allowed to go beyond your own world.*

Be of one mind and accept us. There will be many manifestations of love from us with your acceptance. We have the God consciousness within our hearts of which I speak. We too, were involved in wars and other negative manifestations while learning this lesson. Each planet was unhappy until they tried to be within this God consciousness. When man tries to rule by his own mind of negation, then his planet is always in the chaotic condition yours is in today.

We'll try to be with you while you are reading this book. There are many Truths you will not understand within these pages. But as this book is read, many of us will impress your mind with what is true. When the Truth is understood, you will accept what is said about the Love of God. Since the Love of God is so powerful, you could create positive thoughts throughout your whole planet if you would.

There is such a negation built up within the negative pattern of your newspapers by the minds of those men. *If you had positive thoughts within your newspapers for twenty-four of your hours, the planet could be entirely light!* We could *use* this same power created by you with positive thought patterns and manifest the Love of God on your whole planet.

When your newspapers insist on writing what we call negative thoughts of things, they continually create a negative atmosphere. We are not able to come through this until the pattern has been changed or has diminished. This is truly tragic. Your newspapers are the very thing encouraging the negation around your planet. If your newspapers were to be in the God conscious thought, then the headlines would be positive. This positive thought would create positive vibrations in the minds of your people.

The whole planet could be illuminated if this occurred. But while your people insist on the tragedies of life to read, they themselves cannot be with God. You create this negative thought within yourselves. You will attract these same things to you. Your world cannot be in a God conscious thought until this takes place. So you will continue to be in negation. This is not the way of God to create negative vibration in men's minds.

You of Earth should now learn to be with us in God thought. Those of you who have a full understanding of this thought will be with us when we come to help you take your evolutionary step into your Golden Age. You *must* go forward in thought and deed to manifest the Love of God within yourselves when you reach this point in your evolution.

You will *feel* the love of God in a more conscious manner than you do today. Many of you say, "I love God," but feel nothing for Him. You may feel much more love for your pets or your children even but really *feel* nothing towards God. You will reach this point of conscious thought that the God within is the God without, being manifested through you. When this is realized you will *feel* what I mean. When this does come, you cannot help but feel God is truly the good God your Bible speaks of. You must *feel* this love though to progress to the New Age. In this Age, you must be with Him to enable Him to manifest this divine love *through* you which exists throughout Infinity.

We cannot help but be brothers for we are all of God in God and manifesting God. This is not an *ideal* way of life. This is a *law* of life, to be brothers in thought and deed. This is the Will of God and a law we must fulfill. Realize this and you shall have the love in your hearts that we have for you. The New Age thought will be, "We're all one," and progression will go beautifully.

This future of yours will be so beautiful and so wonderful. Your whole planet will be beautiful as you reach this point. As this thought permeates throughout the vibrations of your planet, everything existing here will manifest God's love. The very trees will feel this love vibration and will bloom in the most beautiful manner you have yet to behold. Every type of plant and flower will be so filled with love. Their beauty will far surpass what now exists. Your way of life will be evolutionary in its progression. By *evolution*, we mean *progression*. This will occur in all the various kingdoms besides the human kingdom. This God-thought will permeate the whole planetary system and enhance it.

Each *plane* of existence is also evolving with your planet and the human plane. When the human plane rises, so do the worlds within and without. The world itself will take on a new look as this is manifested. Then your planet and all within it, will be more receptive to the forces and the beauty within these forces, which God is sending. Thus your entire planet will become the world you've dreamed of.

Your personalities will also change when you receive this new force. You cannot help but be more beautiful with a Christ conscious thought. The light within will shine without. This very light is the vibration of love you will manifest. Your very physical will change into a higher vibratory rate so you may *use* this force sent from God. Your body is nothing more than a *power house* or *receiver* of *life forces*.

Your body cannot receive unless you let it. As you do, your physical make-up will improve. Until the time you *release* this negative vibration from yourselves, your planet will remain in the present turmoil. Everything on your planet is trying to "shake off" this negation. It will continue to be in confusion with the various forces of negation and positive power until there is a *settlement* of these forces. The planet suffers what you suffer when you have a common cold, which is a result of upset balance within. Inner confusion upsets balance of life forces. When you are balanced once again, your cold disappears.

So it is with larger things, the planet is also in a state of confusion and thus "suffering a cold." When this confusion is settled, it will "feel better" and manifest the beauty of which I have spoken. But until you manifest the love of God, your planet will continue to "suffer a cold." It is now trying to shake off this negative confusion, but is not able to do so while you continue to build more negation. There will be turmoil with the various continents and oceans until the destruction which will take place eliminates this condition. This is not to worry you but to tell you *why* your planet is in this chaotic state. You, yourselves, create this negative vibration and it cannot be otherwise since you continue it.

It is within the power of man to create harmonious conditions for himself and for his planet. But until you can feel this God-self within, you will be without the proper balance to maintain harmonious action in all things. When you learn to be within the Christ consciousness of the God-self, you will understand to the fullest extent the possibilities coming to you as this vibrational action is balanced.

There will be complete harmony in all things in this new vibration. Your very planet will adjust to its proper rotation of its axis with greater harmony. This new polarization of your planet will establish the lines of force emanating from the Cosmic Lord of the Central Sun, into the proper channels of receiving. Then too, you will also receive forces now passing you by.

Until the axial activity is balanced, you will want to run and feel so upset over so many little things. This is the resulting factor of trying to polarize your two poles to the proper lines of force so you can receive this energy in the proper centers. This shall be soon and will probably have taken place before this book is out.

This process is now being handled by many of the Cosmic Beings Who have come to your planet to work on this problem for you. This unrest or imbalance will be manifested in your lives as confusion and uneasiness until this polarization of your poles is completed.

Before Earth returns to its proper rotational axis, there will be great turmoil with the various countries and peoples from these countries. As the new vibrations come to you, the old ones, or negative ones, will be greatly aggravated by this new force. So it will seem many things will be very bad. This is a result of the old forces shaking off or fighting the new forces until the proper balance is maintained. The world will be able to live in peace with each country with the new balance.

This will be a great step. Many of you will think the world is coming to an end because of all the bickering and turmoil and ensuing uprisings manifesting this negative resistance. This will not be told to the country that wants to war with you. It is told to you for only *one* purpose—to *understand* this fact!

The negative attitude towards your country is sometimes necessary in order for people to "clear the way," so to speak, to understand what it is your country wishes to do. In the meantime, the countries who have this negative thought towards you, will be very uneasy in their own consciousness. When you understand the *reasons* behind all this, you'll be able to tolerate these situations much more.

When this occurs to you as an individual, then you will also understand why this must be. If you can overcome any negative feelings, you will be more progressed in your God-thought. The way is made clear for the Christ consciousness to enter in.

Many of you will wonder why I tell you these things. The reason is because I must help you *understand* why your New Age may come with such a "bang." When there is negation, this must be *cleansed* from whatever it has entered into. Only after the cleansing process has taken place, can you accept the new forces coming to you and be in better tune with your God-self. You will be living closer to the supreme way of life then, and not the way of man. There is confusion with man, and with God there is the slow but sure way to perfection.

Chapter XII

THE WAY TO THE NEW AGE

Your world today will not remember what has been told until the New Age is actually on its full way. When you of Earth realize we have come to help you through this step into your future, you will be with God. Knowing this, you will be in the Christ consciousness. You may not understand the words I say to you, but with understanding of your *self*, you will understand God since you are a small part of Him. In this small part is the exact duplication of the Plan He is working out. Your own physical being has the Plan to be worked out by you.

The whole Plan of the One Great Spirit is seen in everything in the whole universe. I want you to understand within everything, from the macracosm to the microcosm, there is but *one* Plan. There are many plans to be worked out by individuals through the One Great Spirit and His Plan. You will suffer until you realize this fact. But you will become illumined in your very suffering. When this takes place, the suffering will disappear into the *illusion* it is. You must now take steps to overcome this illusion of self and the world about you.

You must understand, in this world of illusion or of maya, this is not God's Will but of man's will. That is why there is so much suffering. Without the Will of God to follow, you inherit the negation of Earth built up by yourself in past lives. This is not to be alarming, for many good things were also built. These good things will bring better things in your future.

There is the Law of Karma to be considered. Not just negative forces, but the positive forces will also work for you. When you receive these positive reactions or results, you shall indeed know this Law is just. When you receive the negative results, you always cry out, "Why, God, why?" This is not of God's doing but of your very own. When you finally learn

131

the lesson the Law of Karma works *both* ways, then you can reap only good and not the negative.

When you fully understand this Law can be worked out to your advantage, you can use it correctly. This correction of Our Father's good is not entirely known. But this same good He sends, is not *accepted* because our own negative thoughts do not let us accept what is coming.

I like to acquaint you with the facts of your planet so you can see why we must be here to help you into the Golden Age of Opportunity. This shall be your key-note. There is nothing but good coming from God with opportunity, and when man understands this fact, he too, shall be with God. We will be with you. As you learn of these things, please prepare to accept them for what they are. Not as tragedies, or the world in turmoil, but as the world *confused by your own negative vibration* you have built up over centuries of time. Then you can understand what it is I want to teach so well. You will never have to face this situation again, once this lesson is learned.

When this lesson is presented, it shall be a most difficult one. One that will remain within your subconscious to always be maintained as a way of life. Until this event, you must realize the words are not mine, but the words of God. When God speaks to me, I speak to the Instrument and she in turn speaks them for you.

These words cannot be written without the consent of our Father. This book was written to tell you what it is we must do to assist you. Come to us with God in your thought. You will be with us as brothers. This is the Plan of God.

Now, try to be with us, when I tell you why it is your planet must respond to these forces of negation. In the first place, the continent of Lemuria must rise again. Not because the planet must change on its axis, but because this continent is of a *cleaner* vibration than what you are living on now. The Planetary Logos can work with this new vibration to help overcome the negative ones that exist. You may suffer greatly until that time.

But this is only necessary to cleanse yourselves of this negative vibration. Again, this is not of God but the will of man, because these negative vibrations have arisen from this will. Unless you fully understand this is so, you will not comprehend why these negative reactions take place. When you learn what is to happen to your planet, many of you will be fearful. And again I say, *be not afraid, for with this fear, you will attract the very thing you fear.*

You will create a negative aura or magnetic field about yourself. Thus you shall attract the thing you fear. This is merely the law of attraction in action. But if you tell yourselves, there is nothing to fear, I'll be safe, you will attract the positive forces and cannot be hurt.

It is very important only to create a positive thought or force field around you. If you do not, you cannot be with us. You will have to accept us for what we are in order for us to help. When you fear us, you create a *wall* about yourselves of this negative force and attract it as I have already mentioned so many times. Try within your hearts to understand what I tell you. It is for your own good you must create a *positive* field of force so you will not be disturbed or fearful.

This great continent Lemuria, will rise again, When it does, we want it to rise *naturally* and slowly with the course of time. If you continue to explode your atom bombs and what you call hydrogen bombs, we will not be able to maintain this slow process or method of rising. Your very bombs have released certain forces or pressures which were entombed within your planet. These forces have created the greatest hazard yet to Earth.

Within the course of one year alone, the ocean floor will be rising towards the surface of the waters! Many of you will wonder where the water will be going when this takes place. This will be sad for many of you. Water must seek its level and certain areas of your country will be flooded. *This will be fine, if you can understand why this must take place!* These flooded areas will be *cleansed* of any negation built up through the centuries. You can proceed more quickly into the New Age after this has happened. Without this cleansing process, the negative vibrations would continue to control your planet.

Be with your God-self if you want to be in complete understanding of this cleansing process. Before this cleansing process, we shall land and take you up in our ships. You'll be released when the planet is cleansed completely of the negation. Until this time you may not understand why we want to take you up. This will be very necessary. The country you call Russia, today, has many forces working against you. These forces will be so aggravated by the new vibrational forces of love, they will not want to wait to release their bombs. They will be only too anxious to release these bombs over your country to show you they are more powerful.

This is not so in reality. We know what you will be in the New Age. They will only be destroyed by their own negation. (You will not understand this until you can be with God.) Now, as you find out this country of Russia wants to destroy you, you will be angry with them. But let me say, *the country itself is not negative, only the men controlling the country.* This force they are building up for their country will one day be felt and then we can do nothing to help the innocent people involved.

This is not exactly to be in the way of a *warning.* If this takes place the New Age will be beginning, as this is *also a cleansing process* for your planet! Your whole planet will be in chaos when the New Age begins. Not necessarily because of the enemy, but because this negative force will be fighting to such an extent to win and keep one last foothold. However, the force of love is always stronger in the end.

When you realize this is so, you will not be angry with them. They cannot be with God when they do not believe in God. This is the reason I tell you of these things. *But,* if you insist on *hating* these people, then *you will be creating your own destruction!* Maintain the thought of *love* towards them, and you can *conquer* this negative force with the force of love.

The time may be when your country shall be bombed by the Russians and many will be killed, as you would say. But as we say, you shall be taken to another plane of life. The law is, those who are to be taken, shall be.

This is not the Will of God, but the will of man. The will of man creates this karma for each individual. If the God of our system were to say, "This one is to be taken and not that one," then He is not a good and just Father. But if *man* says, "*I* have created a karmic condition, then *I* must be the one to go," then God is not the one making the decision, but the *man* creating the karmic pattern.

My plan is not to tell you that you created this karmic pattern for yourselves, but to tell you *why* this must take place. If you become fearful of this country known as Russia, *you* will be the very instigators of a bombing. There is no danger whatever for the present, that they will bomb you. Remember, you will attract the very thing you fear if you think in terms of negation.

Always try to understand what is really *behind* any activity of this sort. When you can comprehend the idea of negative forces trying desperately to keep a foothold against the love or positive forces, you can be with God in that time of sorrow. Many still may not be able to understand why such a thing must take place. Remember this though, you will protect yourselves if you are with God. We shall come to you *before* this happens and take you with us to a place of safety and relate the true facts.

Many people may be incensed this country of Russia could even think they might rule the world. All through history many countries have thought they could rule the world. Have any of them yet? No, because this is not the Will of God that any man should rule His children. Only God shall guide them.

In the past many have tried to rule your world and were never successful. Why? Because they were destroyed by these same negative forces which *they* set in action. Read through your past history and many of these things will be understood if you can see just this one fact: negation eventually destroys or dissipates itself by *its own action in motion!*

You will then understand this book was not written to frighten you, but to help you overcome any fear you may have concerning this other country. In God's Eyes, the country of Russia is just as dear to Him as yours. God can do nothing if these people insist on building up these negative forces until they "burn" themselves out.

If this situation does take place, you will want to hate these people. Again I say, be of the thought they are *brothers* to you in *reality*. This negative force they are creating is only from themselves and not from God. If *you* create a negative thought, you will also create a *force* behind it. You will be receptive to it if you also hate. But if you *refuse* to hate and only love when this negation comes to you, it will be *repelled* by your love and shall turn from you and return from whence it came.

This thought is perhaps overwhelming to some of you. Only try to consider this, if you send out thoughts of love to some one they will eventually return to you. But if you send out thoughts of hate, they will return to you. This is just a natural law of like attracting like again. If the "like" is good, then you will attract good; but if it is hate, you will attract the evil force within that hate.

The time may be, when your country will be governed by Russia for a period of three years. You will not be with them if you continue to love them in the God consciousness. You will not feel love for God if you continue to hate them. In hating someone you only close the door to God.

I do not mean to startle you, but to merely *prophesy to what path you are now heading,* if you continually persist in building up negative thoughts of your so-called enemies. In this *continuation* of negative thoughts, *you will only work out this prophecy!* If you are of the *same* thought as they, you will only *attract* this force and give them more strength.

Win them over, so to speak, with love and not fear, and you will be the conqueror—with love and not with bombs. This is why I wish to tell you these things. It is most important for you to understand not to continue to create a negative thought form of your "enemies." You can't help attract it by continually building a field of receptivity for their evil force.

Bombs could not affect you in any way if you dispel their evil force with love. When you create hate, *you* will be releasing the very bombs that fall on you. Create a thought of love for these people and you cannot be wounded by their bombs. You can protect yourselves with a shield of love around you. Evil cannot penetrate this shield. They do not understand what love is. Love will protect as well as rule for this is law too.

Be with us and be with God, and *it will not be necessary*

to undergo this karmic pattern. In the justice of God's heart, He wishes only for you to learn a lesson, not to tell you what must be. If you learn this lesson *before* this occurs, *you will not have to suffer the final lesson.* The way to God is not through hate but love. There is more energy with love and more force than the world will have experienced with all the bombs released through the ages. Until you learn love is a *force of God,* you will suffer greatly.

The way to the New Age is with God and love. We cannot tell you this if you want to hate, for you will close your mind to the thought. The world will be incensed if Russia does drop these bombs and in the eyes of the world, she will fall. This is fine for me to tell you; if this does not happen, *you* will have changed this prophecy yourselves. And if you do, the Golden Age shall be entered into without the destruction which is now in your karmic pattern.

If you cannot change your thought, this destruction must take place to fulfill the cleansing of this evil negation. When you find this point out, it could be too late. Try to understand why I wish to tell you these things. *You can and should change these prophecies!* It is within your power to rule the world with love and not fear.

We want so much to help you understand why this may come about if you cannot change your thoughts regarding your so-called enemy. This prophecy must be fulfilled otherwise. Please understand, this is not necessary *if* you fulfill the Will of God with thoughts of love and learn this lesson. See the country of Russia within your God-self, and you *will* change this prophecy to the union of the countries in the United Nations. This will take place some time in the New Age anyway, but if *this* prophecy takes place *before* the prophecy of destruction, you will pass into the Golden Age without the suffering in your karmic pattern.

If it's possible for you as an individual, to enter into the New Age, you will understand why this was told to you before anything happens. If you cannot enter with us, you will not understand. You must learn the way of God is not always the way of man. When man tries to learn something, he creates the hardest lesson imaginable. But when God teaches something, He *guides* gently and with ease. Man himself, creates the very lessons he must suffer through, so he will learn them well. This is unnecessary with God unless you first create these lessons for yourselves.

The way to the New Age will be with God, not man. Until this is realized fully, the wonderful "room" will not be ready that God is planning for you unless you can accept the new forces entering your planet. The forces will be so strong, they will be felt first by those on the path of becoming Gods. But the forces emanating from God will *disturb* those *not* on the path. They will be greatly agitated and want to be destructive. To destroy is to hate, and to hate is to destroy. When one destroys, he will usually destroy himself in the end. This is the prophecy of the *Old Age,* now ending. When the Old Age has terminated, the New Age will begin with love and peace and understanding towards all men.

Chapter XIII

THE WAY TO GOD IS TOGETHER

The way to God will be the way we wish you to follow always. This means, follow the Plan to the fullest and to be with us when the right time comes. There must be *complete* cooperation when we come to you. The job will be great in magnitude and the responsibility also. Many people will not want to come with us and if we force them, then we would not be following the Plan ourselves.

So, by this book, I wish to tell you, please try to be with us in thought and action. The cooperation you give us will make this great but wonderful job complete. Your planet, Earth, shall be the first one in our solar system to be helped by this method. *Never before has this ever happened to any other planet.* So when we do come, we must know you will be able to follow directions.

There shall be a time when our ships will be so numerous, your skies will be darkened by them. But, we cannot come if you fear us. This fear will set up a barrier which we will not be able to penetrate. If you try to run from us, you shall be running into the evil force. We come to you in love and *will not harm you in any way.*

This year will be beyond your belief that this sort of thing could possibly happen to you. Soon, so much will take place. As you read this book, the present plan, will be for us to land in the ships you call "saucers." If you change your thoughts to a more positive channel, this will not be necessary. We will let you progress within your own scope and we shall return to our own planets. You may enter into your future without our assistance. But if this power of negation is not changed to power of love, then we must help you. You would not be able to survive without our help.

Try to remember these words when we come. If you do, you will also remember I said we come in *love.* We will not harm you in any way unless you create a negative force of thought around you by not following instructions. Then, you could be hurt, but this would *not* be our doing. Run away from good and you create your own field of negative force which will attract the same negation.

Before I tell you what our plan is, you must understand this is not the *only* plan. This is now the way we will *probably* come to you, but if this plan is changed, *you* will be the reason we have changed it. But for the present, this is what we will do:

We shall land quickly. Be with us in love. If you wait for us to come to you first, the time will be short. You will have to be rushed to meet the schedule we have set up. But if you should come to meet us, we can land before you reach our landing spot. *You must wait until we tell you to approach our ships!* The ships we fly are surrounded by a *magnetic field* of *force* which could *injure* you if you come to us *before* we tell you it is safe.

Wait for us to land and then wait for our instructions. We shall tell you when to come aboard. Pack a small bag when you see us and we will not have to wait for you to be ready. We cannot wait for you to return to your homes to prepare. That would take too much time. When we can, we'll let you know before hand so you shall be able to prepare. The plan is, we shall announce this intention of action by your radios and televisions and even to some people, by telephone. It is possible for us to intervene on your instruments.

When you hear this announcement, try to be prepared for us. We shall not be able to wait for anyone to pack. The time will be very short. This procedure is necessary to take you out of danger. If you cooperate with us, we will be able to proceed efficiently in the rescue instead of doing it badly. You can raise your vibration when you see our ships by saying the "Lord's Prayer." This enables us to "tune" in to this vibration of the prayer.

Do not expect to see us! We shall be able to impress you with our presence. Because if we were to lower our vibration completely, we could not operate our ships as successfully. We operate our ships with mental power as well as by touch. Our *minds* are actually tuned to the very controls. This is not understandable perhaps now, but we shall later explain.

This is the reason it would be better for us, if we did not

come within your range of vision while we must fly. If we projected to you, we would not be able to use our mental body freely. Come aboard and be with us in *thought* and we'll be with you in love. Even though our presence will not be seen, it will be felt by you.

The best way for you to receive us, *will be to accept what I tell you now.* This is most important that you understand why we want so much to help you. If the Old Age prophecies must be fulfilled because the majority of you cannot change your thought to love, then it will be necessary for us to land and be of assistance. We shall be able to fulfill our duties without any upsets if you cooperate in this rescue. Our job would be handicapped by your not following instructions or wanting to pack at the last moment. We shall not be able to wait. You must stay unless you can come to us within the time allowed. This *time factor* is most important for we must leave the Earth's atmosphere *before* any bombs are dropped.

The bombs will be dropped on your key cities. This will not surprise you for the Russians usually follow a pattern much the same. When they plan this move, we shall know of it. Before they begin then, we shall notify you and pick you up. Should they change this plan, we shall also know of it and we too, can change our plans accordingly.

Should this book be read by the Russians, they will wonder why you are being told this. This is not our concern. When we wish to tell you these things, we are with God. The work we are doing is not of man. Tell them this same thing and they would laugh and make a joke of it. They'd probably say the Instrument is crazy and the usual accusations made of people who tell the Truth. But if you tell them this is so and remain firm, you will be *fearing* them. They will be the card holder to the game of chance. Only tell them we *know* of this plan. They will be amazed you would be willing to let them try it.

You know we will warn you beforehand. They will not particularly believe any of this. *I want you to understand, the whole idea is NOT whether they will bomb you or not, but WHETHER YOU CAN CHANGE YOUR THOUGHTS.* None of this plan would be necessary if you did. The plans could be changed completely if you could accept Russia as

141

your friend instead of your enemy. But if you were to *continue* to tell them they are planning to bomb you, then you, yourselves, would be creating the thought this *will* happen.

I want to impress this on you very clearly. This will not necessarily happen if you try to embrace them with love of our Father. When I tell these things, be with us in mind. We can come in mind and impress you with the Truth. But should you read this and say, "What a lot of hooey!" which is a favorite expression of yours, you will negate this thought of ours to help. We would not be able to plan the rescue correctly. Try to understand just what I have told you. You will then be able to cooperate with us to the best of your ability. And we will be greatly helped in our part of the job if you do.

Be with us now for this is most important for the work ahead, *if this prophecy is not changed by your thoughts.* But if it is, then you can laugh at the plan and say, "Well, I guess that was hooey!" Unless other changes will come we do not know of at present, we'll continue with what we have planned for you.

When we tell you we will be landing, is the time for you to prepare what little clothing would be necessary for a short trip. Do not try to take what you consider valuables. We will tell you these things must be left behind. You can leave with us if you take only the necessities for just a few days. Should anyone come with their arms filled with money, jewels or such, we will have to tell them to leave it where they are and just come as they are. These things will not be accepted by us.

When you want to be the instrument for the news I relate here, try to tell your friends this book is not to frighten people but to be for their *benefit.* It is not the Will of God to frighten. We are to be of assistance when the negative forces begin to react to the new forces coming to your planet. When this happens, the whole world will be uneasy. Many times the people of Earth will be wondering why this is happening.

We shall be with you and try to help you understand what I have told you so far. You will negate the very thing we are trying to do, if you insist on making this out as a funny situation. Live the love I tell you so you can come with us. We will try not to let this be too unpleasant for you.

The plan is, you shall be taken to your moon, the one you have wanted to see so much. You will be very disappointed, I imagine. The moon is not inhabited by people such as you, but they will be there to receive you with open and loving arms. You will be their guests and you must meet them with love and understanding. They were once of your planet and taken to the moon ages ago when your planet was in its infancy. They were not taken back to Earth though. They then became adapted to the conditions of the moon.

Thus, they continued to live there until the moon actually became a dead body. The Logos Who inhabited the moon was sent on to another world. This is the reason the moon is "dead", so to speak. There is oxygen there, of the type you call "thin." It is not too difficult for you to breathe. But if you think the moon is completely without life, this will be a shock to you, for it is very definitely inhabited.

The form of life is not the form of body or plant, as you know it, but are forms to us nevertheless. The forms existing there cannot be seen by your telescopes yet, but if they were to be seen, you could see what I mean. Their forms are not the same as the ones which inhabited your planet in the beginning. They were changed by the conditions imposed on them and made necessary in order to survive in that environment.

When you see the forms existing there, any idea of influencing them and ruling them is very ridiculous. The moon is already owned by these people. They will not let you "take over." They are with us and we shall protect them if the people of your planet wish to take it away from them. The reason these people wish to be with you and help at this time, is because they were once of Earth. They were taken from your planet when the first flood occurred. This was not the flood mentioned in your Bible, but was during the first root-race, before that.

When this occurred, the people were frantic and wanted to leave the planet. So they were taken by space ship to the moon. At that time the moon was very much as Earth in vegetation and form. Now the moon is entirely different from that period.

However, the people of the first root-race were not the same as you today.

They were also changed by the slow process of evolution and adaption to the moon's climate. When the time came for them to return to this planet they decided they were too well established and wanted to remain where they were. Afterwards, they were very sorry but were not able to return. By this time, they were so acclimated to their own little planet, they had to remain in order to survive the life they now manifest.

In the beginning, they were not with God, and learned many lessons, to the extent, they now will only be God-like in thought and action. They understand well, the meaning of God's world. They have created a wonderful civilization for themselves. You will soon see it but until that time, they too, will be anxious to help you. They are not afraid to work out their karma by helping you.

Now that you need them, they need you to repay the debt incited by leaving the planet and by not returning. Since you may be there, there will not be any need to tell you more of their civilization. Except, they now live underground and are not the same from living there for so long. They have come into the growth of new ways of walking, on what you call arms, and not their legs alone. You will see this for yourselves when you come with us.

You will have nothing to fear from us or them. They will be with you completely and will serve you with love and kindness until you can return to Earth. But if you wish to ridicule them or criticize them in any way, you shall be creating your *own* karmic pattern. Perhaps, one day you'll incarnate there to learn the reasons why they look as they do. Their bodies merely adapted to conditions. They will not be beautiful to you, but you must not look at the form. Your thought must be, that you can see the Christ consciousness within their Souls. They too, are children of God and are your brothers.

This is fantastic to many of you, I know, but be with me. Do not continue to say it is impossible for life to exist on the moon. You will one day find out this is untrue and you will be unhappy you were so closed minded. But tell yourselves, this is *possible.* Then you may be ready when this occurs. But if you firmly suggest to yourselves, this is not so, you will close your mind completely.

Try to think this is *possible,* so you will be more receptive to things I wish to tell you about your solar system. Be with us when we come to you for this will be the greatest experience of your lives—but—*this is not for the experience alone.* God is with you and you must realize this experience is for you to *grow spiritually.* Not to be thrilled or excited by this experience, but for you to understand *why* these things must take place. Look beyond the excitement of the moon and know what the lesson is you must learn. You consistently try to overlook these lessons and the time shall be when you must look at them directly. It will not be pleasant for you, but you will bring this upon yourselves. The negative thoughts you have created will suddenly flare up and then you will be suffering and once again saying, "Why, God, why?"

But if you really try to understand there are more things in your philosophy than you have dreamed possible, you will be with an open mind. You can accept the situation without fright or fear. This is not what I wished to tell you, but to *prepare* you for this experience.

This experience will be very wonderful if you would accept what is being done to help you. If you should only take the *experience* as just that and the thrill you receive, you will miss out on the whole lesson we are trying to teach you. Know within, this experience is the lesson of love towards your fellow man, and it is well learned. Try to know, with God, these things are not impossible. But if things of negation continue to be; if man continues to follow his own will; then the way will be that of suffering. This is not of God, but of man's own creation.

We will be with you in time. You can work out this pattern before the necessity of this destructive force and this whole experience will be unnecessary. Then we will come in peace and with brotherly love to help you forward in your future. Many situations will arise needing our assistance when you return to your planet after this big step. Take this into consideration, and the problem of adjusting to a new life will

145

be much easier than if you were brought back and set down any place. We will instruct you on what to do.

Your planet's face will have changed considerably. You will not know where to turn. In many cases, the homes you had will not be there. You must rebuild your cities according to the proper Plan of God. There is the one thought within this Plan that *cities should be located on the proper lines of force,* so they can receive energy without hindrance. Thus, your civilization will continue to grow and be much freer than it is now.

Do not continue to build your cities helter-skelter. You cannot use these forces which will be coming to you for they will be "out of line," so to speak. When we want you to build this city or that one, we would like to know you would accept our suggestions and build in these areas. Not say, "Well, we can't do that for this is not our land, and that person is not about to sell it!" When you cooperate with us to the fullest, you shall be with God and the New Age will truly be beautiful for you.

The forces which will be coming to you, will be lost if you insist on trying to build your cities in the usual manner. You will have to maintain these cities with your old methods of lighting, heating, and so forth. Utilize these forces and you shall be freer with your lives and have more of the abundance God wishes you to have. You can be with us and come to us for advice.

Remember, we too, were once in your state of evolution. Now, we can tell you what we were doing when we started into the new vibrational rate you are now entering. When this is known, the way will be much easier for you. We will be ready to take you with us to our cities and show you what it is you must do. Should you say, "Well, we always did that or this," then we will not be able to help you much. But if this is the way you want it, we shall not interfere with your will.

Let us show you these things and you will be much better off in your living and working conditions. You will be able to be with God more in thought and action. The new forces coming to these new cities will be so strong, they will open up new vistas of opportunities for you to see. Until that time, we will try to come to you with our love and blessings. When we do, only say, "This is fine with us, for we know you were once with our thought and understand why we must change."

Do not continue to say, "We never did that before!" or "We want to do this now." We will not be able to supply you with the needed information you will require to receive our blessings.

Chapter XIV

THE WAY TO THE FUTURE

As you read, try to visualize what your life will be like when you enter into the new vibrations of the Christ consciousness. The new forces will be so strong in vibratory activity and energy, your very minds will be affected to spur you on into this higher consciousness. You will *want* to follow the Plan laid out for you. Your own God-self has that desire.

When your future is here you will understand more of the things I have told you in this book. Until then, try to visualize what it will be like to live in this new consciousness. Your whole planet will be enveloped in the vibration of love. You will not feel the necessity of war, nor will you *want* war. The idea of war itself will be appalling because the vibration of love will be so strongly entrenched, you will think only of peace. The only solution for your problems, as this takes place, will be to consider each side and work them out with the aid of God. If you accomplish this, the sense of brotherly love will be very real to you.

In the past, brotherly love was just the thought of liking your neighbor. But with this new vibration within you, love will actually be *felt*. When you *feel* a thing, it is far easier to understand what it will mean to your world. The world can look at itself in this love vibration and your whole planet will be lit up. The light of love which will be manifested will indeed light up your sky. Many will say that is not the light of God but the light of man. Let me tell you—the light you will see will be the very force of love being sent to you from the Central Sun!

When this love is felt, your skies will be lit up by this same force. You will then be well on your way into the New Age. Until this time, many will want to know what this will mean to them. Try to see what this will mean to your planet as a whole. You will not understand what is happening to you when this step is to be taken, but afterwards, you will understand why it was *necessary*.

You must be with God for we will only work with God in mind. You work so many times without God in mind. This is why you suffer as you do. When I tell you something, I want to tell you only Truth, for Truth can never be denied. If you insist on believing the thoughts of man and not the thoughts of God, we will not be able to come to you without your *fear* interfering. It is not us who make you fear, only the *thought* in your own minds. When I say we wish to help you, we want you to cooperate to the fullest measure so we can be of service. This is not the thought of greed in us. Only the thought you will progress much faster when you accept the Truth that God is with us. Should you continue to believe in the same old manner, "God is no longer with us," many of you will not be able to withstand the new vibrations.

You must then be taken to this other solar system of which I spoke before. But if you should understand what I wish to bring out in this book, you will be ready to believe God is a good and loving Father. Anything that happens to you will be brought upon yourself *by yourself*, by your own mind or the thoughts within your own mind. I do not mean to excite or frighten, but to bring out the true thought you possess within your own God-self.

We, of the solar system, wish only to lend our hand so you can proceed into the new vibration of your Golden Age. We find only barriers between us when you insist this is not so or that is not so. We cannot come to you with love. Continue to live the lives you have been living and we can see only chaos for you. Change your thought to God is good and you a part of Him, and you shall be able to continue into your new world.

In the near future, there will be many new inventions brought forth for you. But most important, the inventions will not be the ultimate of your lives. They will be to serve you and make your living easier. You will see these things coming when you live this Christ consciousness. Then you will understand what I mean when I say this consciousness will *attract* so many new inventions.

Live first the life of Christ and the things of the material world come in a natural way. You cannot help but progress in your civilization. Try to force this progress by inventing bombs of destruction and things of that nature, then this progress is not coming *naturally*. It is being forced by wrong actions. When man learns to find the world of God first, then the world without will come to him in the glory intended to be his.

When men try to outdo one another in scientific inventions, then the inventions can only be for destructive purposes. If this effort were put forth to *utilize* the power of God, the natural forces coming, you couldn't help but express the ultimate in life. It is the epitome of life, to express the Christ within.

If your world continues to try and outdo the other and not work on the "within," the Christ consciousness is forgotten. Only grief can take its place. When your nations rise up against each other, it is not with good or love, but with greed or hate for one another. When this lesson is fully understood by your nations, you shall indeed be in your Golden Age. The thoughts of greed will be undesirable. Continue to force your progression by trying to outdo one another in science and you cannot overcome the will of man. When the will of man is foremost in thought, the Will of God is forgotten. And the Will of God cannot manifest without man's will being subdued.

When we land, we wish only to be of service and lead you to the proper God of Creation. Realize within yourselves, God *is* within, not without, and *not through the ways and means of many of your churches*. You will be well on your way to the understanding we wish you to have concerning the New Age.

Don't try to come into this understanding through the old method of going to church and telling God, "We want this or we want that." You cannot be with God when you ask for a thing. You never say, "I will be with Thee, or I want only that Thy Will be done." You say, "Give me this or give me that," and then *expect* nothing but evil. Say, "Thy Will be done," and *know* only good will come, then you'll receive only good.

There is only love for His children within God's heart. When you were created, the *whole* of Creation was made for you. Think on this many times, my friends. This is wonderful to understand. *The whole of Creation was made for you alone.* This in itself will be your reward when you can learn this one Truth. In that statement lies the answer to your *Beingness.* Try to see this as God sees you. Then you shall understand what it is you came to Earth for; but should you not understand this Truth, you will not be ready for the New Age.

Only the love of God will be expressed through you in the future. *Through man, God makes Himself seen and through man, God expresses the love He has for you.* But when man continues to use the mind of man and not of God, this love is shut out completely. You say, "Why, God, why?" When God's love is manifesting through man, then you too, will see what the rest of the solar system now sees. This planet shall be the last to enter into brotherly love.

There is only cooperation and respect for each other in our solar system. And when this comes to your planet, you too, shall be with us in love and action. Before this time, you must remain in your own circle, so to speak, until you can accept this love vibration within your hearts. When you do, you will only respect each other because God respects you.

I do not mean to preach, but to *teach* you why your world is in its present condition. Learn, this is not of God but of man's own mind. When you accept us, God can come easier to you. If you shut us out, you shut out God. God lies within you and not without. This is so important for you to understand I have to repeat myself. The Truth is, you are also Gods, for you are a part of the One Great Spirit of the whole of Infinity.

Stay alone, then *you* only shut yourselves out from the rest. You alone can bring yourselves back to the realm of God. Come to us with love and we will return this love. You will find peace for yourselves and the rest of your world.

The time shall be when your planet will be the brightest star in our solar system. When this takes place, the rest of the solar system will be so joyous. The music of the spheres will be with us all. Indeed, this one inharmonious note that emanates from your planet will then be in tune with the song of the whole system.

Your planet will be further illumined when understanding of God takes place. When the thoughts of man become one with the thought of God, the very atmosphere or magnetic field surrounding the planet takes on a very real light. This can be seen by other worlds. But when negative thoughts are created, these are seen as black clouds, so to speak, because the light there is *clouded* by this negative force or vibration.

As you learn of this fact, the thought of negative forces surrounding you will be very distasteful. Surround yourselves with the thought of love, then this vibration creates the most beautiful light that exists. This very light is what surrounds the sun. The sun is the wave station, so to speak, of God's energy emanating from Him.

The sun is not the flaming body you suspect it to be. The waves of energy you see are not flames, but only electro-magnetic waves of energy emanating from that vortex of magnetism. When this energy is seen in the physical, there appears to be flames flowing from the sun. Let me try to enlighten you further for it is important. When you see this energy coming from the sun, you see it in the *form of fire,* but this is not so. This energy is so powerful, the very ethers become electrified. As this energy travels to you on the lines of force in *your vibrations,* then it is *translated* into lower, God-like forces to be received by you in the amount you can *withstand.*

Should you receive this energy in full fashion, you would literally be shattered. The "stepdown" this energy takes when translated is very great. Thus, when you return to your rightful orbit, you will also return to your proper lines of force. The energy coming to you will be much higher in vibration then what you now receive. Until you can adjust to this higher vibration of love, you cannot react properly to this before you understand the love is within you. You, yourselves, will be *power houses* for the incoming energy to be expressed through you.

Since you are all relay stations, you will be receiving this energy into your bodies to be sent out to the world as a whole.

Your very bodies are the transmitters of love and other energies emanating from God Himself. It's to be used by man for the progression of man to higher vibratory fields of activity. Man himself will be better attuned to this God-like energy when this takes place. You can then receive the very inventions I spoke of before. You will be better tuned in, so to speak, to the mental power or thought existing on *higher* planes.

You can't help receive but good. When you do receive a thought, you will be directed what to do with this invention or idea necessary for service in your New Age. If you cannot attune yourselves to this new force, you will not receive the good being sent. In all of God's Creation, only *good* is being sent. You benefit by God's very Thoughts.

Chaos usually results when man wants to benefit by man. If you really want to be with God, we can work together to fulfill God's Plan for your planet. Be with us, I pray, for where love is expressed, God is; and where God is, we want to be. Take up your bed and walk, as did the man in your Bible. Realize you are now part of this Creation which was made for you alone.

Before you walk, meditate on these things and *know* this is so, then you walk out of your problems with God's help. You alone, can be master of your Soul—You can, and you will and should be your own master. This is the Will of God. Your future will be here when you do.

The way to God is through your own mind and your own selves. Not through any man or ritual. There is freedom within yourselves because God dwells there too. You can master all things with this God-self. Your planet will be among the stars of God then, and you shall shine in the glory intended for you. Your planet will be destroyed of its own self if you continue to live in the old ways. Understand these Truths and you can master self. This is the secret to change your world— *change yourselves.* This has been told to you by many of your teachers and philosophers, but I repeat it, for it is so.

To change anything which manifests within your lives, you must change within *yourselves* first. When this takes place, only love can be manifested. Only harmony can come to you. When many of you find inharmony, you immediately pray for the *other* person! Pray for yourselves and you automatically change the inharmony to harmony. The *thought* is changed then and the world will be without evil. This lesson will not serve you if you continue to be with man instead of God.

When some of you read this book, the thought will probably be, "What is said could be true, but I can't go along with it." If you really and sincerely look within your own God-self, to find the answer, you will know this is true. But if you say, "Well, I don't know, we'll see what happens." Then you'll be operating on chance. The chances are, you'll fall. When you refuse to think for yourselves, you usually let others do your thinking for you. But if you *try* to think this out, you will be greatly rewarded by a better understanding of God.

Be with us and your Earth shall be illumined. You'll be with God and shall understand the prophecies made in this book are true, *providing* you cannot take the thought of negation for what it is and destroy it. Be not fearful though, *if* this prophecy takes place. You shall learn the lesson set forth. Continue with man's way and the prophecy will surely take place.

Understand what and why I tell you these things and you shall be able to take the step without our help. We love you and you are indeed our brothers in love. We want only to help you. The love coming to you will be felt the world over. Know that we shall be with you if necessary. Find this love within and in this expression you will be Gods.

You must know by now your future is in God's hands. Remember these words for one day they will come to you when needed. Meditate on these things. We wish only to serve you and take you with us to the realm of God. There is only love in this realm. There are no misunderstandings, or thoughts of lust or greed. Only the love of God exists.

The one who writes this book is from the planet, Jupiter. You may not understand the words I speak when I tell you who I am though. In a sense, I am what you would call the God-head of that planet. Should you know of such things, you will be understanding of my words, but if this is new to you, you may not. There is also a spiritual hierarchy on my planet. I hold the same office as your Lord Gautama,* Lord of the World, or the one presiding over your spiritual hierarchy.

When you discover what is meant by all this, you may be surprised I should bother to come to you at all. My office is very high so this book may seem completely unnecessary for me to write. The reason is this, when we came to you, we wanted to be with you but your planet would not accept the people from the ships you call "saucers." So it was decided the God-head of my planet be commissioned, so to speak, to write to you. The authority of this office I hold, must be made manifest to you. Many of you will understand why we wish this to be known.

When my planet is ready to take its initiation, of a Cosmic nature, I shall be with you in thought and send you these words of wisdom I write now. Should you desire to understand to a greater extent the office I hold, you must study your books of occult nature. Then you will learn what is meant by this term. When you do learn this, you will know why I wish you to understand and appreciate this fact: *None of us will be small enough or high enough to be of service to you.*

There are many Cosmic Beings within the solar system, Who are here to be of assistance. Even with the office I now hold, I consider it to be an honor to write this book through the Instrument. She has been associated with me in past lives, on the planet Jupiter, and even on Earth. If she were to remember this, I would not be able to relate this story because she would probably have no fear of criticism. As you learn this, she too, is learning of these facts. The Instrument is not aware of many things from her past. I tell this now because she is worthy of your respect. This will be the greatest shock to her, knowing we were together in past lives.

The Instrument will not remember any of these facts at this time. We will not permit the memory of the past to come to her yet. When she has finished her work here, she shall return to the planet from whence she came. Until that time, the memory of the past will not completely be given to her. If you were permitted the memories of the past, you would not

*This office is held jointly with Jesus, but he is manifesting on a different ray not attuned to the New Age as well.

overcome the life of the present. Because of this, many of you will never recall what you were or what you did. This is not the Plan.

Were you to remember the things of the past, you would not be as ready to work out the problems of now. This is why many of you do not remember and why you refuse to believe in reincarnation. But I say to you, there *is* reincarnation—for life is eternal. When you incarnate on any planet, it has purpose and will teach you the reason you can return to God. By incarnating on various planets, we always learn something from each one, and from each life time we live.

We progress in this manner. We could never learn the many things we do without these lessons. Through all our lives, we will have been everything that is possible for man to be. This is man's will, to learn the whole of Truth and to experience the whole of life. But before we learn this lesson of life, we shall continue to incarnate in our own way to learn these lessons. Each one must eventually return to the Father. When we do, we will have had all the experience necessary to understand what is meant by the "road of life" and by the "eternal struggle of returning."

The Instrument and myself, will once again come to be of service when your Golden Age is well advanced. It is our desire to be of service to all mankind. Until that future time, we hope to be of service now. We can tell you what will be in the future, but if you take care of the present, the future will take care of itself.

The words of God will be with us throughout all eternity. Find time to meditate, be silent within your thoughts. God speaks to you in silence and when the Voice of God is heard, you will recognize that Voice and you shall be with Him. But should you talk and reason within your conscious mind, the Voice of God cannot be heard. You may tell yourselves, this is God, but your own mind speaks, not God. Learn to be in silence. The Voice will be heard and you shall be master of your lives.

To us, the understanding of God is far more important than the flying saucers, as you call such, or the way your world could be destroyed. Understand the Truth as I have told you within your own hearts, then these things would not be important to you either. When we know a thing is so, we will be further enlightened with our problems. We can tell each other what should be manifested.

We'll be with you to help enable you to understand the words of Truth I now tell. If you are not able to understand this knowledge within your hearts which I have given you, you must turn to God by yourselves and learn why such things take place in your lives.

The best way you can cooperate with us is to just be silent when we come and let the Voice within tell you this is right. You'll know why we want so much to be in the love vibration. As you overcome any fear of us, the love vibration will manifest in your hearts. When it does, you will understand the Truth in this book easily.

We shall be friends in time. Should you not find the "true you" within, you will only be creating a negative aura around you. Your lives will be more upset if this happens. If you cannot find the Truth within, the Voice of God will not be heard, for what I teach is true.

The words of this book were planned to be given to you by the Instrument before she incarnated on your planet. Her mission is to fulfill this job of being the "communication center," from our world to yours. The well meaning thought that we come to you with love, will be completely wasted if you cannot find it to be true within your understanding. The most important thing I wish to tell you, is, if you continue to feel fear or hate towards us and your brethren of Earth, you can never take the step into your Golden Age without the suffering necessary for your understanding of this great lesson.

Because God is good, you must realize these things which come upon you, will only be manifestations of your own self. *Your own mind will have created these things for you.* Understand our Father, which is the Father of our solar system, can only give you that which is right and good, and then you will be with the understanding we want you to have so much.

When we take you to the moon many of you will want to say, "Well, this is the biggest thing that could happen to me!" But this is *not* the biggest thing that can happen to you.

When you receive the illumination of the Christ consciousness within, *that* is the biggest thing that can happen to you in any life.

When you understand the Truth of God and *feel* love for God, this will be one of the biggest things in your lives. When this happens to you, your whole world, even the people around you and your own self, will change for the better. Refuse to accept this vibration of love, then *you* must be the one to travel to another solar system of your same vibration. Should you continue to live within the vibration of love, the forces coming would be most unpleasant to your physical and mental bodies. They would shatter you to such a degree; the physical would be impaired to the living necessary in the New Age.

Try to find this God-self, then you will be able to find the true meaning of life. The answers lie within your very self and when this comes to you, this shall indeed, be the biggest thing which can happen to you.

Be with us, we say in prayer, for we wish only to be of service. Your world needs us now, to lead you into the new world of peace.

J.W.

THE END

WHY WE ARE HERE

Our birth is but a sleep and a forgetting
The Soul that rises with us, our Life's Star,
Hath had elsewhere its setting,
And cometh from afar;
Not in entire forgetfulness,
And not in utter nakedness,
But in trailing clouds of glory do we come
From God, Who is our home.

—Wordsworth

THE IMPRISONED SPLENDOUR

Truth is within ourselves; it takes no rise from outward things,
    what e'er you may believe.
There is an inmost center in us all,
Where truth abides in fulness; and around,
Wall upon wall, the gross flesh hems it in,
This perfect clear perception—which is truth.
A baffling and perverting carnal mesh
Binds it, and makes all error; and to know
Rather consist in opening out a way
Whence the imprisoned splendour may escape,
Than in effecting entry for a light
Supposed to be without.

Browning

QUESTIONS, ANSWERS, AND COMMENTS

Upon completion of the book I, as the Instrument, had many questions and knew the reader would also. I have tried to compile those which I thought would be of most primary and general instruction and world wide interest, and which would clarify certain points within the book. I found some of the statements made so interesting I'm sure the reader will appreciate them and also understand the limited space for this section. It is possible to ask questions all day, but perhaps I shall be able to give you all of the desired information at a later date.

Question: Will any other countries be bombed?

J.W.: No, at present the only country in the plans of the Russians for bombing is the U.S.A., to be bombed in eight major cities. No other country, as far as we know, is in such a plan.

Question: Will the space people pick up any other individuals not in the United States?

J.W.: Oh, yes. We have a good supply of ships that can go into the different countries surrounding the United States first. These people, of course, will be in the most danger of any immediate fallout, should this event occur, and will be picked up first. Those who are in countries in Europe or elsewhere, should there be any danger, will be picked up last.

Some of our ships can carry as many as twenty thousand people in the physical. These are the ships you call "mother ships," and are from my planet Jupiter. Some of the ships are large enough to accommodate ten thousand people and again we have ships only large enough to take five thousand. However, the ships that will pick up the people will be the small "scout" ships, as you might say, or the "flying saucers" which will land. Also, we have wing ships which are crescent in shape to take the people up.

It would be very difficult to land these extremely large ships on your planet, especially in populated areas. Some of them are three to five miles in length. The radiation of the electro-magnetic field surrounding these ships is very great and would be disastrous in some localities due to buildings and other mechanisms you have, so it will be the "scout" ships which must pick the people up. But we have hundreds of thousands of this type craft available.

It is very important too that people understand that when these ships land, those who go aboard will not necessarily *see* anyone on board. As I mentioned in the book, we must be able to fly the ships in our normal consciousness, for the *instruments are attuned to our higher bodies!* When they reach the mother ships, we will be seen by your people, for a part of us not needed to control the ship will be projected to them.

Question: Is it possible some may spend a longer period on the moon? (This question was actually answered before it was asked! I have but to have a question in my mind at times and he answers it before I put it into words.)

J.W.: Yes, it is true some of the people may spend as long as three years on the moon. However, this may not take place if the government or the dictatorship for the United States during this critical period is a lenient one. This applies to the people of the United States only. The people from the other countries shall be returned as soon as the planet has settled down and there is no longer any danger of fallout.

The people of the United States may not return if it is decided the form of governing is to be too severe or dangerous to the individual. Then it would be most advisable for them to remain on the moon until this period has passed. It would be very uncomfortable for anyone living under their rule should this occur.

The people from the other countries will be returned as soon as the atmosphere has settled and is safe, possibly a period of five days or so. It would be good for those planning to go with us to take something they are interested in or to work with their hands to keep busy. Idleness causes unrest and we cannot teach them sixteen hours a day. But in leisure time if they had hobbies to work with, it would be very good. We will also supply things of this nature, but should any have a particular hobby they are interested in, I would advise they make some sort of preparation and take it with them if it will not take up too much room.

As I mentioned before, they should pack for a short trip, and now I mention a possible three year stay for some! They will not have to worry about supplies, as all things will be taken care of. They will have a chance to learn many things which will benefit them and I'm sure this situation will not be bad for anyone. It will be a blessing in disguise.

Question: Why couldn't the people of the United States return to other countries, rather than remain on the moon?

J.W.: If they were to return to other countries to live, they would create bad feelings. People cannot progress spiritually with such feelings. Many of these other people would resent them if they were to live with them and not in their own country. This situation must be avoided at all costs, for people must begin anew with brotherhood in mind and not with resentment of somebody imposing in their homes.

Question: Why couldn't preparation be made on this planet for the people?

J.W.: Now, Gloria, do you really think that if you told your government, or any government, like say, Australia, to prepare and build accommodations for over two million people *in case* of necessity, that they would?

Question: How will this affect the primitive peoples?

J.W.: The primitive people in the northern hemisphere will undoubtedly be affected. However, those who cannot vibrate to the New Age will be shunted out of their bodies and taken to another planet also. Those who have a spiritual light showing and have progressed in their spiritual development enough will be allowed to go on. However, it is too bad they must suffer certain tragedies; but again, this will be for their development.

It does not matter what the *mental* development is of a personality, but depends on what their *spiritual* development is as to whether or not they can adjust to the new magnetic field. The cannibalistic ones will be taken of course. The South Sea Islanders and people of that nature, if properly developed, shall continue with the Age. However, in your northern hemisphere, there are not many such people so it will not be a big problem to take them with us if it is at all possible for them to understand they can join us.

Question: Does this mean only the *northern* hemisphere is in danger of fallout should this prophecy occur?

J.W.: Yes, only the northern hemisphere will be affected. This is because the centrifical force in this area will throw off any subversive elements or activity and will not affect the opposite *atmospheric rotation* of the southern hemisphere. The people in South America, Australia and the other countries in this hemisphere, will not be affected by any cataclysmic activity, other than possible floods, earthquakes and things of that nature, *resulting* from what happens in the northern hemisphere. There will, of course, be no danger of fallout.

Those who live on coastlines in low areas would be wise to move to higher ground, and those who live in areas below sea level definitely should move, even though they are away from any ocean. There will probably be an underground movement which will rapidly fill these areas. So it is advisable for these people to move. I believe there are many places in the middle east, especially in Asia, who have situations such as this in the desert areas. These low spots will rapidly fill up by this underground movement. This will not be a cataclysmic effect, but will occur more as if someone turned on a "faucet" some place. Those on low coast lines may suffer tidal waves.

The weather will be greatly affected even in the southern

hemisphere and may turn very cold in some areas. It would be well to have warm clothing on hand.

Question: Are there any instructions you would like to give for the book to any other countries in particular?

J.W.: Yes, for all countries first. When the poles of your planet are lined up to the degree that the oncoming forces from the Central Sun are centered exactly over the receiving centers of this planet, the influx of power will be so tremendous many people not on the spiritual path or receptive to this added influx of power will feel it in such high intensity they will lose their minds.

Do not be concerned, people of Earth, if your friends or relatives and loved ones seem to go berserk all around you, for this is a *blessing* in disguise! Should they be allowed to continue into the New Age, they would literally shrivel up physically and spiritually. The oncoming radiation that your planet will go into in the Aquarian field would be too much for their bodies to take and progress at the proper rate of development.

So it is for a short time only they will seem to lose their minds, as you call it, but in reality, what is happening is a complete breakdown of the alignment of the spiritual bodies. This disarticulation of the spiritual bodies with the physical causes great confusion and so your psychiatrists will say they are insane.

They are not insane in the usual sense, my friends, but are merely within a great state of confusion concerning maladjustment to this new vibratory pattern. If a friend or loved one goes berserk in your presence, calm him or her with music. Color too, is important. Do not have red, yellow, or bright colors about, but soothing colors, the blues and greens. Even lights in the room would help a great deal if of a soothing color.

Use music also of a soothing nature. Definitely not what you call jazz or rock and roll, but the "old masters" as you would say, with a calming effect. This music helps realign the spiritual bodies so they have a more relaxed attitude from this confusion. In this way only will your friend or relative receive temporary relief. At a later date all these dear souls who are not ready to meet the requirements of going into this higher vibration, will be taken out of the physical and released from their dense vehicle so that greater relief will come to them on the spirit side of life.

In this higher dimension, we have wonderful therapy for such cases and beautiful colors not yet known to your physical eye. This will soothe them and help realign their spiritual bodies in such a way they will become coherent again. Until they are told and taught the truth of their situation, then and only then will they leave the atmosphere of your planet and go by space ship to the other solar system. Once again they shall incarnate and learn from childhood up, the various truths of God's laws manifesting in our universe.

After this is done they will receive greater therapy yet, for the people on this other planet know of the situation here and of some of the consequences which may follow and are well prepared for *child* therapy in that day to come.

So, fear not, nor fret not. It is indeed a blessing that they leave first, or they would become too impaired physically and spiritually to even be able to go on to the other planet. If God's mercy was not great, this would not happen. They would completely backslide in evolution to such a state that it would take eons to return to that which they are manifesting now.

I should like to tell the people of Australia this. When your country is in greater harmony and vibration of the New Age, it shall rise up some two to three thousand feet above the present level. This shall be done gradually in some places but quickly in others, depending on the geographical structure and land construction or fault lines, etc. When you hear of this, be not frightened, my friends of Australia. You will be warned in time and we will do what we can to alleviate any drastic or sudden change. Should such a thing take place, we will be there immediately to take you up and deposit you on safer ground or territory.

Now, my friends, this will not happen for many years yet, so there is no need to worry at present. Should anything of this nature occur any place on your planet where there is not a karmic pattern to be fulfilled by the people living there, we will do everything in our power to alleviate the situation and to take you up if it is necessary in our eyes.

Question: What about Atlantis? You have never mentioned it.

J.W.: First, let me say Atlantis is also to rise again, but not until after the Golden Age has completely been passed into. It will be at least 12 years before anything is noticeable to any great extent about the rising of that continent. It will be a slow process and will not rise as fast as Lemuria. When Lemuria makes its final acension, it shall take place in a matter of hours, not minutes, but hours. Thirteen hours was all that was needed for the final submergence about ten thousand years ago.

Atlantis will rise slowly over a period of years and should cause no ill effects. What may be caused by Lemuria's rising will be sufficient to be called cataclysmic, if you wish to call it that, but of course to us it is merely a karmic cleansing. When Atlantis does rise, it will be possible for those in any danger spots to leave and prepare themselves for any activity. However, it will not be, as I have said, until after the Golden Age has begun.

The people of England may feel fearful too when they read this. But again I say, do not feel fearful, for all these things will come gradually, and you will be given much time to prepare.

England, my friends, will disappear once again beneath the waters. I say once again, for it has not always been above. During the time Atlantis is about to rise again, there will be an underwater movement which will occur. There must be a balance of certain forces and lines of construction which will make it necessary for England to be submerged again. This includes most of the British Isles. Not only is this necessary because of land structure, but because of a vast karmic pattern that must be fulfilled. This must take place for several reasons I shall not go into just now. You people will naturally feel sad, but try to look at this thing from a higher consciousness or standpoint, such as we do, if at all possible.

When your country goes under, we will be there to help you. Great preparation will be made years before by your government and your Queen to relieve any drastic changes which may take place. Most of you now living on your small island will be taken to Canada, some will prefer Australia or the United States, or South America, or wherever the individual wishes to go. Canada will become a beautiful, *semi-tropical* climate in the years ahead. The weather will be beautiful and you will not suffer the English fog as you do now.

Canada will open up into a vast civilization commercially, spiritually and technically, which does not seem possible now perhaps, but when the New Age is well entered into there will be many changes brought about by this higher consciousness. Where there is no beauty now there will be, either in climate or vegetation, or in many other ways not necessary to discuss now.

You, of the Balkan countries, may feel alarmed as you read this too, but again I say, if you are not individually involved in a karmic pattern you have nothing to worry about. And of course as we see it, you still do not have anything to worry about even if you are. Each debt must be paid and you should be happy that you have the privilege of erasing a debt.

But there will still be some who cannot understand the law of karma and also will be fearful. To those I say, your very fear will draw that which you fear by the negative magnetic field you surround yourself with. Be with God and all will be well.

Much of the Balkan countries will be submerged also. Again, this too, is because of land construction. Along the coast of Europe, much will go under water, because as Atlantis rises the water must seek its own level and there will undoubtedly be land changes. But as I mentioned before, regardless of whether or not there is a karmic pattern to be paid off, you are within God's love and law and all is right with the universe. These things I tell you now will be better understood in the future vibration. Now, perhaps, the heart will feel faint because the mind cannot comprehend, but the mind will comprehend more and more as the mental bodies are stimulated by this higher vibrational activity.

Question: Do all people on the different planets breathe oxygen?

J.W.: Not all breathe oxygen as you do. They breathe various substances, some containing oxygen perhaps. Some of a similar physical nature to yours cannot stand the vibration of oxygen in their lungs. However, we from the higher planes breathe of the gaseous nature of the plane depending totally on our bodily makeup.

With myself, I can breath oxygen but of the higher ethers of the atomic structure of oxygen. However, we of Jupiter, breathe a mixture of a gas you have never heard of, combined with a certain part of oxygen, and for short periods only we can lower our vibration into your physical level and breathe your oxygen. It would be similar to your skin-divers breathing helium mixed with oxygen. Under pressure, their lungs are better able to assimilate the needed oxygen without ill effects. So it would be with us, but this could only last a very short period of time. In lowering our physical vehicle in vibration, we feel a tremendous amount of pressure. It's most uncomfortable to us and we prefer not to do it.

Question: Will you give me more information on the moon?

J.W.: (To what was in my mind) Yes, Gloria, the moon contains many caverns. These caverns have been so situated that they do exist right to the center of the moon. Now, contrary to the popular belief of your science, the inside of a planet is not hot molten material but is *hollow*. This occurs because the centrifical force of the atoms in the construction of a planet are thrown outward, and thus it is, the center is hollow.

No, Gloria, it is not dark inside, but illumined completely by *natural* light. This light is nothing more than the free energy I spoke of before. The people were given this knowledge so they could light the inside of their small world.

There is really no night or day for them with this continuous light.

When these people first developed their mode of living underground it was dark, of course, and they used fire light. But it was seen there was a need and they were developing well spiritually, thus, they were given the knowledge of using this gift of God. This is also the reason they developed their way of walking on all fours, as you say. When they first began to explore the moon's caverns, it was naturally easier to crawl over the rocky and uneven terrain. And as nature developed their bodies to adapt to this situation, the arms became like another pair of legs although they still retain fingers.

Incidentally, the moon will remain static when your planet moves into the new orbital position and attracts two new moons!

Question: I've read some reports about there being a volcano on the moon. Is this true?

J.W.: The volcano on the moon does exist but this was not caused by underground eruptions, but by *outer* activity on the surface, caused from drawing atomic dust from your earth's atmosphere that has been polluting it. The moon was used as a magnet, so to speak, to draw this atomic debris, as we call it, to its surface. This was done with the full knowledge of the people living there beneath the surface.

They knew of the situation and gave permission because it could not harm them in any way. We are also able to nullify most after-effects that are caused by contact with the various minerals on the surface which produce terrific spontaneous combustion. (Not a good term, but he sent the thought picture rather than words and this was my translation due to lack of a better scientific vocabulary.)

When this occurred, we also took care to relieve the outer atmosphere there of any deadly radiation. Of course, for us, this radiation is not deadly. Our planet has great radiation and our bodies are attuned to much greater and higher vibratory activity than the physical body can stand. The energy that is promoted or precipitated by the occurring explosions on the moon's surface has been utilized by conducting it to machines or dynamos, as you might say. It transfers this same energy that comes from your atmosphere to the people of the moon.

They have artificial light also, but the interior is lit by occult means. However, they do have machines which can utilize this power being sent to them. When they consented to having this atomic debris brought to their planet, they knew they were also repaying a karmic debt from the time I mentioned before, when great floods washed over the then known land areas on Earth. Thus, by housing the people of Earth, should it become necessary, and by receiving this atomic debris, they are able to repay the people of Earth. This is much more involved, but I won't go into it just now.

When Atlantis was in its prime, the people flew to the moon quite often, and many times they did harm to the inhabitants there. They naturally created a karmic debt doing so. Some of these past cruelties have been known to come to your planet by ships during certain lunar positions and have contacted some of your people here and done harm to them. But this has not occurred for thousands of years and is of no importance right now, but I had been thinking of the karmic aspects.

Comment by J.W.: I see you have been reading this book and I have been with you while you read it, but you must not concern yourself with these dark forces. As I said to the class and you (my own esoteric science class) yesterday, "the dark forces" (so called) have been at work on your planet but they will not harm anyone who sheds a spiritual light. This is law and we can see what attracts light. When these "dark forces" are at work, so to speak, we know of this activity. And if it is possible for us to interrupt their work, we do so, but if we see a karmic attraction, we do not.

When the "dark forces" eliminate certain areas by bombardment of certain instruments, we do not let this occur unless we happen to arrive too late, which is unusual. Yes, it is true, there have been cases when planes of your government have been shot down by certain craft but we are not responsible for this. The craft used was not of our group or the Solar Con-federation but under the assumed name of "flying saucers." This will surprise many people who read these words because they will not understand. The ships may *look* like ours but they are not the same, for they are powered electrically and are not sufficient in mechanical structure or operation to fly at tremendous speeds, such as we do. Nor can they fly into the upper atmosphere without ill effects. We know of these ships and usually keep careful surveillance of them. Their origin is known to your government.

Question: Is there a way to tell the difference?

J.W.: Yes. They do resemble ours very much, but there is one way to tell the difference. Our craft have a force field about them. These do not. They are propelled electrically and do not have a sizable force field, hardly any at all in fact. The electromagnetic power that is used does not create a force field, only a slight magnetic field around them to some extent, not noticeable except to your television, radio, or other electrical equipment.

Question: I have heard from another source that your people "project" by machine. Is this done at all?

J.W.: These machine projections are nothing more than a T.V. or telephone, or a projection like your movie cameras have. However, the *consciousness* of the person projecting his image or thought form is intact. This machine is not necessary for most of our people, but a few individuals who have not fully developed their mental bodies or vehicles do rely on these machines.

It is also true these projections can look so real that you would think they are flesh and blood. In a way they are real, to the extent they can walk about, but the body is more like the projection on a motion picture screen. You could pass through it, and it can suddenly disappear when the "switch" is turned off . . . like our mental projections, when we re-lease the *thought*.

Question: Are there evil entities that come to us from other solar systems or planets?

J.W.: There are some who are evil because they have not developed to the Christ consciousness. They have the knowledge of space travel but this knowledge did not come "naturally." It was stolen from those of higher evolvement who had a knowledge of the occult. These people did not have the occult knowledge and therefore they worked to steal it from those who did. It is said that some of your people have been informed these people were of an evil nature. The Space Planetary Control has knowledge of their activity and can pick them up when they make an entry into this solar system. They may not always be apprehended at once, but are soon placed under observation of the patrol and are quickly rounded up if their intentions are not good. They still have lust and greed in their hearts, as do many of the people of Earth.

Question: Is it true the Deros who live within our planet have ships similar to the saucer?

J.W.: The Deros who live inside your planet do have knowledge of saucer-like ships, but they cannot leave your atmosphere. They are watched also and are not allowed to harm anyone, but they are frightening more than anything to your Earth peoples. They have a strong sulfurous smell about them and people who have come in contact with them usually become quite ill from this odor. The low rate of their vibration, even though they are etheric, has degenerated so they are actually below the human vibration and in the *mineral* vibration! They aren't the same vibratory line as the minerals but run almost with it. This is rather difficult to explain, but the difference is great between your vibration and theirs, which has degenerated to such an extent they have become more mineral in vibratory activity, and this low vibration results in nausea for many of you.

They have been manifesting the past few years in a physical type form. They are able to take advantage of the greater cosmic energy coming to your planet. They can build up a lower atomic structure of material but are unable to hold it for any length of time. They had degenerated at the time your people manifested in the etheric, but instead of taking on denser form they took another path and degenerated to a lower vibration of the etheric which was more closely attuned to the mineral vibration. Even the minerals are evolving, of course, and the Deros do have a sincere desire to gain that which was lost and evolve back to a higher vibration.

This has been of special interest to me at this time, because I have been on the council to decide on their disposition before the New Age is entered into. We have decided to help them all we can under the instructions of the Logos of the Central Sun. Since they are trying to evolve along the path, they should be given every opportunity to make that return. Thus, it has been decided they will be taken to another planet that is of such a rate of vibration they can harmonize and evolve with that planet, probably a fairly new planet. (At this point I received a mental picture of bubbling mineral springs and molten lava. It was a weird sight, much as our scientists depict Earth in its new-formed stages.)

This has been an interesting problem to us for it will be necessary for higher Souls to help them out of this degeneracy into a higher and greater light. We are wondering if people like yourself would be willing and/or able to withstand their vibration enough to incarnate in the future to help these people. If their gross vibration cannot be withstood, then it would be better to work from the inner planes or etheric level to help them in their way of returning.

We must take into consideration whether it would be unsuccessful for higher beings to incarnate or not. In our desire to help them, it may be much easier to do it by working on the etheric level than to incarnate into their level. Because of their low state of degeneracy, we are as anxious as they to help them return to greater light and want to give them every opportunity. This is an increasing problem, bringing the various aspects into the picture, but shows that none of God's children ever become too low to be rejected by the higher Beings as long as they *ask* for help. If there is sincerity in their hearts, help will always be given.

Question: What will happen to the animals during this transition?

J.W.: Most of the animals now inhabiting the planet are not in a consciousness suitable for the New Age, so they will be taken from their bodies at the time the masses are taken. They shall inhabit other spheres of life for a time until they incarnate on another planet or sphere of vibrations similar to their growth or evolution.

When you reach the place where the so-called catastrophes may occur, the animals shall be taken. This is not to worry the people, for the animals are dear to God's Heart also. They will be well taken care of on the "other side" by those who look after such things.

The animal is Spirit, as is man, and will one day develop to the human form. But that will not be until the next Round or Cycle of the solar system. Then they will have evolved to a higher degree than they manifest at this time. When animals are destroyed physically on a planet, they are not destroyed spiritually, of course. They will inhabit other planes of life until there is a need for their particular manifestation in other worlds, perhaps outside of this solar system entirely.

When we see the Plan for the animals, we are happy. The same thing will happen to them that will happen to many people. They would not be able to stand the strain of the new vibrations. As their consciousness is raised in spirit, they will be taken to other worlds to incarnate in other forms, perhaps, but will still be of the animal kingdom.

The animals which will inhabit the Earth in the New Age will be different from the animals you now know. They will be manifesting a higher degree of consciousness. Many will be quite lovable enough for house pets, such as the cat which well resemble the black panther you were told about before, Gloria. He will suddenly appear, probably in the South American jungle first. But this cat will be a vegetarian and herb eater. There will be no predatory instinct whatever in him. When he is discovered, men of your science will try to figure out from where he evolved and from what line of a known cat family. However, he will be placed here as an entirely new form of animal.

Your future animals will be very few in number. You will never again see great herds running on the plains or in the mountains. That era of your evolution has passed. Man likes animals in a world, so there will be some left to begin with. You will not need animals for meat any longer. Vegetables of a protein nature will appear and replace the animal meat that has been eaten. Yes, it is necessary for all to take meat off their diet. This is a requisite if they are to enter the New Age vibration.

Some of the animals will be similar to the horse and some to the dog, not as the dogs you know of the present consciousness, but of a much higher consciousness. It will be found they will have highly developed telepathic powers. (Much more than the dog has today.) This will be quite novel for some people, who will enjoy practicing telepathy with them. This will not be for some time though. It may be as long as five years before these animals will become apparent.

Once before in your past the animals were vegetarians, but as the planet became so negative and gross in manifestation, the animals too became gross. They became meat eaters and ate each other. This too had purpose, for again, balance had to be maintained in nature so the animal kingdom would not overrun the human kingdom. It would have been possible for that to happen had not this balance of nature been worked out.

The battle of strength, or the "law of the jungle," as you call it, is now almost over for this planet and will soon be a thing of your past. Animals will no longer seek to kill each other or have bitter enemies in their kingdom. There will be few of them, and man will appreciate the animal life more than he has under the influence of the Picean Age. Many cruelties have been committed by man to animals. Back in your unrecorded history, there were cruelties by the animals unto man. This was acknowledged by man in the Atlantean times by bombing the animal kingdom to destroy it. It was becoming a great hazard to the people.

You will find the Great Wall of China was built for this reason. Also a great wall in South America was built for the

dietary habits, Gloria. Any congestion of the physical is not good during this transitional period, for he physical too must adjust to the new vibration. If it is congested or clouded by eating meat, the higher energies of which I speak will not *penetrate* the physical as easily. Should there be too much of a *resistance* to this energy, the physical body will become ill and new diseases will crop out. Your doctors will wonder what is happening to the people. This will be one of the reasons.

The health foods that have been introduced in your country of late are appearing for a purpose. It has been in the Plan for some time now to try and change the diet habits of the people, especially the American people who have and eat so many unnatural foods. The natural foods are the best there are for the physical body and not the conglomerations and concoctions most of you now eat. If you can change your diet habits as soon as possible, you will find greater strength and vitality with this oncoming force and a more youthful feeling with the *ability* of the physical to *accept* this energy with greater ease.

Now, the women will be happy to know as their dietary habits are changed, weight will not be a problem any longer! The oncoming vibrations will stimulate the physical so there is a "speeded up" process in the atomic vibrations and excess weight will not be as great a problem among your people as it is today. If the diet is not changed, however, from unnatural starches and sweets to the more natural foods, the weight will be a great detriment to the physical and disease will be made manifest on that particular body. Other countries do not have this problem as much as the American people. I am happy to relate this information to them, in the hope some of them will follow instructions and arrest their intake of meat, following a more correct diet of natural foods.

Incidentally, as the atomic structure of the physical is slowly changed, in time your different races will gradually disappear. All bodies will take on a golden or yellow skin color. Your Bible mentions the yellow race will one day inherit the Earth. The Oriental races have mistakenly thought it meant them!

The chapter on Sex is for the most part rather startling to most of us. Since we have been taught from childhood up that certain morals should be practiced in our lives, it is sometimes difficult to analyze intellectually when there is so much emotion involved. I do not think the majority of the people are ready for some changes he suggests in our moral society. Why? Pure and simple . . . EGO!

I have brought out J. W.'s views on sex at a few of my lectures, but discovered I was really treading on eggs. Many were incensed! At first this surprised me, for I was merely relating the point of view of the Space People, but in analyzing the comments and questions, I found it always turned out to be Ego or some form of self-righteousness.

One woman said, "Well, that certainly gives the men a free hand!" Later, I discovered she was extremely jealous of her husband and always suspicious. No gleat love was manifested between them. If he was at home and she away, she would wonder whether he was really home; if she stayed home and he went out, was he really where and doing what he said he was? This attitude made both of them rather miserable, it appeared.

It is nothing but Ego that declares, "He can (*should,* they mean) love no one but me!" Or "We always do *everything* together and never go *anywhere* without each other!" In such cases, I have seen only a great deal of doubt existing in the relationship. Emotion plays a big part but is still based on an easily bruised Ego.

Intellectually, I can understand well the principles J. W. wishes to bring out, but *emotionally* could I myself stand my husband going out with someone else? It is an excellent question and one most women would say they hope they never have to find out! But again, why emotion? Ego. I have always been happy I was never particularly of a jealous nature concerning my husband. Again, why? Jealousy always stems from *doubt* or *self-esteem.* This applies to both sexes.

It is amusing to me to see various reactions from people in telling them of love from the higher standpoint without the necessity of physical contact. The men especially groan and react violently to this, as it is not within the realm of their understanding (of their present consciousness, anyway), to imagine love without physical sex. But unless one has experienced this *divine love,* it *is* beyond the realm of understanding, for there is absolutely no comparison and no words within a vocabulary to explain it.

We are more and more accepting the idea that unwed mothers are expressing a *natural* thing, and it is becoming less of a "sin" for men and women to live together, for this too is a *natural* thing to our analytical minds. However, how long before we as individuals, will be able to replace Ego with *understanding* and emotion with *mental discernment?* It will take greater growth in our spiritual evolution of consciousness.

In talking these higher evolved Souls many times have mentioned, "There are no strangers to us." At their step on the ladder of life, they are able to *remember* who individuals were in past lives and their *personalities.* It seems eventually most of us have lived and loved together, and memory of these associations remain in our subconsciousness.

I recently talked to a Master some eight million years old; meaning he first incarnated in *form* eight million years ago. This is what is termed an "old Soul." Think how many individuals you would come in contact with in that length of time! He remembers all his experiences, although the very first are a "little hazy," he says. Recollections of his associations are concerned with the *individuals,* not the various *personalities* they may have expressed. High souls are primarily concerned with the experiences that helped them develop *spiritually,* not whether they were kings or famous persons. A lifetime as a peasant or slave may have taught them far more *spiritually* than any historical life.

(Incidentally, I had never asked J. W. his Soul Age, as we had never discussed this much, but he is twelve million years old! I think we would do well to heed the advice of one with that much experience. There are comparatively new Souls on Earth at this time. Some only in the 100,000 year category, one reason for their lack of understanding of the higher laws. It is simply not within their realm of consciousness. Compare it with putting a child from kindergarten into a Physics class! We all have to ga through our preliminary training.)

Therefore, discerning relationships from this higher point of view, it would seem very natural for a husband or wife to have an affinity for a *former* husband or wife, sister or brother, or whatever the case may be. Unfortunately, too few of us remember *what* the attraction for someone may really be based upon. The higher you climb in evolution, the "tighter" your life pattern becomes and the more "old friends" you attract. So by *honest* analysis, does it not seem *natural* for such relationships to be made manifest at least once in a person's lifetime?

Even though some of us may not be emotionally prepared for things which may happen to us, whether of a personal nature or of the outward things J. W. has stated may happen, at least we should *try* to understand what is happening from a *higher* (consciousness) point of view and better prepare ourselves for entry and personal growth for the New Age. This will at least be a step in the right direction.

Often I am asked during my lectures, what religion I follow, and, perhaps strange to the reader, I prefer not to identify myself with any particular religion under the heading of Christianity or an Oriental theosophy, but rather to establish *my* religion merely (?) under the heading of Truth. Truth is God and where It exists, whether It be found in the Bible, ancient writings or letters from an old sage or master, various religion, philosophies, or from an old reprobate on the street (for Truth is found in all places, and all things, as God is), matters not. No greater or higher religion can be attained than to know Truth.

Some will be the first to say, "Are you selling Christianity short?" No, I am definitely NOT selling the *teachings* of Jesus short at all, but I surely do the *misconceptions* of His teachings which are hidden under the guise of religion and placed in the category of Christianity. My greater expansion of consciousness is due largely to the teachings of J. W. and my own experiences during my search for Truth. Whenever a teacher works as closely with a student as J. W. has with me, the student often has glimpses of the teacher's expanded consciousness and knowledge and this is a never-to-be-forgotten experience. My whole narrow world of yesterday is gone forever and now, paradoxically, I can see how very little I comprehend of God and our universe in the ever increasing search for knowledge.

God does not love any of His children more because they claim to be Catholic, Baptist, Buddhist, Christian Scientist, or what have you. Any prayer is heard, even from a would-be atheist. All great religions teach brotherly love, yet how often is it truly practiced? The Orientals tend to dislike the Christians and the so-called Christians not only dislike, distrust or hate, but think in their warped concepts they are unique in the Eyes of God. The most uncivilized savage may have a broader concept of life and a deeper, more satisfying faith and reverence toward a Supreme Spirit than is ever taught in our alleged Christian churches. I hope I shall always be able to maintain the attitude when I look at another man, "You are my brother."

If the people embracing *any* religion actually *practiced* their own doctrines, what a change would take place on our planet! Reincarnation has been proven in many ways* if one will look with an *open* mind. It certainly makes any racial prejudice an asinine precept. Just by *honest* analysis, why would a good and just and merciful Father favor one race above another, if we're all children of His? Consider well, how again and again, we are told how just and merciful and good our God is, yet how many prayers daily are sent up for Him to be merciful and just? Do we not believe? Obviously *something* is wrong and now is the time to tear away the old concepts and replace them with the Truth if we are to enter into the Aquarian Age with love, enlightenment and understanding. How beautiful our lives can be if effort is put forth. Nothing good comes without work or perserverance.

Sin is only within the minds of men or in a broken law of God. It is time to stop thinking negatively and calling everyone a sinner, and to start analyzing just where a so-called sin may lie . . . in the minds of men or in a law of God. And it's a good bet there will be very few "sinners" left under this new concept! It will be found there are more imbalances than any-

---

* ONE example—See the Long Lost Second Book of Acts translated by Rev. Kenneth Sylvan Guthrie, written by Luke in the house of John immediately before the passing of Mother Mary in her 83rd year, approximately AD 61. Copy in the Astor Branch of New York Public Library.

182

thing. Then we can start fresh and seek to know the laws of God, find the proper balance, and abide by these. Thus we will create a happier world as God, death and true brotherhood are at last understood.

Now, our world must release the old, worn, false concepts and replace them with Truth, if a more graceful entry into the New Age is to be accomplished. No longer can man try to *fit* "truth" into his concepts because he does not like the Truth or find it appropriate to his understanding of life. We have gone beyond the age of a "simple faith." This faith must be replaced by *knowledge*. The age of *reasoning* (perhaps, incorrectly at times too) is leaving us also and we must develop *intuition* or the more direct method of tuning in to our Godself without the *usual* time-wasted effort of man. All is within the One Mind. We have but to be receptive to receive. But first, we must tear these bonds of materialism and illusion from us so we can be more receptive to Good. Then, our Golden Age will really dawn.

J. W. has stated, it's difficult to be helped unless you *let* yourself be helped. Even a drowning man struggles against his would-be rescuer. It has fallen to my lot in life to be the one who throws you the "life preserver" enabling you to go into the New Age. You have caught it in reading this book. No one can force you to understand, nor do I wish to argue with people why they should save themselves, Truth has been presented to the best of my ability with an earnest desire to help. The rest is up to you.

I have thrown it. You have caught it. Will you swim . . . . . . or sink?

The Instrument
Gloria Lee

Finis _____